RESPECT & REPUTATION

ON THE DOORS, IN PRISON AND IN LIFE

Robin Barratt &
Charles Bronson

First published in 2010
This edition published in 2015 by
Apex Publishing Ltd
12A St. John's Road, Clacton on Sea
Essex, CO15 4BP, United Kingdom
www.apexpublishing.co.uk

Typesetting and layout by
Andrews UK Limited
www.andrewsuk.com

Copyright © 2010, 2015 Robin Barratt & Charles Bronson
The authors have asserted their moral rights

All rights reserved. This book is sold subject to the condition, that no part of this book is to be reproduced, in any shape or form. Or by way of trade, stored in a retrieval system or transmitted in any form or by any means, electronic, mechanical, photocopying, recording, be lent, re-sold, hired out or otherwise circulated in any form of binding or cover other than that in which it is published and without a similar condition, including this condition being imposed on the subsequent purchaser, without prior permission of the copyright holder.

Contents

Foreword	ix
PART ONE	1
Introduction	3
What Respect Means for Door Supervisors	17
What Reputation Means for Door Supervisors	32
Finding the Right Training Course	40
A Few Tips on Good Door Supervision	46
Be The Best You Can Be	54
On The Doors	67
Heroes Are Not Cowards	79
Fight, Not Flight	85
Tough Doors in A Tough Area	89
Do You Know Who I Am?	94
Real Training for The Doors	102
Thoughts On Respect	107
Girls On The Doors	110
How The Sia Fucked Up The Industry	116
Showing Disrespect	126
Stories From The Doors About Respect and Reputation	143
Earning Respect by Facing a Man With A Reputation	168
A War I Could Never Win	183
PART TWO	197
Introduction	199
Going Inside	209
Respect and Reputation	224
Prison Life	230
Respect Where Respect is Due	242

Because of the high level of disrespect in the industry now, this book is dedicated to every single professional door supervisor working the doors today; I respect you and the job you do, for it is infinitely more difficult than it ever was when I worked the doors. However, if you are a scrote or scumbag, or an ineffectual, unprofessional, arrogant doorman that couldn't give a toss about his job and the people you have been tasked to protect... fuck off!

Becci Maple Born: 3 March 1983 Died: 23 March 2009. She loved working for the guys at Alamo Security and her favourite door was at the East Bar in Swanage. Rest in Peace Becci, and keep the idiots from Heaven's gates!

Respect

[rispekt] the condition of being esteemed or honoured: to be held in respect

Reputation

[repyuhteyshuhn] favourable repute; good name: to build one's reputation a favourable and publicly recognised name or standing for merit, achievement, reliability

Foreword

By Bernard O'Mahoney

Out of all the words in the Dictionary, the true meaning of one word has to have been abused more times than your average Catholic Choir boy. To each and every one of us 'Respect' has a different meaning, and it is usually a meaning that we have tailored to suit our personal needs and lifestyle. The Government, for instance, have set up a website called `Respect` to deal with what they deem to be antisocial behaviour. The same selfrighteous bastards also send young men to the other side of the world to Iraq and Afghanistan to meet their deaths in a futile war. Ironically, the very antiwar group that campaigns against this senseless slaughter by the Government is itself called 'Respect'.

Like our hypocritical masters, the common man preaches one thing about respect and then practices the complete opposite. The infamous Kray brothers went to great lengths to propagate the myth that people in the East End of London respected them. In reality the meek that kowtowed to the terrible twins did so because they were simply terrified of them. The smiles and handshakes that greeted the Kray's wherever they went were usually camouflage for genuine fear and resentment. And so it was with my father, a sadistic bully who demanded `respect` but who was incapable of expressing love, affection, or any other decent human emotion to his own wife and children. How can such people claim to know the first thing about respect? When you are forced to live in the shadow of a deluded violent maniac who truly believes that you respect him, you accept all of the fear and misery that you are subjected to for a while. But within us all resides a beast that is rarely unleashed. When it is, it can never be stopped until our tormentor is defeated or dead. At the age of fifteen my father disappeared from my families' home after receiving his comeuppance. Fear had evolved into anger and he was badly beaten by myself and my brother.

He was not the only bully that I have met in my life who confused the meaning of respect with fear. In 1987, I arrived in Basildon, Essex after being released from a prison sentence for wounding. There, I began work at a nightclub called Raquel's where the clientele appeared to be only interested in either fucking or fighting one other. My fellow doormen were at best inadequate with dealing with the battles that raged each night. They were local men who `respected` the local bullies who had earned their reputation in the playground and who were determined to take them to their graves. It was my view, that the sooner that happened the better.

After confronting the head of security about his spineless attitude, he walked out of the club and I took over. Within weeks I had brought in a man named Tony Tucker as my partner. Tucker controlled a large and extremely `influential` door firm that was 'respected' throughout London and Essex. At first things went well. We cleared Raquel's of the local bullies (usually head first via the three storey concrete stair case) and decent people once more began to frequent the premises. In the early 1990's the love drug Ecstasy arrived in club land and Tucker and I found ourselves in a position to control a very lucrative market. Dealers would pay rent to sell drugs in the club and soon we were enjoying a lifestyle that neither of us had ever before experienced. However, the more money we earned, the more concerned I became. I could see beyond the smiling faces that showed Tucker and I `respect` and who wanted to be our `friends.` Meaningless, empty people who wanted a piece of the action to enrich their miserable lives would do their best to immerse themselves in the murky world that we inhabited. I chose to avoid them, Tucker chose to exploit them. He would ply young men with bags of pills and packets of powder. They would then be dispatched to various clubs throughout London and Essex to earn him money. Inevitably some dealers would take the drugs themselves, give them to friends or occasionally get caught in possession by the police. Regardless of their sob story, Tucker would always want his money. If the dealers were unable to pay, Tucker would take great pleasure in subjecting them to cruel and merciless violence. `If I let one off, they will all take the piss, they have to respect me,` he would say. In December 1995, Tucker and two of his associates went to meet one of the dealers that had failed to pay his dues. The dealer, a rather nondescript individual who has never been known to be violent before, had already suffered the wrath of Tony Tucker previously, but he had decided that he wasn't going to suffer it any more. He wasn't angry, he was in fact scared, but the beast that resides within us all had been unleashed. He knew what he had to do, the bully who confused respect with fear had to die. When the Range Rover carrying Tucker and his associates pulled up at a Farmer's gate that night, the middle aged drug dealer approached the car. In his hand he grasped a Spas.12 semiautomatic pump action shotgun. Moments later, Tucker and his associates were dead but the gunman continued to fire into their motionless heads. All of the fear, the anger and the hatred that he had felt for Tucker was finally being expelled. As three men had died, a new man had been born; one who knew the true meaning of respect. Never would he confuse fear with respect because he had endured it. The man had learned that you cannot respect anybody until you respect yourself. To have self respect you have principles, stand up for yourself and treat others as you would wish to be treated. To have self respect you have to love and cherish those closest to you. To have self respect you have to honour the wishes of others. And if you do these things, you don't have to think about giving others respect or earning it, because you will have already done both.

RESPECT & REPUTATION

PART ONE

ON THE DOORS

*Written and compiled by Robin Barratt
with contributions from:*

Mick Lyons, Jamie O'Keefe, Will Bishop, Rob MacGowen, Paul Knight, Steve Wraith, Geoff Carter, Wesley Downham, Ryan Hucker, Jim Thompson, Jim Myers, John Brawn (www.johnbrawn.com), Jeff Stewart, Colin West, Lloyd Smith, Richard Wood, Dave Llewellyn, Ben Elliot, Becci Maple, Masood Kamal, Chris Houghton, Donna Stanley, Steve Strudwick, Karl Spooner, Karen and Zarah.

Introduction

By Robin Barratt

Because I have no real desire to retrain already trained door staff, this book is not about the mechanics of the job. Since the Security Industry Authority (SIA) introduced national training and licensing for door supervisors throughout the UK, most if not all door supervisors have had some form of basic training, although undeniably SIA training is not nearly enough to equip new door staff for life on the doors and in this increasingly violent world. But this book is all about building a reputation and bringing back respect into this once worthy and loyal industry. And what a better world it will then be!

Although your mother may love you, if you are a wanker you are a wanker, simple. And I hate wankers; I hate wankers working on the door pretending to be door supervisors; and I really hate the kinds of wankers who think they are 'someone' and want to cause trouble. Although I fully understand that massive alcohol consumption and binge drinking have a great deal to do with a violent and wankerfilled Britain, if you have a core respect for other people this should remain strong, whether you are drunk or sober. Long gone are the days when doormen had authority and control, and now even stone cold sober people show so much more disrespect for the public and, of course, for door supervisors than ever before. People just don't care anymore. But, aside from the influence of alcohol, it is a plain and obvious fact that in Britain today and in much of the rest of the world there is little respect shown for others or for authority, and people don't care about doing what is 'right'; they are far too preoccupied with getting what they want and doing exactly what they want to even consider the thoughts and feelings of others. And, even worse, people also have little respect for themselves.

At the time of writing this I am living in Bahrain a little country in the Middle East off the coast of Saudi Arabia. I moved out here in the summer of 2009 and have more or less been here ever since, apart from a couple of weeks visiting my family in the UK over Christmas. People ask me why I am living in Bahrain, so here's my answer. Apart from Bahrain being much cheaper than the UK and, of course, sunnier, and apart from Bahrain being recently voted in an online poll as being the most friendly country in the world, one great reason for living here is that there is very little crime and almost no aggressive behaviour. Also, because alcohol is scarce in the Middle East there is no drunkenness, and because there is no drunkenness there is almost no violent crime either. In Bahrain you would never see an 18-year-old girl vomiting in the gutter with her bare arse in the air and her friends around her cheering and egging her on a fairly normal sight on a Friday or Saturday night in the UK. In Bahrain there are no groups of scummy youths standing on street corners taunting and verbally abusing passersby; there are no drunks vomiting in the streets or taunting the police and door staff; and there are no street gangs or violent punchups in bars and clubs. Nobody kicks anyone in the head or punches them in the mouth. There is no 'do you know who I am?' attitude.

Why is this so? I think there are two fundamental reasons. Firstly, and most importantly, from what I have seen and the large number of people I have spoken to, it's absolutely clear that people here have far more self-respect than a lot of people in the UK and are much more concerned about what their family and other people think of them. The Bahrainis respect their extended family immensely and are very conscious about what they think and are acutely aware of the disrespect that any bad behaviour could bring to the family. In the UK we don't seem to give a toss. And, even though there is still immense hardship and poverty, as there is in the UK, out here these problems do not cause people to mug old ladies, graffiti walls or shoplift and steal from their neighbours. In fact it is just the opposite: they tend to support each other and their neighbours in extremely difficult times. For example, the poor here may only have one or two sets of clothes, but they keep them clean and mended and they try to look neat and tidy, and even in the cramped, squalid barracks occupied by many of the foreign construction workers nobody ever steals from anyone else; not ever. And everyone is so polite and friendly. There is none of this scummy attitude that many people have in the UK. In Britain poverty and hardship are blamed for so much, but the social ills of the UK aren't caused by these problems; it's the people. There have been times in my life when I have been extremely poor. One weekend I remember only having porridge to eat because I had no money to buy anything else, but I didn't go out stealing or mugging.

How can we respect other people if we don't have any respect for ourselves? And if we don't care about ourselves and how we behave, how on earth can we care about others?

Talking about the Middle East was not originally going to be part of the introduction to this book, but I am finding the region really interesting and so different to the UK and, like it or not, the British most definitely have an awful lot to learn from the Bahrainis on the subjects of respect and reputation. I can already see some of you holding up your hands in horror at this statement, especially when there is horrific violence in Iran and British soldiers are being killed in Iraq and Afghanistan. But, surprisingly, for the vast majority of people in the Middle East, the thought of behaving in an aggressive, violent or criminal way doesn't even enter their minds. The respect that normal people have for each other on a daily basis and in life generally here in the Middle East is much higher and so very different than in the UK. It has got nothing to do with corrupt governments and fanatical extremists and wars. While I might not always agree with many of the Middle Eastern, Arab and Muslim policies, either religious or social and as a Westerner I frequently have trouble understanding their culture and their very unique ways of doing things we can certainly learn an awful lot from them regarding the control and management of crime, street violence and yobbish, aggressive behaviour, which are almost nonexistent out here but are so prevalent in the UK.

Punishment for even the smallest crime in Bahrain is severe, which is a real deterrent to criminal behaviour. For example, I recently read in Gulf News, the local daily English language newspaper, that a Bahraini man was sentenced to three years' imprisonment for slapping a Pakistani man in the face and stealing his mobile phone. The Pakistani man was not injured, just shocked and upset, but the perpetrator got a massive three years for common assault and nicking a phone! A week or so later I then read that someone jumped out of a recess in a wall and grabbed a woman's breast as she walked by with her husband (I know it's not funny, but I did smile at the bizarre vision of this happening). The culprit ran off, with the woman's husband in hot pursuit. Soon three or four other people were chasing him too, until he fell over and got the beating of his life. After a week or so in hospital, he was then sentenced to five years in prison. In the UK he would've probably got a caution and then sued all and sundry, while the husband and the others involved in the beating would've probably been arrested, charged with assault and more than likely imprisoned. The laws in Britain are pathetic, aren't they? When I go to the gym in downtown Manama, the capital of Bahrain, I leave my wallet, keys and mobile phone on the front desk in the gym, alongside the same personal items belonging to all the other members training at that time. Nobody ever thinks about stealing someone else's things; it doesn't even cross people's minds. I wonder how many gyms there are in the UK where I could do this? And if you follow the King Fahd Causeway from Bahrain across into Saudi Arabia and you get caught stealing something, you get your hand chopped off. Guess what? No one steals in Saudi Arabia!

In the UK, because people have little regard or respect for others, criminals know that they can do almost anything to anyone and that even if they get caught (which is unlikely) they won't really suffer. And this is precisely why there is so much crime and so much injustice and disrespect in the UK. While you may think that long prison sentences for relatively minor crimes and the lopping off of hands are barbaric, isn't it better for one criminal to suffer than for the whole of society to do so? Personally, I don't advocate the lopping off of hands for petty theft, but I wonder how many one handed people there would be in the UK if the British Government did implement this policy and how quickly the crime rate would diminish? Almost overnight, I reckon. I am not a thief, so why should I worry about a harsh punishment for thieves? The only people who should be worried are those involved in stealing! I am not a Pakistani slapping, mobile phone nicker either, so why should I worry about a three year stretch for this crime?

As Westerners we certainly openly criticise some Arab countries for their draconian and horrific punishment practices, yet violent crime in the UK is undeniably out of control, mainly because there are simply not enough severe punishments and therefore very little deterrent.

New York was once the murder capital of the USA and one of the most violent cities in the world, but in the mid 1990s the New York police implemented a zero tolerance policy introduced by Mayor Rudy Giuliani, and the crime rate halved almost overnight. New York became one of the safest cities in the USA. British society is unquestionably crumbling around us and moving very swiftly towards the crime rates seen in the USA, and we need to take control and do something positive about it now. We need to get back respect, firstly for ourselves and secondly for everyone around us.

What has this got to do with door supervision, you ask? Well, our micro world of the doors and the scum that we deal with on a nightly basis very much reflect the bigger world around us. It is violent, there is little respect, and the law is not on the side of door supervisors but on the side of the scrotes who inhabit the streets doing whatever they want to whomever they want with little comeback and virtually no punishment. And something ought to be done to bring back respect.

Before I moved to the Middle East I did an interview for a Norfolk radio station. I talked to the presenter about Norwich, the region's capital and where I grew up, and how violent and disgusting the city was at weekends. With regular stabbings and fights and drunkenness, Norwich's main clubbing area Prince of Wales Road, leading down to The Riverside complex was now one of the worst streets in the UK. I told the radio presenter that I could clean it up and bring respect back in a month, guaranteed; that there would never be any violence on Norwich's streets again no more violent, abusive drunks, no more stabbings, or fights. He looked at me stunned. How could such a marvellous thing be accomplished? Simple. Implement zero tolerance to street crime, a bit like in New York, and for the first few months put hundreds of riot police armed with batons and guns and shields on the streets every Thursday, Friday and Saturday night and give them the power to do whatever they need to suppress violent behaviour. I can almost guarantee that within a month there would be little or no violent crime and that my grandmother could walk through the streets once again at night and feel relatively safe (if she wanted to). But as soon as I said this I must have really upset the many pathetic do-gooders who were listening, as calls came flooding in complaining about my recommending such overtly aggressive behaviour. But it is precisely because of all this nambypamby human rights crap and all these do-gooders many of whom have never experienced a violent street on a Saturday night that the majority of normal, law abiding people continue to suffer at the hands of a scumbag minority; that the innocent suffer because of the guilty. I am not, nor have I ever been, a scumbag scrote who just wants to get pissed, abuse everyone and have a good fight on a Saturday night, so why should I worry about baton wielding policemen patrolling the streets and bashing these oiks over the head if they misbehave?

As I have said, many people now have little or no respect for themselves or for others; they are too consumed with their own lives to care much for other people. We see it every day: society is collapsing; violent crime is rising; muggings, beatings, rapes and murders are at an all-time high; and from the inner cities to the once quiet and sedate provincial villages, violence now prevails. It affects each and every one of us, wherever we live, whoever we are and whatever we do. This is undeniable. A recent online survey showed that just over 75% of people aged between 16 and 65 randomly polled throughout the UK have been affected in some way by violence, or are worried that they could be. Most people in Britain are afraid to walk outside late at night, to get involved in situations they witness, to argue with teenagers hanging around street corners or causing a disturbance, or to open their door to strangers. Why won't the British Government wake up and realise that its people are scared?! Years ago all you needed to do was shout "Stop it!" and the perpetrators would run off; now they're more likely to come over and stab you. Where once the young respected the elderly and we all respected authority, now they tell them all to fuck off and mind their own fucking business. Rarely, if ever, would we hear of a pensioner being beaten for just few pence in their purse, or of kids being stabbed, or of people being killed in broad daylight while protecting the innocent or their property, or just for standing their ground and standing up to yobbish behaviour, but now we hear reports day after day after day, in an unrelenting stream, of the most distasteful behaviour perpetrated by people that just don't care.

Without sounding too apocalyptic, I believe our world is crumbling in around us, and I am saddened by what I read almost daily in international newspapers about respect, or the lack of it, and am disgusted and appalled by what I regularly witness on Britain's streets. I am also saddened by the attitude and apathy of the younger, inexperienced door supervisors, many of whom should not be working the doors anyway, about the job they do. But for those genuinely conscientious and professional door supervisors, if you can work towards achieving a degree of respect from your customers and colleagues, and can develop a good reputation, then for sure it will roll over into life generally. Everyone I met while writing this book has said that working the doors has taught them so much about people and life as a whole, and that the skills they have learned on the doors have helped them immeasurably in their everyday lives. Learn to respect people in a world of nightclubs and bars, alcohol, drugs, prison, gangsters and violence and it is almost guaranteed that you can respect other members of society.

So what is 'respect' and how do we get it back?

Actually this question is almost impossible to answer, as respect means different things to different people and, of course, at different times. Respect is such an ambiguous word too; it defies a fixed definition and emotion and can therefore be such a difficult concept to understand fully. However, time and time again, the one thing that has continuously stood out when putting this book together is that if you respect others, in whatever capacity and whoever they are, you will almost always be respected in return. This has been said to me by 'old school' and 'new school' door supervisors, wrestlers and street fighters, hard men, martial artists and prisoners. Everybody has said exactly the same thing, over and over again, and it's absolutely true: respect others and respect for you will follow. And, of course, the opposite is also very true: if you disrespect others and treat others badly, this will always come back to you too. Although you may not agree with everything that I, Charlie and all the other great contributors to this book have written, this is the one thing that is absolutely guaranteed: disrespect others and disrespect for you will follow.

From short paragraphs and brief statements to short stories and standalone chapters, apart from myself and Charlie, there are many other people who have also contributed to this book, but there are no contributions from academics sitting in stuffy bookfilled libraries hypothesising over behaviour theories and remedies or fatarsed, balding government ministers that rarely venture out of their superficial, enclosed world of money, power and the elite, let alone have any real, meaningful contact with violence, the streets and the people that inhabit them. Neither is anything written by anyone remotely close to the SIA, which I (and many others, I might add) believe have single-handedly destroyed the door, security and close protection industry over the past few years… but more on that later. From door supervisors to former gangsters and excons, this book is written and compiled by the real people who genuinely do understand what our world is all about; the world of the streets, the world of alcohol, clubbing and the doors, and also the world of prison for if you choose to lead a violent life and a life of disrespect it is almost certain that you will be spending at least some of it behind bars.

As I am sure some of you will know, I do not mince my words and I am known for speaking my mind and telling it exactly as I see it. I am not always politically correct (I don't even try to be sometimes), and I have been know to have upset quite a few people over the years with my opinions and attitude, as well as my frankness and brutal honesty. I tend to say what many other people are actually frightened of saying, and so for some this book might be slightly controversial and contentious.

I am the first to admit that in some cases an 'old school' doorman was certainly not a good one. There were definitely more bullies and hard men working the doors before SIA licensing kicked in than there are now, so undeniably the SIA has done a good job in this regard. Doormen (for there were very few doorwomen back then) were known to be tough and aggressive, and in many venues they handled even mildly aggressive situations in a swift and usually violent manner. This was never a good thing and without any doubt something had to be done to professionalise the industry. However, in my opinion, 'new school' is no school and today, instead of standing up to confrontation and doing 'what is right', many door supervisors crap themselves and run a mile in any such situation, leaving their colleagues in the shit and their customers in real danger. I have experienced this myself many times, as well as hearing it from colleagues and friends working the doors in almost every kind of venue in every town and city across the UK. Where once there was loyalty, trust and respect, now there is an almost complete disregard for your team and for other door supervisors and contempt for the industry in general.

However, for the record, let me state quite clearly that I don't advocate violence. Violence is ugly, degrading, disrespectful and sad and it can completely ruin someone's life, both physically and emotionally. To be punched hard in the mouth or kicked in the head or violently assaulted in any way by anyone is horrible. As Mike Lyons, a well-known doorman running many of Wigan's clubs and pubs, said to me when we chatted about the subject over a coffee just before Christmas 2009, "Violence is shocking, Robin. It insults and abuses to the highest degree. Sometimes, sadly, it is necessary, but it is horrible." Mike has had his fair share of battles in his time and yet even he agrees that violence is not a good path to take. In this book I am certainly not advocating a violent path, but, as Mick rightly said, sometimes the fear of violence is absolutely necessary to control the uncontrollable.

Almost every single door supervisor I spoke to while writing this book said that there is little or no respect or loyalty on the doors anymore; you look after 'Number One'. As a result, many good, experienced door staff have left the industry. Of course there are still many excellent and very close door teams working out there that would back each other up no matter what, but generally, because of the poor quality of door supervisors currently working the doors since SIA licensing took over, the professional, tight door team has almost lost all significance. Door supervisors no longer respect other door supervisors and there is no longer a comradeship within the industry. And, incredibly, every single door supervisor I spoke to, without exception, said that there is little or no respect or regard from the customers towards door supervisors anymore, and many of the stories in this book highlight this fact, some disturbingly so.

I have never been, nor will I ever be, a violent person, and so I am not boasting when I say that even in my middle age I can still hold my own in most aggressive and violent situations and I won't back down and I won't give up. But I would always prefer a nonviolent resolution if at all possible, as I have seen the consequences of the most extreme acts of violence, both on the doors and during my career in close protection in places such as Bosnia during the conflict, Africa and Russia. I am not frightened of violence, but I am scared shitless of its consequences, as I have seen people horribly disfigured and disabled because of one random act of madness. I hope that by reading this book you will also choose to take a nonviolent path if at all possible too.

People that know me would also testify to the fact that, although I have lived in a sometimes brutal world, I am not a naturally aggressive or violent person. However, in certain situations and at certain times I would absolutely and openly advocate the use violence and intimidation, and admittedly I have, on very rare occasions, had to use the most extreme forms of violence myself to solve situations that I have been completely unable to solve in a nonviolent way and where there has simply been no option of walking away or turning back. Also, at times, I have had to use violence to back up colleagues on the doors or out in the field as a bodyguard, when again the options of not helping or of walking away just did not exist.

I realise that for many people even the concept of advocating violence is abhorrent and is a subject that should not even be written about, let alone discussed, and there are those that simply do not believe that violence can be a remedy in certain situations. Sadly, these people are generally lawmakers and politicians, human rights activists and moralists, judges and anyone else that lives in a tightly controlled, elitist cocoon, who simply have no idea what the real world is all about but who readily judge and characterise those that do. Even most law enforcers agree that violence can sometimes be a remedy and a form of control. Ask most police officers whether giving a good hiding to a scumbag would be a good thing and I think most would definitely agree. But would the general public agree to the police promoting the use of violence on lowlife street scum? If not, why not? Many years ago, before I started working as a doorman, I caused trouble at a local nightclub and got beaten senseless by the bouncers, and guess what? I never caused trouble in that place again. In some cases violence teaches people a lesson. Fact.

So by writing this book I am hoping to help bring back some of the respect that is missing on the doors and show you that building your reputation does not mean through bullying, intimidation or acting like a thug or scrote. You can build yourself an awesome reputation through professional behaviour and how you treat others. As this book speaks out against violence, it might seem a little hypocritical, contradictory and, I suppose, unorthodox that my co-writer is Charlie Bronson, tagged as the most violent prisoner in the UK and someone who has built his reputation on intimidation and extreme violence. However, apart from the fact that he makes hilarious and completely off the wall contributions, it is solely because of Charlie's extremely violent background that I wanted to write this book with him and no one else. He is neither a murderer nor a rapist nor a paedophile. Charlie is behind bars and has been kept in solitary confinement as a Category A prisoner for over 30 years solely as a result of violence. It is because of Charlie's reputation that the prison system continues to treat him badly, and because he is treated badly he continues to be violent, and so the cycle continues and has done for most of his adult life; there is no escaping the prison system for Charlie. He has respect and undeniably he has an awesome reputation, but has this really paid off? Is leading an extremely violent life and spending the rest of your days on your own, behind bars, and alienated from your loved ones, family and friends, really worth it?

I will let you and you alone decide the answers to those questions.

With this new generation of young prisoners with attitude we have new prisoners that no longer conform to the once defined prison structure and hierarchy, and the rules of prisoner conduct, respect and attitude towards fellow prisoners. Even in prison it's a case of everyone for themselves and many just don't give a toss about anyone else. Where once there was respect amongst criminals, now this has all but vanished too. Moreover, where prison officers once treated prisoners with a degree of respect, now I hear that this has also disappeared. Both prisoners and the prison system have changed, and not for the better.

When reading this book you should always remember that respect must be partnered with reputation; having one without other is ineffectual and, quite frankly, pathetic. It is no good having the reputation of being a hard man but with little or no respect, and there are a number of stories from door staff highlighting this point. Neither is it any good commanding some respect from your peers and customers without having a very good reputation. You must strive for both in order to be successful and professional.

As mentioned, this book hasn't been written to conform to the beliefs of nambypamby human rights activists or to consider the feelings of the frequently pathetic and often ridiculous lobbyists for political correctness. And it will certainly piss off a few Christians and moralists too when I discuss violence, control and intimidation, and those situations where I do occasionally advocate fight not flight and definitely not turning the other cheek. I fervently believe that people should stand up for what is right, hold their ground and react to injustices, bullying and intimidation. And I certainly believe that people should never bury their head in the sand because they are either too scared to do anything or too worried about the political or social implications of 'getting involved'.

When I first started putting this book together I carefully considered the direction I should take. Option one was to write honestly and openly, chronicling exactly what I really think and believe, regardless of whether it is politically correct and regardless of whom I might upset. Option two was to toe the line, so to speak, and take into account correctness, morality and the feelings of others and consider carefully what should and should not be said. Should I write what I think others would want to hear, or should I write about what I really want to say?

Over the years many people have written to me saying that they have a book inside them (figuratively speaking and not literally, of course) and asking my views on being honest and open. I always replied by saying that I believe the most important thing for any writer to do is to write about what they know and to state the truth as much as realistically possible anyway and to always try to write about what they genuinely believe in. Why? Because for many people writing is a form of therapy; maybe as closure on an event or to purge oneself of demons. Perhaps writers are looking for forgiveness or to preach or teach or pursue a personal ambition or goal. But whatever the reasons for writing, if you fervently believe in something and if you can logically and rationally demonstrate your beliefs on paper, it is almost guaranteed that others will agree, believe and understand you too. And that must always be your ultimate goal.

The truth is absolute and can never be discredited. Lies almost always surface and almost always come back to haunt you later, and unless you are stepping into the realms of accusations, defamation and libel you can actually write about almost anyone and just about anything; you do not need permission to write about what you really believe in. But if you write rubbish it will soon become apparent and transparent, and very quickly you will lose credibility, believability and, of course, respect. Writing should come from the heart and you should only write because you really feel moved to do so. In general writers, like most artists, singers and actors, scarcely make a living from their work, and without another job most full-time writers struggle day to day. So it stands to reason that, if you are willing to suffer financial hardships because of your beliefs, then you should not compromise by writing rubbish; you are sure to regret it later. I have met many people who have totally regretted writing certain things, not because they have written the truth, but because they have written lies. Books are immortal; they will be around forever.

And because I preach honesty, of course I must practise it too. So when I started writing this book, unequivocally and without question, hesitation or doubt, I chose option one. I have written what I really do believe in and, in doing so, you will either like it and agree with me or you will not. But that is your choice.

Oh, there was one other reason, of course: Charlie would kick my fucking arse if he read bullshitting, lying, superficial crap in a book with him in it!

Stay safe.

What Respect Means for Door Supervisors

By Robin Barratt & others

Before I started putting this book together I chatted to quite a number of door supervisors across the country, both novice and experienced, about their thoughts regarding respect for and from their peers and also for the door supervision industry in general: what does respect really mean to men and women working on the doors today? Although there was definitely an understandable difference of opinion between the older, more experienced 'old school' door supervisor and the younger, less experienced 'new school' doorman, almost all of the replies were based on more or less the same principles, even though there was an age gap of 30 years between some of the doormen. The feedback was both interesting and enlightening. It tended to mirror my thoughts and feelings on the subject exactly, and it actually shows that for many people in this industry who respect their job and their role the core values are the same. In the next chapter I will also discuss what reputation means for door supervisors.

The last person I spoke to before finishing the book was Mick Lyons. It was just before Christmas 2009 and I was in Wigan at another meeting when I called Mick to ask him if he fancied meeting up for a coffee. I had never met Mick before, but I had known about him since 1999 when I was working the doors in The Mirage nightclub in Standish, Lancashire. The Mirage was part of the Moat House Hotel group, and Mick once had the door. Mick is one hard fucker and was well known as someone you just didn't mess with, and at that time he and his team were notorious throughout the area.

For weeks we had been expecting Mick and his crew to turn up for battle, as a few months before I started at The Mirage Mick's team were sacked and the subsequent door team were 'done in' big time. At the start of the evening, unbeknownst to them, one of Mick's team entered the club as a paying customer and then opened all the exit doors. Mick's heavily tooled up team poured in and quite literally put all of the club's doormen in hospital, where some remained for weeks. It was a really nasty affair and it deeply shocked the staff and management.

Although we had heard a rumour that this disagreement had something to do with a large amount of money owing to Mick by the head doorman, at the time the real reasons were not clear and so I was asked by Jon Maddocks of JKM Security in Doncaster to work the venue and help front any problems that the club and its staff might have with Mick. The club's management wanted an outside door team, as they no longer trusted anyone from the local area, and anyway no one locally would be prepared to front Mick and his crew after that incident.

We were literally as nervous as fuck and on major alert for months, fully expecting Mick and his team to turn up again en masse and armed and do exactly the same to us, and none of us really wanted to spend the Millennium in hospital! He didn't turn up, of course, but we were paranoid: walking back to our cars at the end of the evening in twos and threes with baseball bats under our coats; patrolling the exits every few minutes with knuckledusters in our pockets; and carefully vetting almost everyone that came in, especially if they were on their own and looked like a doorman!

We were constantly on edge, but slowly the weeks and months crept by and nothing happened. Eventually we heard on the grapevine that Mick did not have any grudge against us, apart from taking a door that he knew he would never get back, and that it was purely a personal grudge with the previous door team. When word reached us that he would not be visiting and everything would be fine we all sighed with relief. We had enough work on our hands with the normal weekend Standish scrotes and none of us wanted to battle against Mick and his team as well.

So, almost ten years later, I wanted to meet the man I had heard so much about and had been somewhat foolishly prepared to stand up against. We arranged to meet for a coffee before I made my way back to London.

Time and time again I have said that the hardest bastards are almost always the most respectful and polite, and Mick was no exception. I recognised him immediately. He was certainly 'old school' in his appearance and definitely looked as though he'd had a few hard battles in his life (no offence, Mick!) Now in his mid fifties, he was still an excellent martial artist and boxer and looked as though he could mix it with the best, and it was obvious that he still kept himself in very good shape.

We sat down, ordered our coffees and chatted for a good couple of hours about Wigan, the doors past and present, and the notorious incident at Standish, amongst many other things. I wish I'd had more time, as we had a great deal in common and lots to talk about. Apart from my asking a few questions for this book, he actually did most of the chatting and he had me in stitches with some of his tales of the characters he had meet, especially in Wigan (some of whom you will read about later). "Doing the doors in Wigan," he said, "is always good for a laugh." On the more serious topics his views and philosophies were very traditional and they were ones that every single door supervisor should listen to:

I don't believe you have to be shown respect to give it; I think you should always give respect first. If that person does not give it back then he or she has got the problem, not you. You can only be reasonable with reasonable people. But somebody has to start the ball rolling otherwise everybody would be having a standoff. I think the bigger man gives respect instead of expecting it to be shown first.

Mick makes an incredibly important point that all door supervisors should take on board: that the bigger man is the one that gives respect first. There will be much more from Mick later.

Earlier that year I also met up with another hard bastard while I was living for a spell in Spain. Robert MacGowan was born in January 1952 in the market town of Kendal, in the north of England, and after a difficult childhood he left school at the age of 15 with no qualifications and followed his father's footsteps into amateur boxing. He became a father at just 17, and over the ensuing years he fell foul of the law on numerous occasions, generally after barroom brawls. Along the way he earned extra income to support his family as a bouncer, bodyguard and bareknuckle street fighter. Robert is humble, articulate, considerate and quietly spoken, yet at the same time you really would not want to mess with him. There will be a lot more from Robert later, but he sums up respect in just a few well-chosen words:

Respect is everything; respect for yourself and respect for people around you. If you have this then respect will follow you and will stay with you long, long after you have finished working the doors.

Colin West is another humble yet very experienced doorman and he told me:

It is crucial to have the respect of the immediate team you work with, as well as other doormen and women working on the doors in venues in and around the locality. Without this respect the door team just doesn't function very well at all. A lot of what is asked of, and given by, door supervisors is done purely out of respect and for no other reason. Respect is earned by other door supervisors seeing you doing the job properly, being professional, standing your ground, watching their backs and keeping yourself calm and measured in tricky situations. This is how the respect is earned on the doors, but in life generally we don't always have the chance to display these qualities and ordinary people don't know what we, as door supervisors, go through every night: the abuse we take, the combat we engage in. Over a period of time, as we work with door supervisors, we see all their skills and see how they have our backs time and time again; sometimes we might even owe our lives to them. I was unfortunate enough to be working at a club where a doorman was actually shot inside the venue after the door was rushed by well over a hundred people. Not for one second did I ever doubt the people working with me that night. If I had, I would have been unable to perform my job. The advice I would give new door staff is always treat people how you would like to be treated. Be firm yet fair, but above all be reasonable. Never be manipulated or corrupted. Defend yourself, your coworkers and your door and never confuse fear with respect. People who respect you will do most anything for you; people who fear you will eventually turn on you.

That's excellent advice from a true gentleman and veteran of the doors. Again, more from Colin later.

Jim Thompson, a retail security guard by day, is a relatively novice doorman compared with Mick, Robert and Colin, and has only been working on the doors since November 2008. He started off working for Regency Security at a place called Rocco's and at the adjoining Mercy nightclub, one of Norwich's largest venues situated on the notorious Prince of Wales Road, once voted one of the most dangerous nighttime streets in Britain. When he left Regency Security in March 2009 he joined a company called Hyline and works mainly on the back door at the Squares club, stopping people from trying to enter via the rear exit. Even though he is fairly new to the job and is still learning the ropes, he offers some very good advice to other novice door staff:

Normally I work on the front door for the first hour or so of the evening, when it's fairly quiet, and then generally I get sent to the back door where I have to stop the crafty buggers getting in for free. One person would pay to enter and then go to the fire exit and open the doors, letting in seven or eight of their friends, which apparently happened an awful lot before I was posted there! They still try, of course, but not so often now that they know I am there almost every night. From my experiences of starting work as a door supervisor I believe respect from fellow door supervisors really is very important. But I don't mean acting hard on your first night and telling everyone that you're a boxer or that you do martial arts and that you fear nothing… all that crap! On your first night I believe you should talk to the other door staff and be truthful and tell them if you are a little nervous. Everyone is nervous on their first few nights on the doors, especially if you have never worked the doors before; it's normal, so don't pretend you are not! My first ever shift as a door supervisor I turned up a half-hour before my shift so I could meet everyone. I was told I would be the only man inside, but if I needed help there would be two other door supervisors on the door. This made me feel much better.

Ben Elliot is also a novice doorman and has only been doing the job for about three years. He has worked in Southampton,

Poole and Bournemouth, and it was actually his partner Becci Maple, a seasoned door supervisor, who introduced him to door work. He says about the job:

You earn the respect of your fellow door team by doing what's right, even against the odds, and consistently doing well and proving yourself. For example, if there is a fight that needs breaking up, it's better to jump in and do something than to stand around doing nothing. This is how you learn to respect your team and gain the respect of your colleagues. Some guys in our team work really well on instinct but they don't seem to work well when they have to think about what to do! If they just react they seem to do the right thing every time. It can be easier when your natural reactions take over without the complications of thinking too much about what's going on around you. But this only happens with experience. A bad or inexperienced doorman stands around watching a situation develop and wonders what he is going to do about it; a good doorman just reacts and deals with it immediately.

Although novices, both Jim Thompson and Ben Elliot do offer some really good advice to new and novice door supervisors, and what Jim says about being honest, open and truthful with your colleagues is spot on, because if you start lying and making things up about yourself you then have to keep up the charade, which becomes harder and harder. As we all know, one lie becomes two, and two become four and then you find yourself lying to cover up the first few lies and on it goes until you eventually get found out. Then any pseudo respect from your colleagues that you have built on those lies suddenly disappears. What will they think of you then? A cunt probably! Also, how are you going to feel when, after developing a good working relationship with your team, they suddenly realise that perhaps you are not everything you have made yourself out to be? You will feel humiliated and they will feel betrayed.

I cannot even start to recall the number of complete twats I have found myself working with who boast and brag and come up with such complete crap about themselves it's actually embarrassing. I remember one female door supervisor at The Rectory in Wilmslow boasting on her first night that she had worked as a Russian interpreter in the army. She didn't know I spoke a bit of Russian (my wife is Russian and I lived in Moscow for a year), and when I asked her how she was in Russian she couldn't answer – she couldn't speak a word of the language! Needless to say, she didn't turn up for work the next day.

I admit that when I first started working the doors in the early eighties I was in awe of the people I would be working with. When I arrived at the Ritzy staff room on my very first night I was as nervous as fuck, and on looking around at some of the 'old school' doormen sitting there cursing and laughing with their colleagues I remember asking myself what the fuck I was doing there! They didn't even acknowledge my existence on the planet, let alone the fact that I would be working on their doors, and even before my first ever night I wondered whether this was the job for me after all. There were some big, hard fuckers and a lot of fuckers that didn't look that hard but still you wouldn't want to cross them. And then there was skinny, pimply me, in my early twenties, just wanting to do the doors over the summer for a laugh and to shag as many pretty women as I could. But even in my naivety and innocence I knew there and then not to try to make myself out to be someone I was not. Luckily, my mentor Robert (Bob) Etchells took me under his wing and showed me the ropes and the rest is history, so to speak!

So if you are new to the doors, talk honestly to your team: tell them you are a bit nervous; tell them you might make mistakes; tell them that you don't have much experience. Sure, there might be a few arrogant door supervisors that will take the piss and blank you, but I would like to believe that most will not; most will help you, guide you and mentor you and will not put you into any situations that at first you might not be able to handle. But don't ever tell them that you are some hard fucker and have done this and that and battled here and there, because if it isn't true then you will fall from grace pretty quickly and look a complete cunt. Like I have said, hard men never have to prove they are hard.

Richard Wood has been a doorman for about six years and has worked many places, including the King's Arms in Calne, O'Neill's and Reflex in Swindon, as head doorman at the Sir Daniel Arms in Swindon and on the front door at Revolution in Swindon. He firmly believes that working the doors has given him some great skills and life experience, and he offers some very good advice:

Getting respect from fellow door staff is a process that can start long before you ever step foot on a pub or club door. It will start the moment you approach the head doorman or security company for a job. You can bet that you will be judged on every facet of yourself: your build, presence, communication skills, and any of the other key skills that are necessary in this business. You will find that if you are ticking these boxes straight away your first night on the door with a new team will be a lot easier, because the head doorman or company will already have told the existing team about you; he can verify your credentials and, more importantly, sow the seeds of the most important tool in the doorman's arsenal, your reputation. A reputation can be earned without being particularly hard or fierce. I should know this more than most, as before starting my career on the door I had only been in a handful of fights in my life. Reputation can sometimes be carried solely on the pretence of being hard or handy in a fight. It is part of the mystique that surrounds the enigma that is the 'bouncer' and it can be earned and developed in many ways. Within weeks of starting a new door you should find your niche within the team and be able to form an effective and cohesive unit whether you are in a team of two or twenty. Loyalty to your team and the staff in your venue will be noticed and respect will be gained from them. This respect will be yours and stay with you up until you do something to lose it, so be warned!

A real veteran of the doors, Jim Myers, has been a door supervisor for over 22 years and started working the doors at Monroe's nightclub in Union Street, Plymouth, where he developed his reputation of being good at his job. He then worked the Quay club, Fanny's Wine Bar and the Conservatory Wine Bar. He also worked in Butler's in Exeter and then at Destiny and Elite up in Ellesmere Port, where, working with some real hard bastards, he learned a slightly 'different' way of working. Eventually he moved back to Exeter and joined Shadow Security Services, where he currently works as the operations manager, supplying door supervisors to pubs and clubs throughout the southwest of England. Jim has slightly more down to earth advice:

The only way to get respect from your fellow work colleagues is to keep your gob shut and not boast about previous battles. After years of working on the doors you get to hear loads of shit about the battles people have been in, and then learn two weeks later that the story has changed. I would also advise new door supervisors to meet and greet people nicely, as they are the first person that the customer sees, and of course to keep their gob firmly shut when it comes to cockiness and attitude. After working the doors for nearly 23 years, you do gain a reputation! I hope I have earned a good reputation for being fair and reasonable and a fucking good door supervisor. Anyone can be a jack the lad with attitude, but, when it comes to taking a load of shit on the door, door supervisors really are a breed all their own. And the only way to earn respect is to stand your ground when the shit hits the fan, fight tooth and nail if you have to, and back up your mates when you're needed even if you get a hiding! You must always back your work colleagues up to the end. Your reputation has to be earned and should never be taken for granted; and remember, you cannot gain a reputation overnight. Admittedly, sometimes it's extremely hard to show someone respect, especially if they are an utter knob, but I would like to say that at least I do genuinely try to treat everyone with respect. But there is definitely an invisible line you have to draw that they must not cross, and you have to treat it as a game. But it's a very one-sided game, as you must always be the winner!

After 19 years as one of Norfolk's best-known doormen, in November 2009 Karl Spooner retired from the doors and finally hung up his black suit and earpiece for the very last time. But, as he quickly pointed out, he has actually retired a few times before too! However, he hopes this is for good, as he has retrained and is now working as the general manager of the Mustard Lounge nightclub in Norwich, although he confesses, "It's always tempting when the shout comes over the radio to get involved, and I have to admit I have occasionally slipped back to the doorman's role a couple of times since being manager!"

Karl started working the doors when he was just 18 years old at The Highwayman nightclub in the sleepy village of Sheringham on the Norfolk coast, "which wasn't as sleepy as I had thought, especially at the weekends and especially in the summer, when

tourists flock from all over the UK to this little pearl of Norfolk."
When The Highwayman closed two years later, at only 20 years of age he then formed his own security company and ended up supplying a number of door staff to venues throughout the region:

In 1994 I started working with a team of around twelve others, five nights a week, at The Ritzy in Norwich and stayed there for a couple of years until the head doorman Carl moved to Rick's Place and asked me to join him, which I did. I ended up staying at Rick's Place for four years until, on the request of my girlfriend at the time, I retired (for the first time). But you know how it is: on a Friday and Saturday night, sitting bored in front of the telly with a cuppa, wishing you were standing with the boys again. So by the end of 1998 I was getting the black suit out of the wardrobe once again, this time to work for Steve Barber at Chicago's on Prince of Wales Road, Norwich. At that time the door team at Chicago's was legendary in Norfolk: Steve Barber, Barry Clarke, Paul Andrews, Lee Wilson, Paul Cordy, Neil Wyman, Martin Bell and, of course, myself – all known faces and well respected in the city. After another couple of years it was time for another break from the doors, but that didn't last long either and I was back working a trendy new bar called Orgasmic. Next was a short spell at Yates's and on to Devil's Advocate Lap Dancing Bar, which was by far the most visually interesting and entertaining venue to work at. And then just one night's work filling in at Ice Nightclub in Thetford turned into three and a half years!

Karl offers some excellent advice for door supervisors:

Because of how the industry is now and what door supervisors have to put up with from both customers and fellow door supervisors, for a good door supervisor respect and reputation mean everything. They are the basis of this particular sector of security and the basis of being a professional door supervisor; without either respect or a reputation you are nothing but a waste of time and space. I think it's harder to gain respect now, as you have to have many more attributes and skills than you needed 20-odd years ago. Back then respect was mainly all about how quick your fists were and how quickly you dealt with trouble, but now things are very different and respect now comes from being nice, being diplomatic, being understanding, being professional, knowing your job, understanding situations and dealing with them effectively and preferably without violence. There is still an element of respect in being the first one in and the last one out when it kicks off, but being respected as a door supervisor now means so much more, because there are so few respected door supervisors in the job now.

Masood Kamal, a doorman and professional bodyguard from London, is very philosophical in his views about respect:

For me, earning respect from fellow door colleagues and close protection operatives is considered important, vital and crucial. Respect is earned through giving respect and treating people and individuals how you would like to be treated yourself, not trying to portray yourself as a so-called 'hard man' in an attempt to strike fear into the hearts and minds of your fellow work colleagues by doing that you may well and truly be out of a job faster than you ever would have got into one.

Head doorman Will Bishop, who has his own fascinating chapter in this book, gives some great advice to door supervisors too: *As a head doorman I guess things are a little different for me, in that I have to lead from the front, so I need to command a greater degree of respect from both my colleagues and my customers. As a head doorman respect and reputation are the two things that keep you in your job and keep you in one piece. I know my guys would not work for me and back me up if there was any doubt in their mind that I might bottle it or stand back when they needed me.*

Dave Llewellyn is probably one of the only disabled doormen working the doors, so his is a very interesting perspective:

Basically I lost my arm at birth, so I have never known any different, but doing the doors you do come across very narrow-minded people! I've done martial arts and Thai boxing for about five years and I have been working the doors now for about a year. I do get a lot of people taking the piss and comments like "What's he gonna do with one arm?" or "There's no (h)arm in him!" and many times I am asked what the fuck a disabled person is doing working the doors, so for me trying to gain respect is even harder. But I'm slowly getting known and respected around the places where I work and many people are now respecting the fact that disabled people like me can do the same job as them. Now a lot of people know me as the cocky onearm doorman whom they don't wanna get on the wrong side of, so it's slowly getting there.

It must be tough for Dave having to put up with even more shit than is usual in this business, so respect to you, brother, for doing what you do and overcoming your hurdles to do a job you love.

Lloyd Smith wrote:

My dad always taught me to show everyone the same respect that I would like them to show me and I've found this really does work. After spending 25 years training and studying martial arts and a few years working on the doors, I know that acting hard has never got anyone a good reputation. The best thing is just staying calm and using common sense and this has served me better than being brutish. And even now, 20 years after I stopped working the doors, I still get remembered and greeted with a smile and a nod.

Scott Taylor first moved to Aberdeen when he was just 17 years old and got a job as a glass collector, but his sheer size proved a hindrance in this role, so after helping the doormen out one evening he became a door steward at the same venue. He worked there for a while and then moved to The Cotton Club, where he stayed for two and a half years before being offered a position at a rival venue called The Ministry of Sin. Later he became head doorman at The College Bar, where he worked for ten years before taking over as security manager at Soul, which became the most popular bar in the city. At the same time he continued to oversee security at The College Bar and at another venue called Babylon, and he has some valuable observations regarding the role of managers and the dangers of the job:

One of the biggest problems I've faced over the years has been bar and club managers sticking their necks into the middle of a conflict that I've spent a good deal of time calming down and getting under control. One wrong or heated word from the manager, who's suddenly being extra brave because he's standing behind three door supervisors, restokes the fire and the proverbial hits the fan. I've lost count of the times I've nearly had my head kicked in because the hundred pound 19-year-old spotty manager suddenly took a brave pill and let his mouth loose whilst cowering behind a wall of muscle. Employers need to trust that the men (and women) on the door are capable of dealing with conflicts themselves, and are able to carry out the policies of the bars without having to stand over our shoulders the whole evening and overruling us at every turn. A lot of these managers are young folk who started in the venue as barmen, and over a couple of years have clawed their way up into management. As much as they may be well trained in bar management, conflict management is a different area entirely and one that can get them into a lot of trouble! I'm a firm believer in avoiding or defusing conflict as much as I can, and my staff are of a similar mind-set. The popularity of our venue proves how well these measures work, yet there are always times when talking won't work; when the aggressor is too determined to fold your head inside out and no amount of sweet-talk will convince them otherwise. Sadly, despite the extra training we now receive and the extra level of legitimacy our profession now enjoys, we will at some point have to face and resolve a serious conflict that can put us at serious risk. I was lucky enough that in my first couple of years on the job I was guided along by some well experienced guys who took the time to show me the ropes and how to deal with situations that can swiftly spiral out of control. No amount of training can prepare you for the first time you face a riot in your venue, but guidance and support from those more time served lads can help you get through it and learn from it. Having said that, however, I'm still learning after nearly 17 years in the job! I've had a couple of experiences where I've had people trying to intimidate me because of the job, from other security agency bosses arriving at my venue threatening to take my knees out, to people attacking my home because of something as small as throwing them out of a bar. As much as you can say that these things don't upset you, it's something that nobody wants to happen to them, especially in their place of work. However, that's the nature of our job and why we have to grow bloody thick skins to compensate! Sadly, violence and intimidation are a large part of our jobs, and I know very few door supervisors who haven't suffered some form of injury through their years on the doors. Yet we pick ourselves up, dust ourselves off and pick yet another white shirt out the cupboard to replace the torn and bloodied one. The best way to eliminate the violence and intimidation we face on a weekly basis is to take out the common denominator from the equation: alcohol! But I think we all know that's probably never going to happen!

Steve Strudwick, now retired from the doors, started work in the early nineties for Luminar Leisure and got his first big gig at Utopia in Calcot. He then moved to his local town pub, "which turned out to be a bit of a mistake, because people that I thought were my friends actually turned out to be freeloaders; wanting free entry, free tickets and to jump the queue. It can sometimes be a big mistake working the doors in your local town." (as many doormen would say it is not always the case!) Unfortunately, Steve's reputation as being a little too heavy-handed got the better of him and he was eventually told by the police that it would be in his best interest to work elsewhere. He then moved to a little club called Charlie's in Newbury and worked at Chicago's for a while as well,

… where we probably had the best door team in Berkshire at the time; fair, but we didn't take any crap. But this was to mark my eventual demise, as one night I had an altercation with a very aggressive pisshead, who ended up in a coma. He got a hefty out of court settlement and I got told by the CID to get another job! So I eventually hung up my badge in 2002. We still all talk about the good old days when you could get away with almost anything, and I remember when I was shown around my first club the head doorman said to me, "I have a very strong team and if anyone gets hurt because someone wasn't doing their job then they will get served up." I think back to those days when the doors were run on fear rather than respect. Over the years doormen's attitudes have definitely changed and now female door supervisors work most doors, something not heard of in the '90s. Back then, every door team I worked with had the attitude of hit first and hard and ask questions later; sort of, if they don't move then they can't do you any harm! The longer you work at a club or pub the better the regulars get to know you and what you are about. Most customers just wanted a good time and to feel safe, but there were others that just wanted a piece of you. I definitely think that to a certain degree if you give respect to someone then you deserve to get respect back, but there are a certain element of scum out there that see respect as a sign of weakness and they look weak in front of their mates if

they show a doorman respect. So you do have to tread a very thin line sometimes and be very careful. It takes a certain type of person to be a really professional doorman or doorwoman. I've worked with some hard looking big lumps that have hearts the size of peas and average looking, average size door supervisors with hearts like lions.... To be honest though, I'm glad I'm out of the job now. When I look around the clubs and pubs in my area I feel sorry for the security. It's a tough job now, and one false move could mean you are suspended pending prosecution. This is why the world is in such a mess no respect anymore.

It is evident, based on the feedback from all the people I have spoken to and from all those who have contributed to this book, that respect for door supervisors is crucial and means absolutely everything. Many, many times throughout my career as a doorman I have worked alongside team members that are both cowards and cunts who, instead of backing me up in tough situations, have hidden or run off; the very same people that I have laughed with, drunk with and made friends with. One so-called hard, tough giant of a doorman I worked with in Standish hid in the gents' toilets while the mightiest of all rucks was going off inside. To this day I am at a complete loss as to what must have been going through his tiny mind while he was sitting on the crapper as we fought outside the toilet door. There are many door staff like this in many venues around the UK, and sadly it seems that the number has grown. As Karl Spooner rightly said, because there are so few respected door supervisors in the job now, respect is even more important to professional door supervisors.

I have always believed that a door team should also become really good friends, because for good friends you will always go that extra mile. You might think twice about breaking up a fight between two strangers, but you won't think twice about helping out if you recognise someone involved as a friend, and I believe it should be exactly like this on the doors. You respect your friends, so therefore you should respect your team. Without respect for your team you're on your own, and being on your own on the doors can be very dangerous.

What Reputation Means for Door Supervisors

By Robin Barratt & others

I have worked the doors for almost 20 years, sometimes as a full-time occupation, working continuously five or six nights a week, week in and week out, year in and year out; at other times it was part-time in between close protection assignments and running security training courses for the former Worldwide Federation of Bodyguards (WFB), until 2000 when the WFB was sold to an Icelandic subsidiary of Securitas (and eventually closed). The good thing about door work was that I could take time off as and when I needed and at relatively short notice to pursue my career in close protection, and because close protection was never really a full-time occupation I always had the doors to fall back on.

As a doorman I have worked alongside naïve, newly trained novices as well as some of the hardest fucks on the planet. Although I have not always succeeded, I have tried to make a real effort to respect almost everyone that I have had the fortune (and, in some cases, misfortune) to work with until, of course, that respect is betrayed. Sometimes that respect is lost the first time a doorman opens his mouth and at other times it is never lost.

I think, or hope, that I have commanded a degree of respect in return. And I also believe that over the years I have developed a good reputation as a professional and fair doorman.

As we have heard from both experienced and inexperienced doormen, the real key to obtaining respect is showing respect to others first. Someone (who will remain anonymous) once said to me that he would only ever respect other people if they respected him first, but it seems that most others believe this to be a seriously flawed argument and fundamentally wrong, as it is undeniably the start of a never-ending downward spiral; i.e., if you don't get respected you don't give respect, and because you don't give respect you don't get respected, and on and on it goes. As Mick Lyons rightly said, it's the bigger man that gives respect instead of expecting it to be shown first.

A doorman friend of mine once told me about a very difficult time of his life when everything seemed to be going wrong. He split from his wife, he lost his job and couldn't pay the mortgage, and he even had a car accident! Understandably, because of his problems he had a bad attitude to everyone around him, but also because he had a bad attitude things kept going wrong! He told me that as soon as he started to smile and treat people nicely, things started to change. He is now doing very well, and he said that the turnaround was due solely to his change in attitude.

On the doors, and in life, if you treat everyone as though they are cunts and you are rude, obnoxious and arrogant towards people and generally have a bad attitude, it is almost certain that you will get exactly the same back, and this point is highlighted extensively throughout this book. And, of course, the opposite is also very true: if you are polite, friendly and sympathetic, it is almost certain that you will also get the same in return. Sure, there will be a few times when this doesn't happen, but generally, as the saying goes, you reap what you sow. Respect is all about sowing good thoughts, so always try to sow good thoughts and you will almost always get good thoughts in return. Remember this, both on the doors and in life generally, and you won't go wrong.

And what about your reputation as a doorman or doorwoman? And what does having a reputation mean for door supervisors?

How good you are as a door supervisor is not about the number of people you have floored; well, not anymore anyway! Neither is it about what you say or how you brag, as we have heard time and time again. Building your reputation entirely depends on what you do, on your position and role, and how you treat others around you. How many times have we seen a bully or an intimidator and thought, what a complete cunt? We may know about their reputation as a hard man or fighter, but we certainly don't respect them for it; in fact, it is very much the opposite. It's no good having an awesome reputation if nobody respects you.

As I have said, always remember that reputation must always go hand in hand with respect and you cannot have one without the other. And also remember, nice venues don't employ hard men that have a reputation but little respect.

Even in the fairly provincial town of Norwich, there are still a few 'old school' doormen who are known and recognised as real bullies. They are undoubtedly hard men and can fight a good fight, but nobody really likes them and they find it hard to get work. Even after many years on the doors and having proved their fighting ability time and time again, they still feel the need to intimidate, bully and take the piss out of other less experienced door supervisors or those weaker than themselves. Even in the gym they strut around, loudmouthed and with attitude and arrogance, bullying their way onto equipment and snarling at others in their way. These people certainly have a fearsome reputation and no one really wants to cross them, but they definitely have little or no respect. And I am sure that there are many people exactly like this in almost every town and city across the UK; hard men that still feel the need to prove they are hard men. In this day and age of licensing and litigation, most venue managers are wary of these people and are reluctant to employ them; no manager wants a bully on his door.

Apart from my initial job application for the Ritzy nightclub back in the early eighties, I have never applied for any other advertised door supervisor's position, whether at a bikers' bar or gangland club. I have either been asked, referred or recommended by someone in the industry. Once you eventually prove yourself as a 'professional' you will be asked to work anywhere and with any team, without ever having to apply for positions, fill out long-winded application forms or have tedious interviews with HR managers who are generally a lot less experienced and infinitely less reputed than you are. However, if you have a bad reputation it will be hard to find work and, if you have a reputation of being a hard man but have little respect, the work that you do manage to find will generally be in shitty venues with shitty customers and a shitty manager who has little respect for you or your customers.

Is this what you want? If you do want to work on the doors at these venues for the rest of your career, then great, good luck to you, but I think most people don't.

I am going to say it again, and not for the last time: real hard men never have the need to prove it.

Certainly being asked to 'clean up' a venue is very different today than it was back in the eighties and nineties when we could sort out a venue with relative impunity, using whatever methods were necessary in accordance with the manager's requirements. Most club managers actively looked for a tough team, especially if the venue needed a lot of work, and back then managers really did expect you to do the business. A venue was only safe if you could fight hard, and proving yourself as a doorman (there were very few doorwomen in the job at that time) generally meant having to prove yourself with your fists on the ground in a fight too. A doorman who couldn't (or wouldn't) fight was simply not a good doorman. Looking back at all the teams I have worked with in all the different venues, almost everyone was a good fighter with very few exceptions. Back then a doorman would not survive in the business for long if he couldn't fight and there was simply no place in a door team for those who wouldn't. The violent environment, the management or other members of his door team would quickly force him out.

Now, of course, it is a totally different story. On most doors these days a real fighter is probably a bit of a rarity and is someone you would unchain in a real emergency, so working on the doors now really is an entirely different job with an entirely different crew. However, I still believe that gaining a reputation for being a professional door supervisor remains more or less the same. At the end of the day, when the shit really does hit the fan and violence erupts, I believe (and an awful lot of people would contradict me on this fact) that a good doorman also needs to be able to mix it when needed. A good doorman should be able to stand proud alongside his team when the going gets really tough and until the bitter end, if necessary. No exceptions.

If you are working the door but can't mix it, then you are not only putting yourself in danger, you are also putting the rest of your team, your customers and your staff at risk. And I think that the fact that many door supervisors now really have no idea how to handle themselves is one key reason why there is so little respect on the doors anymore and why there are so very few really professional doormen with reputations. These days it seems that a doorman who can't scrap, or won't scrap, either runs or hides and leaves their so-called friends and colleagues in the shit. Again, you don't have to be the best fighter in the world, but you do have to be loyal and trustworthy and never give up. Sadly, with the demise of the fighter, it seems that loyalty on the doors has all but disappeared as well.

Once again, Mick Lyons says a few words about this subject, and, although controversial, I believe they are absolutely true:

To get respect from fellow doormen you must obviously head from the front in all aspects of the job. From fronting aggressive gangs or individuals with reputations, you must always show that you are in charge of the situation, even if at times the odds may be stacked against you. You must lead by reading problems before they start, being proactive instead of reactive. Let them see that you can defuse altercations with a few well-chosen words rather than wait for the wheels to fall off the bus. You should also lead by being levelheaded and cool, as well as courteous and friendly, which in turn gives a feeling of confidence in your ability to handle the situation, no matter how heated the problem becomes. This should then run parallel with the respect you show in life in general, by being humble, polite and fair and being the same person all of the time, treading steady and strong. Not everyone is strong and can stand their ground; the physically weak need somebody to look out for them and to shield them from potential bullies, and for a good doorman spotting these potential problems can save untold embarrassment to people. A good doorman should protect the weak, not just on the doors but in all walks of life, and when you do this the rewards are great and those people never forget the favours, and the stories about you, your reputation and the respect you have for others are passed on in a positive manner. When working the doors I have never ever taken a backward step because I knew that if I did the problem would be twice as big the day after, and that the gossip would be both exaggerated and demeaning to myself, my fellow door staff and the club or venue. A professional doorman stands his ground, always, and never backs down. You can have a good reputation, a bad reputation or just a reputation! But remember, if you have developed a reputation through doing either good or bad things, after a while your reputation can actually become a burden. And one thing's for sure, it can either last a lifetime or be crushed in an instant, so think very carefully before you decide which one you choose. I tell all new door staff to treat people respectfully and fairly, and in that way you build a reputation by proper values and behaviour. Of course, being a hard man or tough is useful for being a doorman, as it is beneficial in some hard venues, but only if those qualities are used correctly and are not used to take advantage of anyone. But they are not the beginning and end of it all. You can build a reputation without being a hard man but by being proper, caring, sensible, using dialect, putting people at ease – all can be beneficial in building your reputation without being hard or tough.

And these words come from undeniably one of the hardest men in England and should be taken on board, whether you work the doors or not!

Colin West shares the same viewpoint:

You can certainly have a reputation without being a hard man. I have never considered myself a hard man. I'm a big guy, I've dabbled with martial arts and I'm under no illusion that anyone of any size could take me down at any time, but I believe I have a good reputation amongst my peers, which I believe is gained from being a good leader and leading from the front, never asking anyone to do anything I wouldn't do myself and never ever backing down. I would rather die fighting than live as a coward knowing a colleague had got hurt, or worse, because I had 'bottled it'.

Both Ben Elliot and Becci Maple are of the same opinion regarding building a reputation:

Having a reputation really means to be known among your peers to do a good job or to be ready to go down if needed. Knowing when to fight and when not to is a skill in itself, and if you make the right choices it can also help develop your reputation. You can have a reputation without being a hard man or a nutter. You should have respect for everyone unless you have reason not to, or they have given you reason not to.

Chris Houghton, who has been doing the doors for over 12 years, says:

I learned the 'old school' way of being a doorman and it has kept me safe even to this day. I still use 'old school' rules if and when I need to, but I will always try to talk someone down if I can. But these days people are so drunk that it doesn't always work and so I've had to 'sleep' people out and in some cases when really pushed I've had to use force, but as long as me and my crew are safe I don't care; its certainly not my first choice, but if I really have to beat someone up to stop them causing trouble, then I am afraid I will. The problem today is that troublemakers and drunks know that door supervisors can't do anything too much to them, unlike in the 'old school' days when they got taken around the corner and given a good hiding and taught a good lesson. This is where the respect for door supervisors and for other customers has gone wrong, because troublemakers and drunks know they can get away with doing whatever they want.

Like a great many people I have spoken to, Chris believes that respect towards doormen and women went out of the window when the SIA licence was brought in:

They charge you through the teeth for the course and £245.00 for a licence and then they tell you that you can't do this and you can't do that. By the way, told to you by people who have never had to work on the frontline of a club, pub or event and who have never dealt with people fuelled with booze or drugs or giving you shit and verbal abuse. Standing there takes balls and guts and I have every bit of respect for all door supervisors, whether good or bad.

I agree with Chris. In practically no other job in the world do you have to stand there and take verbal abuse, be spat at and be threatened and humiliated. If I walked into a clothes shop, spat at the assistant, called her a fat bastard and a cunt, and said let's go outside for a scrap, I would be arrested immediately and probably fined, if not imprisoned. Everywhere you go now there are signs saying that verbal abuse towards staff will not be tolerated in post offices, banks, hospitals, doctor's surgeries, etc., but not on the doors to nightclubs and bars! And yet this happens every single night to door staff around the UK. Somehow this is considered acceptable and nothing is ever done, and if a door supervisor gets to the point of 'enough is enough' and does something about it, he or she loses their job straight away. Is this fair? Of course not.

Again, to reiterate, I do not agree with violence. However, back in the eighties and nineties calling a doorman a cunt and spitting in his face led to some very serious consequences, which generally meant you limped for a while and never wanted to do it again! But now you can do it to almost any door supervisor anywhere, whenever you want, and nothing is ever done. Is this right? Of course not.

I would like every door supervisor reading this to demand that a sign be put on the main door of their venue stating that verbal or physical abuse of any member of staff will not be tolerated. I don't mean a paper one that cannot be seen, but a proper professionally made sign on the outside of the front door that every member of the public can read. Do it now, please, and let's start to change the tide of disrespect towards door supervisors.

Finding the Right Training Course

By Robin Barratt

Many of you reading this book will have completed your SIA door supervisors compulsory training already and might be either working the doors or waiting for your badge. But for those of you who are considering becoming a door supervisor and who have not yet undergone any training, please read and follow this guide carefully.

It is vitally important for you to train with the right people, and I believe that many SIA approved door supervisor training courses teach extremely dangerous practices and are actually putting door supervisors and customers at real risk. Undoubtedly, some door supervisor training courses are excellent, but others are simply appalling. Some trainers have firsthand experience, having spent many years actually working in the industry, but some other trainers are textbook only, having never once stood on a nightclub door or worked with a team of door staff. This is an absolute fact.

What I say in this chapter should have been said years ago when the SIA was being established, and my goal here is to highlight the dangerous flaws in some training courses. In commercialising door supervisor training, the government and the SIA have legitimised training companies that operate purely for financial reasons and are run by people who have never set foot on a door and have no idea about the job or the industry. This chapter is controversial and is bound to piss many established training organisations off, but do I give a toss?

Regardless of background or experience, it is a sad fact that almost anyone can now teach door supervisors. Trainers just need a teaching certificate and no experience of the actual job! So finding the right training course is a vitally important first step in your career on the doors as a professional door supervisor. If you are not interested in being professional, then firstly you should not be reading this book, and secondly, again, fuck off.

In this alcohol fuelled, volatile industry, working on the doors can be extremely hard work and often dangerous, and in such an environment you could easily find yourself in violent and intimidating situations. Train with the right company and the right instructors and you will benefit from their experience and knowledge in dealing with and countering these kinds of difficult situations. Train with the wrong company or instructors and you could be putting both yourself and your customers at great risk.

One of the first things you should do is check out the company and their background. Apart from SIA accreditation, what other professional accreditations do they have? Are they a known training provider? We have discussed respect and reputation, so are they respected as a door training company (not a general training company) and do they have a reputation of training professional door staff (not scrotes and scumbags fresh from the dole)? They may be handy because they are based in your local town or village, but if they haven't got a good reputation then don't train with them. Be a professional and choose your training provider wisely.

Once you have chosen the company, then look at the instructors. Are they experienced? There is a huge difference between those instructing from a textbook and those instructing from actual experience on the doors. How can someone who has never worked the doors instruct you on how to work the doors? It's impossible! How can someone who has never set foot in a nightclub tell you how to work in one? How can anyone instruct you in how to deal with a crowd of unruly knobs whose only intention is to cause you or your customers hassle and harm if they have never once been in this situation? Sadly, there are many, many courses (with many colleges or generic training companies) where the instructors are perhaps highly qualified and experienced teachers but have never actually worked in the industry, and I strongly suggest that you leave these courses well alone. Make sure that your instructors have real world, on the doors experience; anything less could prove dangerous (but not according to the SIA!) So before you hand over even one penny, ask your course provider what experience the instructors have and their background. If they refuse to answer (and many will), evade the question or don't give you the answer you would like to hear, think twice about learning with them. It may get you your badge, but do you really want to put yourself in violent and difficult situations that you are not equipped to handle?

As well as experience, make sure that your instructors are suitably qualified to teach as well. Again, it's great having experience, but if the instructor is crap his experience will be useless. In the UK all instructors need to have a recognised teaching qualification, and full details of the ones accepted by the SIA can be found on their website. Some training providers will have a number of instructors, but not all of them will have the approved teaching qualifications. Do not sign up for a course where the instructors are unqualified. Check this out before you pay your fee.

It is a legal requirement to give everyone a cooling-off period once a deposit is paid or a contract is signed, so make sure that you visit the training school and meet the directors and instructors within seven days of taking this initial action. You wouldn't commit to buying a car and handing over the full amount without seeing it first, so don't do it with your training. If you are at all unhappy, taking into account the guidelines above, then ask for your deposit back and find somewhere else to train. They are legally obliged to return it to you and, if they refuse, threaten to take them to a small claims court. Your future career is at stake here, so taking a half day off and losing a few quid in petrol is much better than wasting your time and money on an unsatisfactory course that could put you at risk.

Also, ask the training facility for both trade and student references. Would you employ someone if they can't or won't give you a reference? Of course not! All good training courses should be able to provide these references and if they cannot, or will not, do not train with them, simple. You can also ask around on website forums or go and speak to actual door supervisors to see what training companies they would recommend. There will be lots of suggestions and a few companies will eventually stand out.

When training for any trade or profession, very few people worth their salt will actually opt for the cheapest and easiest way in, and I would like to think that most people reading this book will search for the best training available with the most recognised course provider, even if it does cost an extra few quid. As the saying goes, you pay for what you get. If you pay peanuts for a door supervisors training course it is almost certain that you will get monkeys to teach you, as professional, experienced and well qualified instructors will never charge peanuts for their skills. Would you? It is far better to have a qualification from the most prestigious college than from a two bit college that no one has ever heard of. And as a door supervisor it is important to be excellent too, both for your safety and the safety of the people you have been asked to look after. To be a professional door supervisor and to do the best job that you can possibly do, your training must be the best too. It must be relevant and specific to the actual job of working the door, as well as excellent in terms of delivery, content and structure. So take your time and choose the right course carefully.

That said, unfortunately there always will be scumbags who are not really interested in being professional and just want the cheapest and quickest route into the industry. These are what you call in the profession 'muppets' and 'jacket fillers'. It is also a sad fact that almost anyone can attend and pass the door supervisors training course, obtain a licence and work as a door supervisor. All you need is a criminal record check, and the exam grade is so low that it is virtually impossible not to pass! Whilst this might be great for the individual who wants a quick and cheap way onto the doors, this has led to a huge number of door staff in a job for which they are unprepared and inadequately trained, thus again putting themselves and their customers at risk. Don't be one of those people!

Also, get yourself physically and mentally prepared for both the course and then for the job. The course is not physically demanding and even a fat, unhealthy, unfit slob can easily attend the course and pass, but the job itself is demanding and can be fairly physical, so get prepared for it. Tens of thousands of people obtain their SIA licence without ever having gone to a gym and without a single shred of control and restraint or self-defense training. At the time of writing this book, self-defense, control and restraint are still not requirements for an SIA door supervisors' course, even though you are almost guaranteed to encounter violence and intimidation within your first few days on the door. Would you want to employ someone on your doors if they were overweight, unfit and unable to defend themselves or their customers in an emergency? No. So then why would you expect someone to employ you? When faced with violence and intimidation, do you have the real skills to deal with them? Saying, "Yeah, I can handle myself," is not enough, and I have seen many door staff injured because they've had the arrogance to say this without the necessary skills. If you're going to be a professional and develop your reputation you must keep yourself fit and work out and go to regular weekly classes in some form of close quarter, unarmed combat. Personally, I believe that this is absolutely fundamental for the job, because there will be times when talking down situations simply will not work and then what? Stand back, call the police, watch it kicking off and wait till they arrive?

Hands up all those door supervisors reading this who consider themselves professional but still do not have any skills in terms of dealing with a medical emergency, or who have never been to a gym or dojo?

I also believe that all door supervisors, especially head door supervisors, should be First Aid at Work trained as well. It costs a couple of hundred quid at the most to take your qualification (although in many cases it is discounted or free) and four or five nights of your time, but as a professional this is essential. Every single time that someone in your club gets injured it will be the door staff that will be called on for help. Can you really look these people in the eye and say, "Sorry, mate, can't do anything for you"? Get properly trained for the job!

Over the years I have seen a great many door staff injured and maimed and have heard of a few door supervisors even losing their lives simply because they had little/no experience or training in dealing with extremely difficult and violent situations. For example, early in 2009 a 21-year-old doorman was stabbed to death in a 'respect' row after he refused to allow a group of revellers into a nightclub. Mohamed Kaleem Rafeek from Old Trafford, Manchester, was subjected to a frenzied attack in Rusholme, another suburb of Manchester. Known to friends as Kaleem, he had been working on the door at the Mansion nightclub in Manchester city centre and had told colleagues that he had encountered trouble earlier in the evening when he refused to admit a group into the venue. When he finished work, along with another doorman from another nightclub, Kaleem went to Rusholme for a curry and they both came under a frenzied knife attack by the same gang, comprising up to eight men. Kaleem was found bleeding heavily on the ground and he died at the scene. His friend, just 22 years old, was also stabbed repeatedly. A senior police officer said, "It looks like some sort of respect issue. He out muscled somebody on the door. They came off worse and they weren't prepared to let it lie."

Kaleem stood up to the gang and now he is dead. Get the best training possible right from the start, and then train, train, train. Become a real professional.

A Few Tips on Good Door Supervision

By Jamie O'Keefe

In between Stimulus and Response, Action and Reaction, is space. Within this space you have the power to choose your reaction. Use this space wisely and become a good Door Supervisor.

Jamie O'Keefe

Defusing Situations

To use an analogy: defuse a bomb and you save a lot of damage from being done. Defusing a situation will prevent the chain of events escalating into something more ugly; also it will give a positive professional image of security.

In a club scenario where two individuals or groups have a grievance with each other, it's like a bomb waiting to go off. You must separate them before you even enter into discussion, so that you can deal with them individually. It is your job as security to prevent the people on your premises from committing a crime, and you must remember that you are not acting as judge and jury. You must manage, defuse and control incidents of abusive and aggressive behaviour, minimising the threat to the safety of other customers, members of staff and security.

Aggressive and abusive behaviour can come in the form of threats, verbal or physical abuse, or a physically aggressive attack. If a situation has developed and you try to sort it out there and then with both parties present, it will escalate in no time at all to a level that could have been avoided. Haven't you ever seen how the police separate and divide parties that have a grievance with each other? This way you can get each individual's story of what has happened, without the other party interfering and kicking off. If you work together with other security staff, you should be able to put this into operation quite professionally and without appearing to take either party's side. If you are unfortunate enough or stupid enough to work on your own, as I have done many times when necessity and stupidity have become one, you will have to take just one of the parties aside. Make sure that they are out of range of the other aggrieved group and try to sort things out that way. I can honestly say that I have never failed to resolve a situation when I have separated groups or individuals in this way.

Most people who have a grievance just want you to listen to them in the hope that you will be swayed by their side of the story. If you do not use this 'separation' system to defuse a situation, an explosion of aggression that could have been avoided will likely ensue. I ended up looking like a bruised apple at one club because my co-doorman preferred to deal with a situation on the spot as though he were some sort of hands-on agony aunt. He wrongly assumed the role of judge and jury and took the side of one group while the other aggrieved party was present, resulting in it kicking off. The group who realised that they did not have the support of the doorman had nothing to lose. They knew that they were going to be asked to leave, so they decided to go out in style. They kicked off with this doorman, leaving me no choice but to go in and pull him out. His life meant more to me than the cuts and bruises I suffered as a result, but all this could have been avoided by defusing the situation, as outlined earlier, before it escalated.

On a lighter note, I must have forgotten to wear my Black Belt that day or maybe they weren't aware of my grades (ha!) because they weren't the slightest bit intimidated by us. Still, fifteen against two doesn't quite balance out, does it? Where possible, always respond to abusive and aggressive behaviour in a nonthreatening way, keeping your speech and manner restrained to a level that will reduce the likelihood of the situation escalating. If you do see a situation escalating, seek assistance from another door supervisor. Not only will this action minimise the risk to others, but also it will provide you with a witness should things go further than expected.

Finding a Good Team

Finding a good team is like finding a good soulmate. I've been doing security in all shapes and forms for a large part of the last fifteen years and yet only for five years of that time was I with a good team. Circumstances forced us to disband as a team a few years ago, and I have never been able to recreate that ideal combination again.

In sport, managers are responsible for finding and selecting good individuals for the purpose of combining them to make a good team. However, in security things don't quite work like that. You get sent to a venue and have to work with whomever you end up with that night. Apart from my old team, I have only ever come across one or two other security guys worth their salt as security. By that I do not mean one or two who could have a good fight, because I know loads that can, I simply mean being good at the job of security. If you cannot find or become part of a good team, you will have to try to form your own team by getting together with other good guys whom you have come to trust, one by one, weeding out any idiots in the process.

My own particular method was to work to a very high standard and do my utmost to be as professional as possible. This would always make the workshy, lazy types and the amateurs stick out like a sore thumb. I would set a standard to which others would have to adhere and would never drop my standard to fit in with anyone else. I always felt happy with myself, knowing that the customers, staff, and my fellow doormen felt more at ease when I was on the premises taking care of business. It might sound as if I'm blowing my own trumpet a little, but believe me, my attitude is no different from any Premier League footballer playing alongside fourth division players. They would not lower their standards, but rather would try to encourage the others to raise their standards so that the whole team could put on a more professional show and achieve better results.

I would always communicate with other security and staff when working. This would ensure that all staff, security and customers were aware of any risk. In turn, this would reduce any risk to security whilst promoting a good, positive image for doormen everywhere. Have a think about how others would expect doormen to be in terms of professionalism and make sure that you meet this standard as a minimum, and also make sure that you are performing to the standards you expect from other doormen. Set a standard that is above every other doorman that you have come across and then you will be halfway to creating your own effective and professional team.

Getting a Game Plan Together

"I love it when a plan comes together," said Kev, after we had successfully secured tens of thousands of pounds in cash against the threat of at least two gangs that we knew were plotting to rob the venue. Getting a game plan together is very important no matter at what level of security you are operating.

When I worked with my old team for those five years, we would sit up all night working out fail-safe plans, routes, decoys and backups, etc., trying to cover every eventuality that we could think of in order to take proper care of the contract or job we would be taking on, however big or small; even a door job at a tent gig in the middle of the woods or similar. This way we were prepared for any drama that might rear its ugly head. Any security guy without a game plan that just turns up for work, hoping to deal with serious events on the spot if and when they occur, is just a joke. Imagine if you were a customer facing being glassed or having a heart attack or caught up in a fire, bomb scare or gang fight, etc., and you had to rely on the club's security to take care of business and your safety and they had no game plan. Pretty grim, eh? Your game plan will differ from venue to venue, according to the layout of the premises, the amount of security in place, the type of event, etc., and to put together an effective game plan you will need the full cooperation of every team member. If you find that they are not interested or are just a waste of space, get your own game plan together. Here are some points to get your brain ticking in terms of what potential situations a game plan might need to cover:

- There is a fire.
- A customer gets glassed.
- Controlled drugs are found on a customer.
- A sexual assault has been committed.
- A knife is pulled on you.
- A suspect bomb package is found.
- A customer has an epileptic fit.
- An aggressive encounter kicks off between two individuals or two groups.
- A robbery takes place in the office.
- A customer refuses to be searched.
- A customer asks for your details.
- A thief takes a purse from a customer's bag.
- A guy sprinkles something into a girl's drink when she goes to the toilet.
- You are challenged to a fight – one to one.
- You are offered money to throw someone out.
- The manager tells you to take a customer outside and beat him up.
- Known criminals, troublemakers, or banned people arrive at the venue.
- Status/Profile/Authority

In what other circumstances can you get a job without many qualifications, with limited reading or writing skills and with poor communication skills and yet get power and control over hundreds of people each night? Becoming a doorman gives you all this and more: the power and authority over customers; the ability to refuse entry; the authority to eject people from the premises; the power to demand a certain type of behaviour from customers; and so much more. Door supervisors have status in their own little world, a kind of respect that they could not get elsewhere. Many would not last five minutes in quality positions working for the police force, the fire brigade, the army and the like, because to make the grade for any of these positions you need to put in time and effort with a lot of studying and learning. So what could be more attractive than to become a doorman? With just a short, basic training course you can just walk into the job and instantly gain power and authority. It is in regard to this area that many doormen lose my respect, as they become bullies with a badge. I hate bullies in all walks of life, but none more so than those that abuse their position of trust. I have always considered myself to be one of the good guys and would never stand by and watch another doorman physically victimise a customer. There is no need for it. Maybe it's 'being in charge' that makes the job so appealing to these people, and that's fine if that status isn't abused. If you really do want to be a doorman a proud doorman rather than a bully with a badge try to contribute a little more to the profession than simply, "if your name's not on the list, you're not coming in."

Communication Skills

Even today's doormen are not exactly renowned for their communication skills and could do with a little help in order to improve in this regard. If you go through life communicating with others just on one level, that being the only one you know, you will discover that some people find you hard to understand or boring to talk to, or they will see you as stupid, ignorant and uneducated. On the door, it can make life much easier if you try to communicate with the customers at a level that they can understand. This equates to creating a type of alliance between yourself and the customer. Also, if you are polite and courteous with customers, you will be doing justice to your company, club, and all other doormen. Many customers like to think and feel that they are friends with the doorman. It creates a comfort zone in which they feel they have a personal guardian angel that they can call on if they need assistance. Customers are far more at ease when they can communicate with a door supervisor who operates with sympathy, sincerity, impartiality, understanding and confidence. A nice personality helps too.

One golden rule I have is never to discuss sport, politics or religion with customers. This avoids many potential problems. Also, don't make the mistake of thinking that you should lower your level of conversation and communication, as a parent does when speaking to a child. It may be that you need to raise the level of your listening, talking and understanding skills. One thing that I have learned through life is that your ears and eyes can save you from a lot of trouble, as opposed to your mouth, which can get you into a whole heap of trouble if you use it unwisely. So use your ears and listen to people. Imagine that you are holding a conversation over a walkie-talkie, where you can't talk over the other person but have to listen and wait until they stop talking before you speak. I think patience is the name of the game here. If you listen carefully to someone, you will be able to understand much more easily exactly what they are trying to put across. Although their problem may seem trivial or mundane to you, the fact that they have chosen to share it with security means that it is obviously a big problem to them. Talking over someone without listening to what they are trying to say is not communicating. The message you are giving is negative and dismissive: I'm not bothered about what you have to say; it has no importance to me. That approach will not get you anywhere. Have a little patience and understanding, try not to butt in or appear disinterested, and try to be attentive, respectful and genuine. It is not always easy to deal with people's emotions, which may include guilt, uncertainty, embarrassment, anxiety, hostility, distrust, resentment, nervousness, etc., especially when mixed with a little alcohol and peer pressure.

Something that stops many doormen communicating effectively is their ego that tough guy, macho thing. I don't subscribe to that world, so I found it quite easy to communicate with people. I would never take it personally if a customer said something a little out of line, so long as they didn't stray too far over that line to the point that the intent behind it became impossible to overlook. If a customer unknowingly puts themselves, the staff or security at risk due to the way they are conducting themselves, explain to them in a clear, calm and understanding manner what they are doing wrong. Don't just jump to a conclusion and act irresponsibly that's ignorance, not professionalism.

A good measure of success is when a customer says, "Thank you."

Be The Best You Can Be

By Robin Barratt

Are you content being just Mr or Mrs Average (average meaning typical, common or ordinary; for example, 'the average door supervisor couldn't handle such a nightclub'), or do you pride yourself on your appearance and on the work you do? Do you care about your door team, the management, the staff and the customers? Are you genuinely interested in keeping those around you safe? Can you honestly hold your head up high and say to yourself, "I'm bloody good at what I do"? Do you want other door supervisors to look up to you, to hold you in high regard and to respect you? Do you care what others think? Is it important for you to be excellent? Is it important for you to be professional?

If you answered 'yes' to those questions then you have true self-respect and I applaud you for it. Without self-respect you are nothing, a nobody, a muppet.

These are just a few key questions you have to ask yourself, not just at the start of your career on the doors but all the time, each and every night you put on your jacket, clip on your badge and set off for work. From carpenters to lawyers, everyone should want to excel at what they do, at their trade or job. I don't hear carpenters say that they are average, second-rate or mediocre and bumble through their job hour by hour, day by day. Nor do I hear lawyers say, "Yes, I am a lawyer. Hire me, but I'm not very good." I believe that almost everyone wants recognition, credit and respect for what they do from their peers, their colleagues and, of course, from their employers. Almost everyone wants to be seen to be the best no one wants to be Mr (or Mrs) Average. Do you?

I have worked on a great many doors at a whole range of venues across the UK, from the fairly provincial Norwich in

Norfolk, where I started my career, to the city of London, where I had my own small security company and employed some of the biggest and hardest fuckers imaginable. I have worked on the door in the rough and tumble mining communities of Mansfield in Nottinghamshire and Standish in Lancashire where fights are part of a good evening out (for girls as well!), and on a number of different doors in Greater Manchester, where I came across more gangsters, gangs and wannabes than I ever thought possible. And over the years and along the way I have met some really excellent door supervisors: ones that I have admired and respected; ones that are professional and that I have most certainly looked up to and learned from. Years after working with them, some have remained my friends and I have maintained contact with many.

Sadly, the opposite is also very true, in that I have met many bad, ineffectual, unprofessional door supervisors; ones that I wouldn't waste my spit on; ones that are arrogant, that are bullies, and that display contempt for those around them. I have also met door supervisors that are clearly not capable of looking after themselves, let alone providing security services to the general public in a licensed venue, and that should definitely be in another profession.

Recently, via Facebook a friend sent me a few reviews that he had read online about some of Norwich's nightclubs and their security. I have edited out the bits that are not really relevant to this book, but the following excerpts provide a really good example of what customers actually see when they visit certain clubs or pubs:

Optic

Optic is the nicest club in Norwich. It ticks all the boxes and I don't mind paying for that, but the big old boy we had (on the front doors) took his work a little too seriously and although I appreciate they're there to do a job, a little customer service wouldn't go amiss, but once past the gorilla on the front door, there was a super friendly female bouncer inside…

... I've only got one thing to say about Optic the bouncers. If you're prepared to pay top whack for entry, top whack prices for drinks and then have your night spoilt by overzealous bouncers then this is the place for you...

Mercy

Used to be a fun place to go, nice décor, but recently the door staff have seemed very rude and stuck up, and it's put me and my friends off going in…

… Still love Mercy on a Thursday night and the music is great too, but found a couple of the 'security' staff rude the last couple of times I've been, which I didn't think was very appropriate.

Chicago's

Chicago's You'll meet friendly faces who you can talk to, the bouncers are discreet and the drinks aren't too expensive.

These are just three examples out of the many clubs and pubs in Norwich, but they really do reveal what impressions customers get when visiting a venue.

Let me give you my honest feelings about door staff, based on my personal experiences as a paying customer at pubs and clubs around the UK (and I'm sure that you will have experienced exactly the same thing too). There have been times when I have been out with friends to clubs and pubs where the door staff have been self-important and rude, have blanked me, and have been bad mannered and foulmouthed. Now and then they have even tried to prove to me that they are hard by being arrogant and attempting to stare me out. I don't know whether they know or recognise me, or whether they just do this to everyone, but it seems as though they are really trying to prove something. Why? What do they hope to gain? And my opinion of these door supervisors? Utter cunts. Do I respect them? Do I fuck. Do they have a reputation? Yes, of being cunts. Would I floor them without hesitation if they were in any way aggressive towards me? Without a doubt. Quite simply, if you have no consideration for others and do not treat others with respect, whoever they are, then they in turn will not respect you. Thankfully, this doesn't happen that often and many door supervisors I meet are actually great and I can have a laugh and a drink (nonalcoholic of course, ahem!) with most, but when it does happen I really do feel like punching their tiny fucking lights out and teaching them what respect is all about; not specifically respect for me, but respect for everyone. And if I feel like this, then for sure most other people feel the same way too. As I said earlier, if you treat people like cunts, you will get treated like a cunt. Surely it is better to be nice to people initially, and then, if they respond with nastiness, deal with it as it happens rather than start off by being nasty to everyone and by doing so invoke a nasty response in return? To me that makes much more sense and makes for a much nicer working environment.

Professional door supervisors undeniably stand out from the crowd. They have an air of confidence and ability and they command respect. A professional door supervisor has made a concerted effort not to be average and has tried to develop a reputation as someone that genuinely cares about his or her venue and its customers. An average door supervisor does none of these things and just turns up for work because he or she has to – fills a Saturday night, doesn't it?

If you walk round clubs and pubs on a busy Friday or Saturday night you can definitely spot the professionals, who stand out from their less professional colleagues. I have been to many nightclubs where this is apparent from just a brief glimpse of the team. You can see almost immediately who are the good ones and who are the bad; who are professional and who are not; who should be there and who should not. Of course, I have been proved wrong on a few occasions and the timid and pathetic looking doorman has actually turned out to be a real hard bastard in a kickoff', but generally it is pretty easy to tell who will be there when it gets rough, and who will be hiding in the toilets. Unfortunately, in this day and age, an experienced professional door supervisor working for a big, national security company has little choice with whom he will be working on any particular evening or at any particular venue and very often has to put up with a variety of ineffectual 'jacket fillers' turning up either to cover for absent regulars or, in many cases, just to make up numbers. Almost every head doorman I have spoken to has confirmed that this is true. Sure, there are venues where the whole team is a great outfit and it rarely changes, or where any new door supervisor coming into an established team is carefully vetted before they start, but this does not happen very often. In the current climate of massive, impersonal security companies with hundreds if not thousands of door supervisors on their books, jacket fillers are frequently sent wherever they are needed. So professional door supervisors frequently have to work with inexperienced scrotes who are only there because the dole paid for their training and if they hadn't complied their benefit would eventually have been stopped. And there is little the professional can do about it.

It seems that venue managers turn a blind eye too, or no longer seem to care an attitude that actually baffles me. If I were a venue manager who was expected to pay a hefty invoice from a security company that had supplied me with a less than effective team, I would certainly do something about it. The problem is that many venue owners and managers are actually scared of the big door firms, the people that run them and the power they possess, and their view is that so as long as there is no trouble a few jacket fillers on the team now and then won't make much difference. So invoices get paid and no questions are asked – until, of course, something does happen, but then it's too late.

I have noticed, however, that over the past couple of years this trend has been changing. Regional, independent venues once again are asking for smaller, regional, independent security companies to provide them with a more personal, customer focused security service, rather than the impersonal management and constantly changing teams of larger firms. It would also appear that some security companies are purposely staying small and concentrating on giving good service to a select group of clients rather than expanding and losing control. For instance, my good friend Wesley Downham runs FGH Security, and they have a core key market that they focus on maintaining. In doing so, they have built themselves an excellent reputation and year after year have won many awards for their service. I first met Wesley many years ago on the doors at the Tiger Tiger nightclub in central Manchester, and since then he has gone on to build a great little company, together with his partner Peter Harrison. Their area is mainly north Lancashire and south Cumbria, and it would be uncommon for them to take on a venue much further afield that they could not easily control. To this small independent company, providing a good service and maintaining a great relationship with the venue managers and owners are much more important goals than expanding nationally or making a stack of cash.

It would appear that venue policies in terms of employing security are slowly changing too, with pubs and clubs reverting back to the eighties and nineties, when many venues employed their door staff directly. For example, after a long series of failures with various national security companies, a good friend of mine who runs a big independent nightclub in the Midlands now prefers to employ his security directly again. He is very specific with his requirements and by employing directly he has much more control over his team and, as a result, infinitely more loyalty from them. His venue is packed night after night and has an excellent reputation as a really safe place to go, so it definitely seems to be working, especially when you hear some of the comments from his customers. And if the large security companies continue to employ muppets and jacket fillers and offer an ever changing, impersonal service, I can see this happening more and more.

Being excellent at anything takes consistency, time and dedication, and being an excellent door supervisor is no exception.

So ask yourself this important question: are you one of those door supervisors that stands out in a crowd because of your professional attitude and manner, or are you one of those that are seen as just jacket fillers? Who do you really want to be? It is easy to become complacent and lazy and not care. It is easy to get through another night doing as little as possible, but is this really who you are? I hope not.

Apart from writing books on the subject of doors and security, I am still very much involved in the day-to-day life of the industry and still frequently get asked to find door staff for pubs and clubs and to consult now and then. And if I can't do the job, I generally know someone that can. I am also occasionally involved in training new door staff. Sure, I could have jumped on the training bandwagon a few years ago when the SIA introduced compulsory training and licences and made myself a lot of money, but because I was so against the SIA at the time and really felt let down (along with most other people in this industry) by the way they had handled things and completely fucked things up, I decided that conforming to something I really did not believe in wasn't for me! But now I really do enjoy running my private courses on Gaining Respect and Building a Reputation for New Door Supervisors, and every single time I stand in front of a group and look out at the rows of new door staff sitting in front of me, I honestly want to see door supervisors that one day I will eventually look up to and respect. It really does give me immense pleasure and pride to think that in some small way I can help contribute to their professionalism and good attitude.

When I stroll down 'nightclub alley' in some godforsaken town or city, stepping over ugly, fatarsed birds swearing and cursing and vomiting in the gutter (strange, isn't it, that only ugly, fat women get blind drunk, half naked and vomit in the gutter, and you never see gorgeous, slim, well educated women stoop so low?!), I don't want to see scumbags standing on the door thinking they are hard, or pimply students picking their noses or fat lumps of lard trying to get laid. I want to see good-looking (not in the 'handsome' sense, of course, but smart and well groomed), polite and respectful door supervisors running a tight and well controlled door. When I go into a venue I want to feel welcomed by the security and thanked when I leave. I want to look at these door staff with a little bit of admiration and I suppose a wee bit of awe. I want to feel that they can handle themselves both verbally and physically if a group of scrotes decide they want 'in'. But, more importantly, I want to know that they can look after their customers and staff if a fight breaks out inside their venue and they have to go in and sort it out, or if a fire breaks out and everyone has to be evacuated. I don't want to question whether they would be scared shitless, stand and watch until the police arrive, or hide in the toilet. I would want to know that, without any hesitation or doubt, they would steam in and deal with the situation effectively and efficiently and then return to their post with a smile on their face as though nothing had happened. This is what I want to see from the door staff I meet and talk to and this is definitely what I want to see from all the door staff that I train and send out to venues across the UK. I have no time for cowards; I have no time for time wasters and cheats; and I certainly have no time for people pretending to be something or someone they are not. In my book, if you are content to be Mr or Mrs Averagedoorsupervisorwhocouldn'treallygiveatoss then you should fuck off and find another job, because I have no time for average door supervisors – they are a danger to themselves, to their team and to everyone around them.

But I honestly don't really believe that there are too many people currently working the doors who would be pleased to be classed in the 'mindless muppet' category. Nor do I really believe that there are many door supervisors going to work every evening who genuinely see themselves as just jacket fillers. Fuck, how totally humiliating it would be if you actually knew you were a muppet and just filling in until a 'proper' doorman came along! Conversely, however, most people would confirm that door supervision is now full of such muppets and jacket fillers, and that there are more of them working on the doors now than in the entire history of door supervision! So this can only lead to one real and lasting conclusion: muppets and jacket fillers are happy to be muppets and jacket fillers and genuinely see themselves as being good door supervisors! This is really bizarre! So you are content with being just average (and therefore a knob) and everyone knows you're just average (and therefore a knob), and yet when you look in the mirror you actually see nothing average or knoblike. Therefore, you must either be blind (in which case you shouldn't be on the doors anyway) or have one hell of an ego and attitude and, as we have said before, having an ego and attitude is definitely not a good way to gain respect.

So a really important part of becoming a better than average door supervisor is to take a long, hard look at yourself and ask yourself honestly and truthfully: am I really a good door supervisor and, if I am not, do I want to be? This is a crucial step. Take it and you will go on to great things; disregard it and you will remain a cunt because you simply cannot be someone you are not. If you don't want to be good at your job, then find another job, because you cannot lead your life being average and knowing that you are average. Strive for more. You can do almost anything you want to do if you want it bad enough. This is a fact. But you simply cannot be anyone you want to be. This is also a fact. You are who you are. You cannot be a hard man if you are not, nor can you be a wimp if you are a hard man. This is part of the reason why there are so many idiots and wannabes on the streets trying to be someone they are not and making an arse of themselves and everyone around them in the process.

Let me be really honest with you: I was not a good doorman when I started; in fact I was crap. I couldn't fight my way out of a paper bag, I wore jumpers under my shirt to make me look bigger, and all I wanted to do was to shag as many pretty women as I could (and quite a number of the not so pretty too, I have to add). I started my long and often turbulent career on the doors one gloomy afternoon as I was wandering through my hometown of Norwich. I was unemployed, a dropout and completely broke, and I saw an advert for door supervisors in the local Job Centre window. I honestly didn't really know what a door supervisor was and genuinely thought it was like being on the door at a hotel, opening and closing the doors, greeting people and being polite. I reckoned I could do that job, so I popped in and they told me that the position was at a new nightclub called The Ritzy and the adjoining upstairs bar called Central Park. The premises were currently closed and under refurbishment and they would be opening in the place of the old and notorious Samson and Hercules nightclub, which had quite a reputation. I knew the Samson well and often drank there as a teenager, well before my eighteenth birthday. The Samson was a numbers place, and your age and attitude didn't matter much so long as you had a few quid to spend on beer. As I briefly mentioned earlier, I was beaten up by the bouncers there one evening when I was about 17. I was being a knob and larking around, as you do when you're that age, bizarrely thinking I was some tough man. I went too far and the bouncers dragged me out the back and gave me a good hiding, leaving me bloodied and probably crying like a baby in the gutter. Funnily enough, I never misbehaved in that place again! Like many teenagers trying to prove themselves, I had a couple of fights but they never lasted very long and I was always the one that got floored pretty quickly. I didn't know how to fight. I was never abused as a kid and my family were never violent; in fact, I didn't really know what proper violence was. Anyway, the job wasn't as a 'bouncer', it was a 'door supervisor', so it was nothing to do with 'bouncing', and of course I applied. I was sent to meet the general manager, who immediately took me on.

The excitement of the club scene in the mid eighties was undeniable and The Ritzy was just going to be a few fun filled months over the summer while I looked around for another job, as I had other grandiose plans for my life.

Within the first few hours of my very first night I found out that working as a door supervisor at The Ritzy was going to be violent, but surprisingly I also quickly found out that violence didn't actually bother me that much; I wasn't scared of it. In fact, it wasn't long before I got used to it and it excited me. I longed for something to happen a fight or someone to throw out, and when nothing happened I was disappointed and bored.

Twenty or so years later I was still working as a doorman (unfortunately, though, the shagging of the pretty women had long since stopped). So how did I move from being a naïve twat whose sole reason for working the doors was to shag, to a professional and respected doorman? Simple. I was humbled by the team I was working with.

Back then the team that opened the new Ritzy nightclub were a strong, tough, hard team that pulled no punches and that didn't suffer fools gladly. And I was certainly a fool, so either I learned quickly and proved myself or I was going to have a real tough time. I decided to shut my big mouth and learn as much as I could and follow my mentors, and it wasn't always easy. I followed what they showed me and learned how they operated, and, although I didn't always get it right and it took a while, slowly and surely my reputation developed and I became part of the team. And the team at The Ritzy back then was awesome. This is what you must do too if you want to gain respect and reputation and become a professional door supervisor.

This is not meant in any egotistical or conceited way whatsoever, but when I stand up in front of a class of students or when I'm chatting with my colleagues on the doors I want people to say:

You know that Robin, well he's getting on a bit now, and a bit old school, but he's polite and respectful and almost always prefers a nonviolent way if at all possible, but even though he isn't far off his pension, he is rarely fazed by some of the scum that roam the streets at night, can still handle most situations and will always, always back you up to the very end if necessary, without question.

Well, words to that effect anyway! I want to earn the respect of those that don't know me and have never heard of me, as well as continue to earn the respect of the old-timers who know me and have worked with me over the years and around the world.

And this is what you should want, too.

Being average is definitely not the way to earn respect. Nobody ever says, "Oh, he's an average doorman and I respect him for it." No one ever says, "Fuck me, he has a mighty average reputation when the going gets tough."

So, to be honest, if you really are content just to fumble through your job night after night being Mr or Mrs Average door supervisor, a muppet or a jacket filler, then don't bother reading any further because, as I have said before, you really are a waste of space and you shouldn't be working the doors anyway. And if you were really and truthfully honest with yourself you would probably agree with me anyway.

Listen, you do not have to be experienced, nor do you even have to be any good at first, but you must want to be good, to be willing to learn and to follow others that are more experienced. Most importantly, you must also remain modest and humble as you grow and develop. People will then see you as the quiet one, always willing to learn, who follows orders and is always there when the going gets tough, rather than as the ineffectual, loudmouthed braggart who knows nothing and hides every time it kicks off. Actually, it is okay to start off in this industry as a Mr or Mrs Average, or even a Mr or Mrs Below Average Knobhead, so long as you have the goals and the desire to become a professional and respected doorman eventually.

It is a fact that some people are born great, stand out in a crowd, look good and can handle themselves with little or no formal training. Sadly, however, the opposite is also very true, in that some people are definitely not great at all, disappear in a crowd, look pathetic and will run a mile from any confrontation. You cannot change your genes and you cannot change who you are; sure, you can change certain things, but not who you fundamentally are. Yes, you can poke your arse with steroids and turn yourself from a 10-stone weakling into a 20-stone musclehead, but if you are naturally afraid of confrontation then having strength and muscles won't change a thing. This was highlighted to me when I worked in Standish. A huge doorman started working the door, but he ended up hiding in the toilets when the mightiest of all kickoffs erupted. He certainly looked the business, but he was ineffectual and a coward.

Learning a martial art will not make you someone you are not either. You may study for years and have great technique, but on the streets in real-time aggressive situations even the most skilled martial artist can become overwhelmed quickly. Again, this was highlighted in Wigan when my friend 'onepunch' Neil floored two boasting, arrogant blackbelts with just one punch on each (but what mighty punches they were!) It isn't the technique or the skill or even the knowledge that is important, it is who you are and, conversely, who you are not.

Also, you will only get a good reputation as a door supervisor if you know the job backwards and inside out. As in any job, the more you know the better you become, and the better you become the more professional you are, and the more professional you are the more powerful you are. Your first compulsory SIA door supervisor training course should only be the beginning of a career on the doors, and like any professional you should develop your career by constantly learning, growing, experiencing and attending other addon training courses, in particular self-defense, control and restraint, first aid, advanced conflict management and cuffing. If you are serious about being a professional then you should be serious about gaining knowledge about the industry.

What matters most is that you are honest with yourself. It is okay not being a door supervisor, but it is not okay being a door supervisor when you should be doing something else, because this not only puts you at risk but also your customers and your team. Whoever you are and whatever you desire to be, the most important thing is to try to be the very best you can be, and if you are a door supervisor you should strive to be the very best door supervisor you can be – and accept nothing less.

On The Doors

By Will Bishop

I started working the doors at The Vintry, St Albans, in 2002, after the venue doorman came up to me and asked if I could cover a shift on a Friday night, their busiest time. As with every venue, there are certain people, like myself, who get on the right side of the door staff and get to know them well (and manage to jump the queue!) I had been a regular there since around 1996 and I knew a lot of the customers. I had also run one of the gyms in town and trained their staff at a couple of the other gyms, so I knew a lot of the guys from that. A few times I had helped them out with breaking up fights when I knew the guys involved and also had given assistance when difficult customers were asked to leave the premises, especially if their friends were intent on leaving too, armed with bottles and glasses. On one occasion, a mate of someone ejected tried to bottle one of the doormen, so I grabbed the bottle from his hand and, shall we say, helped him on his way! I think they respected me for this. As I got to know the door team better, I started to socialise with them after work, and I would stand my ground alongside them should an ejected customer try to seek revenge when they were off duty. Becoming part of the team seemed a natural progression and they eventually decided to give me a chance. On my first night there were a few kickoffs and I just got on with it. They asked me to do the doors on the following Friday and Saturday, and soon I was doing Thursday nights too.

People have often asked my reasons for doing the job, and there are several. First and foremost, and I think you'll agree that it's as good a reason as any, although my day job was paying okay, I'd been spending around £80 a night getting pissed as a customer at the venue, and the extra money for the part-time door work plus the money I saved meant that I was about 20 grand a year better off! Also, I've never had to queue and have rarely had to pay to get into other bars and clubs, so that's a pretty good perk as well. You get to enjoy the job too, and get the chance to meet a lot of people, far more than you would normally on a night out. Also, it has been a great fallback for me when changing day jobs, as I have been lucky to be able to take extra door shifts and work at other venues and still earn money while going to job interviews in the daytime. Everyone has heard about the girls doormen get while working the doors, but, while I can confirm that this does happen, they are not stories for this book!

Undoubtedly, working the doors has been a good test for me too. I'm a much stronger person both physically and mentally from doing the doors, and, while I never go looking for a fight, the adrenaline and excitement of a big kickoff and throwing several guys out, or getting the better of a lump that's much bigger than me, admittedly gets addictive. One of my doormen affectionately refers to me as an 'action junkie' due to my keenness to help out on the doors either side of me and, I guess, because of both my professional courtesy and the fact that I've got quite efficient at taking people down cleanly and restraining them effectively. And yes, I love it!

In addition to The Vintry at St Albans, I have also worked at quite a lot of other venues, including Lloyds in Watford. This bar is where I've spent most of my time and I've only been away from it for the odd month now and then. I was made head doorman after two months there, and I've been head doorman for three different door companies because the management kept me at the venue each time they changed the door company. I've been lucky, as this really has been an ideal bar for me, and even though I've been offered the head doorman position at a bigger Lloyds bar nearby, as well as places on several other doors, it would take a lot for me to leave. I've been through it all at Lloyds: a 20-man brawl, a bunch of squaddies going mad, and numerous idiots trying to come in tooled up with weapons and just about everything in between.

For a few months I also got to work Sunday nights at After Dark in Dunstable. This was a nice extra little earner. People often say that to describe Dunstable on a weekend all you have to do is drop the initial 'D' and it's true! The club had a bad reputation in the area, but what club doesn't have fights at the weekend? Personally, I really enjoyed my time there. I got on well with the management and they even tried get my services full time, so there was no hassle from that point of view. Two of the guys inside had covered shifts on my door, so after the first week I got to run the inside of the club. The guys on the front door were solid. Believe me, there was never a time that I needed to back them up and on the few occasions that I was called to the front door I might just as well have gone and made a cup of tea instead! They sorted everything out extremely well on their own. If you don't let idiots in, you'll have a hell of a lot fewer idiots to throw out at the end of the night! I'd happily go back there.

I got to do the urban nights at the Base Nightclub in Hatfield. I always believe it's good to test yourself now and then and take yourself out of your comfort zone, and by being one of the few white faces, if not the only one on occasions, in a packed club was certainly a good test! I remember one night I had to escort a drunk girl off the dance floor, down the stairs and out of the club. As I was walking her out, a big Greek guy grabbed at me and started shouting at me to get off her. As I pushed him away he kicked off and we had to drag him out as well, and he was no lightweight. As is always the way, when you're removing a boyfriend, friend, husband or brother the girls always seem to regain enough soberness to attack us too. As we were dragging him down the stairs we met the head doorman, Jason, coming the other way. Now Jason must weigh 20 stone, but the Greek guy kicked him hard enough to send him flying backwards. Short of banging the pair of them out, these two (who had now been joined by a couple of mates) were definitely not wanting to leave. I don't think the Greek expected me to put him to sleep! His mate certainly didn't and was shouting repeatedly with a worried voice, "I can only see the whites of his eyes. We'll leave but let him go!" From my experience, if you let someone go after they've kicked off and been restrained they'll fight again. "When he wakes up, he can leave," was my reply. Unsurprisingly, this is exactly what happened. I think the manager was a little shocked at seeing this 16-stone unconscious lump in my arms, but it's sometimes better to be safe than sorry.

Surprisingly, the quietest door I've ever worked was at Hertfordshire University. I got to do extra nights there now and then and a couple of months away from my usual door too. There were maybe four scuffles and each time I ended up being the guy who restrained and removed the participants. Students on campus are usually more drunk than the average town drinker, but they're also softer. If they cause trouble they risk getting kicked out of university, which is far more of a deterrent than any door staff. I did the doors for the Champions League final in their sports bar, and I bet I had a much easier night than most doormen working the packed bars full of Manchester United and Chelsea fans. I even got to watch some of the game too! I also worked their Summer Ball and looked after DJ Sammy and DJ Slide when they guested.

Other venues where I've worked include Batchwood Hall, O'Neill's and The Waterend Barn, all in St Albans, The Whitehouse in Luton and The Moon Under Water, Walkabout, The Flag and Destiny in Watford.

Over the years I have gained a few souvenirs from dealing with idiots on the doors, including breaking three or four fingers and the odd knuckle. I got a cut lip a couple of times and have taken a few bangs to the side and back of my head, chipped my elbow, been stabbed in the arm with a bottle and sustained a fractured cheekbone (and I worked the next night after that, but the black eye that went with it made it a little conspicuous). I've been put on my arse once, when a guy caught me with a cracking shot. (I'd question someone's honesty if they said they hadn't ever got caught by a good shot at some point in this job.) In my case, I got up and choked the guy before handing him to the police. Also, I'm forever mindful that if you do underestimate someone you might not be getting up at all.

Despite the risks, do I have any regrets about doing the doors? No! Doing the doors is one of the best decisions I've ever made.

It's a great job and most of the time I love it, and it has taught me a lot about respect and being respectful.

In everyday life it is possible to do a normal nine to five job without respect, and often people get by on popularity and the ability to fit in rather than through gaining the respect of their colleagues. In many cases it really doesn't matter what people think of you so long as you do the job and get on with others. We all know people like that those that we like but perhaps don't respect that much; the friendly idiot or the guy that is always clumsy and makes mistakes or forgets things. However, as a door supervisor, reputation and respect make a very big difference. In door work you can't make mistakes and expect to stay on your door or in the job.

Ability is the fundamental word that sums up reputation. Reputation can only be gained by your ability to handle different situations. Before I started doing the doors, the industry was very different and doormen were generally perceived as thugs; the local hard nuts that were asked to take over a door because the venue basically needed someone who could fight. Back then, respect was mainly earned by how many people you had beaten up, and there was a real perception that doormen went to work looking for a fight. Today things are very different, and the average doorman is very different.

A lot of the 'old school' doormen have gone, and since the SIA badge was introduced a lot of fresh faced, spotty 18 and 19-year-olds, without either the skills or experience to do the job, have suddenly materialised on the doors. I was 22 when I started doing the job and over the past few years I believe I have earned respect by doing it as well as I possibly can. I believe my respect has come from a mixture of doing my job properly, not treating the customers like shit and, perhaps most importantly, dealing with fights and trouble quickly and efficiently.

When I took over my door we had a fourman team on Fridays and a fiveman team on Saturdays, whereas now we have two and three respectively. The door team before me had taken a good kicking from the locals and, although busy, the pub had a lot of problems. Don't get me wrong, this was not a shithole on a broken estate; it was a badly run door without any respect from the locals. When I first started there were a lot of fights, maybe five or six a night and involving up to thirty people. The previous door team had let the locals dictate what was or wasn't acceptable and the troublemakers would generally be allowed back in a couple of weeks after causing riots and threatening the doormen. However, we changed all that over time, by showing strength coupled with respect for the locals.

When I started at the bar I'm working now we had the same issues and the same lack of respect. I was working with someone that was on my team at the previous venue and we got on well. He was what you would call 'old school', and although he was maybe a bit long in the tooth he was used to the shit hitting the fan. On the first night that we had worked together at the previous venue there had been a big kickoff between two families and a load of Asians and I had his back and handled myself well. There and then he had decided that I was a 'proper doorman'. Ever since then we had the kind of understanding that you need between doormen; he imparted his knowledge and advice and in return I made sure that no one had his back more than me. When we started at the new venue I looked at what was wrong and remembered how the first bar had been run badly. "Fancy sorting this out?" I asked him. "You know how much shit we're going to have to deal with here?" was his response!

The first issue we tackled was the dress code, and most customers thought we were being real arseholes by banning football shirts and tracksuits. We gave people the option of going home to change, but invariably they never returned. The same applied to baseball caps, hoodies and Puffa jackets. Customer could come in if they took them off, but if they put them back on again they would receive a warning. If it happened again they would be thrown out, and if they came back again dressed the same way they would not be let in. Simple. They then knew the dress code. We had a few months of regular kickouts and had more arguments on the door than you could ever imagine, but slowly and surely the message got through. Some people never really gave up trying, but those that were borderline eventually behaved. It was all about putting in the hard work at the start to pave the way for an easy future.

There are a lot of people who will give you a degree of respect just because you are standing on the door dressed as a doorman. Some may even be a little wary of you. However, this does not mean that everyone will respect you. The uniform may help, but it is who you are and what you do that will make you a good doorman. The trouble is that too many young lads now start in the job and immediately think that everyone will kiss their arse or do whatever they say, only really finding out when it all goes wrong whether they really have all the skills they need for the job. And then it's usually too late.

It sounds logical and sensible that door staff should never drink in the bar in their own venue, but too often young doormen will go out drinking in the place they work because it's an easier route to the girls eager to bag a doorman. Drinking in the bar where you work can leave you open to a lot of trouble, so it's always best to try to keep your distance from the locals. By this, I don't mean be rude to them, but there is a fine line between acknowledging them, which they will appreciate and which makes your life easier, and getting too matey with them. When that line gets crossed, they feel that they can take liberties, their justification being, "But you know me! And we're mate's, aren't we?"

Maybe as a doorman I'm now more paranoid, but if I'm on a night off I still watch my back and my surroundings carefully, as it's much easier to take a doorman out if he's off duty and half cut in a busy club or fumbling for his car keys in a dark car park.

I strongly recommend that all young door supervisors listen to the older doormen. Although they may not always be right, there is usually a reason why they have lasted so long in the business. There is no substitute for experience when working the doors, and in time you will get used to spotting trouble before it happens and identifying the less obvious cokeheads and dealers, who are used to hiding their activities.

If someone is known to be a hard man then usually they will command a cautious approach at the very least, but you can build a reputation without being particularly hard. However, when it comes to the doors you most certainly do have to be able to handle yourself. In the past many of my customers have come up to me and said that they were surprised after I've flattened someone or sorted out some trouble. They treated me with respect because, in their perception, I wasn't an arsehole, but their surprise indicated to me just how much you do need to be able to back it up when you have to, and the following example illustrates this.

One night when someone was giving one of the bar managers grief at the end of the bar. I asked to speak to him and he was dismissive. I then told him we needed to speak and he was dismissive again. The situation inevitably escalated until eventually I had to restrain him, but he went mental and I ended up throwing him on the floor. As I stood over him he changed tack. "That's assault!" was his main response. He obviously thought that I wouldn't go so far as to put him down. As I was telling him to pick himself up and leave, a guy jumped through the surrounding group of people and tried to push me. I pushed him flying and he started shouting, "Fuck off!" and "Get off my mate!" while swinging punches at me. I told him to help his mate up and fuck off, pushing him back and telling him not to be an idiot. I called for backup but the radios weren't working, so I was on my own. The first guy tried to grab me as he got up and the second came back swinging at me again. As one punch glanced my face I decided that I had no choice and elbowed the first guy in the ribs hard. He winced and let go. The second one came swinging in again, so I caught him with a jab, knocking him off his stride, and followed through with a heavy cross to his nose, which I could feel shattering as I twisted on impact. The punch sent him backwards and into the cigarette machine a few feet behind him. The first guy paused and the manager, who had been watching all the time, ushered him out. The second guy eventually went out too with a bit more effort. As I waited for the police to arrive, I looked at him with his crumpled nose bleeding from both the middle and the bottom. "Hit me again!" he goaded. "Once was enough," was my calm reply.

The reason I mention this story is that for weeks people talked about the incident. Don't get me wrong, we've all worked doors where nightly fights have been commonplace, but in quieter venues where fights are less common something like this gets noticed. The young lads ask you where you box, and the older lads make respectful reference to it.

I wouldn't consider myself a violent man, or the stereotypical thug, but experience and common sense have taught me to be respectful of my surroundings in these situations, and when you need to act physically you must deal with it hard and efficiently. That said, things have changed. If you batter everybody that kicks off you'll either be out of a job or probably end up on the receiving end of some kind of retribution, and the most likely scenario is that you'll lose your licence pretty quickly. These days you have to learn to temper your... erm... temper. If you put someone down then that needs to be it. Finished. End of. And I've always been brought up never to 'do someone on the deck', but in a heated situation when you've just smashed someone out for bottling your colleague, I'm sure it's hard for some people to hold back.

I think there's a big difference between fear and 'bricking it'. Anyone that says that he has no fear the first time he sees a knife is bullshitting you. I guess I'm lucky that in the last decade I can count on one hand the number of knives I've seen, and the number of guns on the other. Luckily, I have never been stabbed or shot at. Fear gets the adrenaline going and the heart pumping and it sharpens your reactions. That's the good side. It can also make people freeze and hesitate and can cloud their judgement. You can do all the training in the world, read books on psychology and build up a few stone in the gym, but you only really know how you will react in a confrontational situation when it occurs. I'll be honest, before I did the doors I have frozen in such situations that kind of 'rabbit in the headlights' scenario when you don't know what move to make next. I guess it depends a lot on the upbringing you've had and the situations you get into as a child. What has made a big difference to me as a doorman is that from day one I've always believed that if you freeze, back down or bottle it, that's it; go home and retire. If you keep calm and stand your ground, the worst that can happen is that you may take a few punches or even get dropped, but I'd rather that happen than 'bottle it'.

The most frightened I've been was probably when I had to square up and I do mean up to a 6ft 4 ins,18 stone ex-squaddie bodyguard, ironically nicknamed 'Tiny'. This guy had kicked off with a couple of Asians inside. The moment that someone tells you they're going to do something, that's the last thing you'll let them do, so when someone that size says to you, "Get out of the fucking way! You know I'll go through you!" the reactions sharpen and you try to anticipate their next move. You can't back down, so you stand your ground and go through the options in your head. In his case, he knew he had a size and strength advantage over the rest of the doormen. At that moment I was the most worried I had ever been but I never showed it, and when he repeated his demands for me to get out of the way I think he was surprised when I said, "You know I can't do that, soldier. You know I can't stand down." Much as I think he knew he should win, I think the fact that I didn't back down saved me, and playing on his thoughts of soldiering and loyalty to his unit made him pause and think.

That incident sticks in my mind more than the hundreds of kickouts, dozens of fights and various other situations, because I maintained a level head and it kept me in one piece. Ninety per cent of confrontational situations are purely bravado, upping the stakes to see who will back down first, and very rarely do people go 'all in' when it comes to risking their health or life. More often than not, if someone kicks off with you in front of his mates it's exactly because he's with his mates that he's doing so. When you drag him out he usually freezes, unsure of what to do. I believe that you both subconsciously and consciously condition yourself to adapt to this sort of situation. I've had six or seven guys kick off with each other at the same time inside the doors at the front area of the bar and I've gone into autopilot and literally thrown them out one by one, knocking the bottles and chairs out of their hands at the same time. Looking back at these situation, if I'd been thinking rather than reacting automatically I would've been more concerned for my welfare than I was.

I consider myself part 'old school' and part 'new school' as a doorman. I know the ins and outs of the law regarding what I can and cannot do in situations, and I do use psychology in my job and in how I run my door. What you say and, more importantly, how you say things makes a much greater difference than people realise.

A lot of people think I'm being anal or an arsehole when I shout at them to keep the doorway clear or to keep the drinks in the smoking area. Maybe I am, but there are reasons for my actions. In regard to how you express yourself in these situations, the tone of your voice, your gestures and your body language are all tools that you can use to gain a degree of social compliance from the customers. These are points of contact that let the customers know who you are and the personality you project. I've always liked doing the front door and seeing every customer that comes into my venue. This not only allows me to project to them who I am and why I'm there, but also gives me the chance to gauge what they're going to be like when I let them in by observing their actions, language, tone and reaction to me.

I've always believed in being respectful to others, but, at the risk of sounding like an old man, the levels of respect in the street and often on the doors from new customers have deteriorated. It's just down to standards of manners slipping and the diminishing consequences of people's actions. A lot of my customers talk to me, show me respect and come and find me if they think there may be a problem that the door staff inside the venue might not have spotted. They will also feed me information as to why things kick off and any outstanding grievances between people. If I'd been too arrogant with them, or too weak, that level of respect just wouldn't be there.

That said, some guys I've worked with or met have got respect from how they look. It's still true that people generally think twice about causing trouble if someone is a 20-stone hulk. I did work at a bar with one black guy who must have been nearing 20 stone, was tall and had a good natural shape and he could have been a good doorman, but he never lasted as when it came to the bit of the job where you have to earn your money he was nowhere to be found. The team working for me now are a mix of doormen I've known from my early days in St Albans, another head doorman from one of our other venues, and a younger guy who is also my biggest doorman what he lacks in experience, he makes up for in bottle; he always stood his ground when I helped him out with fights when he worked at the venue next door.

I wouldn't ever have a doorman back if he bottled it, would you?

Heroes Are Not Cowards

By Robin Barratt & others

A coward is a person who lacks courage in facing danger, difficulty, opposition, pain, etc. A coward is someone timid or easily intimidated. For example, the door supervisor was a coward for allowing those troublemakers into the venue; the door supervisor was a coward for not stopping the fighting.

Are you a coward?

I think as a society we are now controlled, monitored and restrained far too much. We are quite literally frightened of doing what is right, frightened of being just, fair and honourable, and bloody frightened of getting involved. We are being told time and time again that if we see an injustice or trouble we should walk away, call the police or simply ignore it. But by not standing up to injustices we allow society's miscreants and scum, its bullies, intimidators and knobheads, to rule and get away with doing more or less whatever they want, and society is degrading as a result. Personally, I believe in doing what is right and fair and standing up for your beliefs when you witness or are involved in injustices.

I believe it is better to be a hero than a coward. What do you believe? Read Jeff's story below and then answer that question.

Jeff Stewart is a doorman and has a reputation for not backing down. Like me, he completely believes in doing what he thinks is right. But this philosophy both wrecked his life and almost cost him his life. Here is his inspirational story:

It all started ten years ago when my mother and father purchased their first house in a part of Rochdale called Sudden. At the time I was 19 years old and, along with my two brothers, I moved with them. I soon made many friends – well, people I thought were friends and met a lovely girl who had just turned 17, and after a couple months we became an item. She had a lot of friends around the area and as I was with her I got to know quite a few of them. Everything between us was fantastic for about two years. And then, during a night in, one of her sister's friends, who was just 13 and sleeping over, sat there and started crying. She told us that her stepfather was raping her and her two sisters each weekend when their mother was at work. As you can imagine, quite a few emotions went through my body at the time anger, disgust and distress and at the time every inch of me wanted to kill the sick bastard. These girls where 13, 11 and 8 and she said he had been doing it for about 12 months. I had to do something. I couldn't just ignore it, turn a blind eye and let the bastard carry on, especially as I now knew about it. So I immediately called the police. They came very quickly, the stepfather was immediately arrested, and the children were questioned by specially trained officers. And because me and my girlfriend were the first people to be told about these crimes, we were also questioned and our evidence was gathered and statements given. The stepfather and his family lived about three doors down from us and the word got round that we were the ones who exposed his behaviour. His family and friends spared no time in trying to make life as difficult as possible for me so that I wouldn't give evidence against him. Malicious rumours were put around that it was actually me that had done these sick things to those innocent children, and in less than a week my reputation as a paedophile was around the town. My girlfriend and I split up and I was told by the police to leave the area and live with relatives until they managed to sort it all out, which I did. My parents stayed but were tormented and verbally abused. The court date came and I was called to give evidence. Of course I willingly went, but had to go with a full police escort and was taken the back way into the courthouse. Exposing a crime, especially as sick a crime as this, had literally left my life in tatters. He was found guilty and given three life sentences for his crimes and I eventually returned home. Everything was fine again and even a few people that had initially pointed the accusing finger at me came round and apologised. But a little later, when I thought things had got back to normal I got attacked in the streets and ended up in intensive care for three weeks. At one point my family were called, as the doctors said I wouldn't make the through the night. Now seven years on I have pulled myself up and have moved on with my life. I work the doors and I now have the reputation of a being a bit of a 'hard nut' that wont back down. It's true, I won't back down but I am not a hard man, just simply a family man that wants to live my life and do the best I can for my wife and son.

Would you do the same thing? Would you give up your life for the lives of those children? Would you refuse to back down, even though the consequences could ruin your own life? Would you suffer humiliation and physical pain for someone else?

The past is the past and I don't wish to dwell too much on what life was like on the doors 20, 15 or even 10 years ago, but in my opinion, and from experience, many doormen today are not fighters and I honestly do think that this is a very good thing. I am really glad that we no longer have teams of hard, tough fighters running today's doors. With the mayhem on the streets today, adding to it with aggressive, fighting, arrogant, egotistical doormen would turn that mayhem into complete anarchy. And, sadly, I think the word 'fight' is very different today than it was years ago and when I worked the doors. Back then, you had a good scrap and whoever won, won. And whoever lost, lost. And that was the end of it, simple. In all the years on the doors and in all the fights I've had – and I've had many I think I only saw two or three blades. That's an average of one blade every seven years! People never carried blades. Now it is a different world entirely and a good scrap could, quite literally, end your life. Sadly, scrotes and scumbags are lazy cunts and cowardly and would prefer to end things with a blade than to fight like men one to one. And they know that if they get caught with a blade they won't get much punishment either. For example, a 22-year-old scrote called Christian Soares was found to have a double-edged blade in his trouser pocket when door supervisors searched him at the Talk nightclub in Southend in early 2009. Soares was given a four month prison sentence, suspended for 12 months, and was ordered to carry out 180 hours of unpaid community service. The judge told Scrotes, sorry Soares:

It is obviously a nasty weapon that could clearly cause a very serious injury if used. The fact it is such a nasty weapon is one of the aggravating features of this case, in my judgement. Another aggravating feature is you had it on you in a nightclub, a place where incidents can happen and people can do things in the heat of the moment... Take my advice: never ever carry a knife in public again.

What planet was this judge on? This was Scrotes' oops, done it again I mean Soares' second conviction for carrying a knife! Does the judge really expect him to stop carrying because he was told to do so?

People carrying blades are pathetic and yet the ironic and surprising thing is that they actually look in the mirror and think they're tough. How can they be tough? Surely they are the complete opposite? They examine their weapon with pride, as though it somehow makes them a real man, but the opposite is true; a real tough man can mix it without the use of a weapon; a real tough, hard man doesn't need a blade to prop up his ego. I can, therefore, with the huge amount of cowardly cunts roaming the streets tooled up, completely understand that door supervisors today are scared. I would be scared too. But being scared should not mean being a coward. The heroes of the First and Second Word Wars, The Falklands, Afghanistan, Iraq, etc., were scared shitless, but they went into battle being heroes not cowards.

What happens when you've told a group of scrotes that they are not coming into your venue and they refuse to listen to you? There are just the two of you on the door and there are five or six scrotes rearing up outside, all ready for a scrap. You know you're outnumbered and you don't have much experience fighting; in fact, you've probably never had a real fight in your life. In addition, your partner on the door only qualified as a doorman last week. What the fuck do you do?

A)Let the scrotes in and run like fuck?

B)Let the scrotes in and call the police?

C)Stand your ground?

For those of you that have chosen options A or B, you can also fuck off home now, as this book is about building your reputation and is not about the unrealistic and inappropriate conflict management skills that you are taught in your pathetic and totally unrealistic SIA endorsed Level II Door Supervisors course. On the course your instructor, who has probably never been in such a situation, would have told you to put your hands up and shout, "STOP, STOP, STOP!" Farcical, isn't it?

I have been in this situation many, many times and when I have exhausted all calm, polite options and avenues of cooperation, I have always stepped back, clenched my fists at my sides and shouted, "Okay, come on you fuckers, let's do it!" And then you wait. Do not make the first move; you must let them move first. If you make the first move then, firstly, you are putting yourself in real danger, as they will be defending themselves instead of attacking you, and surprisingly in these situations defending provokes more rage than attacking. Also, if you make the first move it is almost certain that it will kick off big time. Secondly, if you make the first move you are opening yourself up to arrest. So don't say anything else, not a word. Don't do anything else. Don't even step forward (as they might think you're going to attack), but just wait. This is a big risk and, of course, you could actually get fucked but I have done this many times and I cannot think of one single occasion when it has kicked off big time. Each and every time they have eventually left. This is not textbook door supervisor training shit, it's about gaining a reputation, standing up to a team of scrotes and being willing to have a 'shout' with them, no matter what the odds.

Most people will probably choose to let them in and call the police, and this is exactly what they might also tell you to do on your SIA training course, but at any of the venues I work that simple is not an option. No scum are going to walk past me on my door, and nor should they be allowed to. At the end of the day, none of the scrotes actually know who you are and what you are capable of, and even scrotes don't want to end up in hospital, or worse. This is about not backing down and, regardless of the outcome, it is pretty good for your reputation. Running, hiding, calling the police, letting scrotes into your venue because you are scared of them is not.

As a door supervisor stand proud, don't back down, and don't let people intimidate you. You are worth much more than pathetic, lowlife scum like them.

Since leaving the doors full-time a few years ago I have been asked many times to clean up venues in rather rough places where today's modern doormen struggle. Cleaning up a venue 'old school' style now is so much harder than it ever used to be and, to be honest, I would struggle. Firstly, I am far too old, but mainly I would struggle with the lack of respect afforded to today's door supervisor, with the realities of violence on the streets and with the laws and tough conditions imposed on today's door supervisor. It doesn't mean that modern doormen don't do a good job; it's just that the venue, local conditions and laws limit doormen in terms of what they can and can't do. Today's doormen would simply walk away rather than lose their badge. Sad but true.

But whatever you do, don't ever be a coward.

Fight, Not Flight

By Robin Barratt & others

In case you don't know, the word 'flight' means an act or instance of fleeing or running away; hasty departure. For example, the door supervisor ran away when it kicked off.

In 1929 Harvard physiologist Walter Cannon first described the 'fight or flight response'. Actually, the technical term is 'acute stress response'. Basically it's all about the 'firing' of neurons in a section of the brain called the locus coeruleus. Normally, when a person is in a calm state, the firing of these neurons is minimal, but where there is a perception of danger, trauma or stress these little buggers start firing wildly, preparing you to either fight or flee. The more intense the perception of threat (and this, of course, varies from person to person and from threat to threat) the more they fire, resulting in a host of other biological reactions including the release of adrenaline, noradrenaline and cortisol into your bloodstream. These act in other physiological ways, including the acceleration of heart and lung function, paling or flushing, a general effect on the sphincters of the body (in other words, crapping or pissing yourself), the release of nutrients including glucose for muscular action, the redirection of blood from the stomach and digestive tract to the muscles, the dilation of blood vessels for muscular action, loss of hearing, loss of peripheral vision (tunnel vision) and shaking, amongst many other things although you are pretty fucked if you suffer from all of these at once! In reaction to a threat our awareness of our environment intensifies, our sight sharpens and impulses quicken, and we become prepared. Although with training it is possible to control some of the physical reactions to stress, many of these signs are hard wired into our brains and are primitive and automatic, designed to prepare the body to fight or run like merry fuck. And one amazing reaction to stress is that our sense of pain diminishes too we can be stabbed or shot and sometimes not even know about it.

It is a fact that males and females throughout the animal kingdom, including humans, tend to deal with stressful situations differently. In humans, men are more likely to respond to an aggressive emergency situation with aggression, whereas females are more likely to flee, turn to others for help, or even attempt to defuse the situation. But, of course, as door staff we have seen that this isn't always the case, especially where alcohol is a factor. Men can be seen cowering and cowardly while the women are battling like deranged vixens.

By its very nature, the fight or flight system bypasses our rational and logical mind and can cause us to perceive almost everything around us as a possible threat and to view everyone as a potential enemy. As door supervisors this can easily and frequently result in an overreaction to a potential threat before it actually develops into an actual threat. All door supervisors have experienced precisely this. Perhaps we've had to escort someone quietly out of the club for a minor misdemeanour, but their friends suddenly surround us and now we see them all as being a potential threat and things quickly escalate out of control. We consider ourselves in real danger even though in reality we probably are not and push one aside in order to get away; he falls, hits his head and dies. A few seconds of madness results in a lifetime of misery. Making clear, logical, meaningful choices becomes almost impossible, and recognising and understanding the consequences of those choices is impossible. Uncontrolled fear causes us to focus only on the immediate and nothing thereafter.

Mick Lyons told me that fear in confrontational situations has got to be channelled in the right directions:

Anybody who tells you that they have never been frightened in door situations is either telling lies or just plain daft! It is the way you deal with that fear that makes the difference. Your fear heightens your senses, tunes them in ready for action, physically or verbally. If used properly, fear can make you strong, careful and prepared for what lies ahead.

Colin West remembers his first fight on his very first night on the doors and how experience helped him control the fear:

I remember my first night on the door: big fight, local hard men, feeling complete fear, then adrenaline, then feeling alive afterwards. And after that, every time I dealt with confrontation the fear seemed less and my confidence grew (never overconfident or cocky though). I remember one time there was a 1010 (big kickoff) call on the radio when I was in mid conversation with a young lady. I responded, dealt with the incident alongside my team, and returned to my conversation as if nothing had happened. Sure, the fear was always there, but buried deep, and as time passed and my experience grew I was so accustomed to it I hardly noticed it. However, having taken a few years off and recently returned to the doors, I can confirm that fear does come back as severe as that first night (well, almost!)

Richard Wood makes some interesting points about harnessing fear and using it to your advantage:

Fear in a confrontational situation is a natural, involuntary response. The key is how you turn it to your advantage. The normal macho response is to suppress it, or even deny that fear was there in the first place. However, the thinker can accept that the fear is going to be a part of the job and harness it to sharpen your senses, increase your awareness and prepare your body for any impending situation. Fear is not uncommon in the rookie doorman, but this usually subsides with time served and is eventually replaced with something more important: respect. Every situation on the door, no matter how mundane, is worthy of respect, and failure to show this will result in loss of respect, your job and quite possibly your life.

Once the fighting, or fleeing, is over, and the threat is gone, physically and mentally we slowly return to a state of calm again. And, of course, for most door supervisors there is a sense of euphoria, especially if they have come out on top in a major battle or have handled a really aggressive situation successfully.

At one venue I went over a year without any incident at all; at another venue I fought two or three times a night, every night. It is virtually guaranteed that at some point every single door supervisor at every venue will experience some form of violent confrontation. And I honestly do believe that this should happen to each and every door supervisor, whether male of female, young or old, within the first few weeks in the job. A violent confrontation should be part of their training and their apprenticeship, as how they react and behave will define their potential for being either a real professional or a coward. As I mentioned earlier, a door supervisor does not necessarily have to be the best fighter in the world, but he or she must never back down, no matter how tough or violent it gets. Backing down, just once, will destroy any reputation and any self-respect a door supervisor might have had. We all want to work with someone that we know will be behind us no matter what. And if you consistently prove this time and time again you will earn yourself a very good reputation.

Over my 20 or so years on the doors I have had hundreds of fights and, like anything you do time and time again, you eventually get good at it. However, there are certainly many, many people who are infinitely better fighters than me, but I got a reputation because I always stood my ground, no matter how much the odds were stacked against me; I never once backed down; I never fled. My instinctive reaction was not to flee when I encountered violence, stress or aggression but to stand my ground, stand up to it and be prepared to fight if need be. And because I never gave up or backed down, and on many occasions had to battle real hard, I can honestly say that I have never once had a really severe beating. I would literally do whatever I could to survive. Of course, I can be beaten by many people, it's just that I have not allowed myself to be, and I believe that this should be the same for each and every doorman/woman standing on the doors today.

Never allow yourself to be beaten.

It is because of this fact alone that I have worked the doors for as long as I have, and not because I was some hard bastard. Go out on the doors with the belief, "I will not be beaten," and you will survive and become a very good doorman.

Tough Doors in A Tough Area

By Steve Wraith

Steve Wraith is one of Newcastle's best-known doormen and has been working in the pubs and clubs on Tyneside for 17 years. He is a company director of Players Inc Events, the author of the bestselling book *The Krays The Geordie Connection* and a professional actor represented by Sam Claypole at Claypole Management. I have great respect for Steve and what he has accomplished in his life so far. Who says doormen are uneducated and mindless? Like many 'old school' doormen, he started the doors after helping the local doorman out one night.

I used to go out in Newcastle a lot with my mates and they were always getting into rucks. I was always quite tall and inevitably ended up wading in and stopping my mates making a fool of themselves. I'd simply grab my mates and pull them away from the situation. One night Gary, the head doorman at Masters bar in Newcastle, noticed me and said I should do it for a living. I just laughed. Six months later he asked me if I fancied working at his bar because a doorman had broken his wrist in the leadup to Christmas and couldn't work. I needed the money and it was only three nights, so I said, "Why not?" Seventeen years later I'm still standing in the cold taking crap off people who can't take a drink. But mostly I enjoy it! Masters bar was a right dive! It was a typical end of the night bar. It got rammed from 9.30 p.m. till 11 p.m. when everyone got kicked out that's if they hadn't been thrown out first! An easy place to pick up a 'slapper' or get slapped! The first ever team I worked with were a great bunch of lads. Gary was the head doorman and John Lillico was deputy head and he's still a good pal now. There was a doorman called Irish, because, well, he was Irish and mental. The other members of the team were Davey,

Buzz and Paul and were all sound lads and very experienced. We were all good at our job and made a good team. We mixed well, socialised together and as a result knew each other inside out and respected each other totally. Trust was never an issue, which was very important.

My first night saw my mates come in and they kicked off with some lads from a neighbouring town. All parties got kicked out. The lads from the other town knew me and turned their attention to me and the other lads on the door. The police chased them, but they were back the next week tooled up. The lads at Masters were a step ahead though, and we had a reception committee from a couple of other bars waiting for them. Never had trouble with those lads since. Funny that! But working the doors now has changed beyond recognition. The licence has really taken a lot of good lads' livelihoods away. Also, we now have a lot of substandard door staff as wages have come down, good door staff have left, which has attracted general security guards into the game. Cameras can help you, but they can also be a hindrance too. I believe that the increase in CCTV has actually made our job harder; more restraint has to be shown. You have to have the patience of a saint with some punters. The CCTV can show you pushing someone away after he's just called your mother a cunt. Sadly, CCTV doesn't pick that up and visually you look like the guilty party. The SIA started off badly but seem to have their house in order now; my renewal only took eight weeks this time around! To be honest, I struggle to think of many good changes to the industry. The bad things are less hours, reduced pay, CCTV, paperwork, too many inexperienced door supervisors, too many youngsters with attitudes and, of course, the SIA badge causing the loss of so many good door lads. However, saying all that, I suppose the SIA are a step in the right direction at least, but we all really need a reliable union to represent us. Only then will we stop being taken for granted and start earning the money we deserve. People generalise when they think of door supervisors, but we have the upper hand on them from the off and we should use that power. Imagine a union calling a strike on New Year's Eve if our demands weren't met for better pay! I also think that all door supervisors need to go on an extensive restraining course, not just a two day course that the SIA are currently aiming to introduce, but proper ongoing training; also, first aid training, of course. I just think that the whole training at present is inadequate and Newcastle Council's course before the SIA was a lot better and it also meant that there was a rapport between us and the police from day one; something we need, like it or not. Life hasn't always been easy up here on the doors. For example, The Hoppings fair would visit Newcastle Town Moor for a week every year in June and, apart from bringing bad weather, it would bring a whole lot of trouble in the form of gypsies. Personally, I think that 'travellers' are the worst type of gypsy you can come across, although, as a Newcastle fan, Sunderland fans do come a close second! From my own experience 'travellers' are always looking for bother with anyone who so much as looks at them, and this particular night was no different. It was a quiet Thursday and a couple of door lads were late arriving and so there were only three of us on duty. We had already let in a group of lads on a stag night from Edinburgh (have you ever seen a sober Scotsman? Neither have I!) The gypsies looked alright and arrived in dribs and drabs and, because we were fairly quiet, we had no objection to letting them in. It took all of five minutes before the alarm was ringing. "Fight in Bar One," came the call over the radio. Sure enough, the Scots and the gypos had been introduced and Paul and I had a riot on our hands. Johnny, the other lad, had to stay on the door as standard practice. There was a ruck of about 20 blokes punching and kicking seven bags of shit out of each other. Paul and I got amongst it and pulled them apart as best we could. I pulled a few back, sovereign rings and all, while Paul weighed into the kilt wearing warriors. Our backup arrived in the shape of Simon and Vaughn and we eventually managed to get them all outside. It was like the Wild West! Blood and snot were still flying as we ragdolled the lads up the stairs and out onto the street. It was one of the very few occasions that I have actually had to hit someone at work a record I'm quite proud of, as like most doormen I like to go into work, earn my money and go home without any bother if I can help it. But these gypsies were from the school of dirty fighting. One gypo decided he fancied a bite of my arm, but I managed to pull my arm free before he drew blood. I caught him with a cracking uppercut. I followed that with a straight left. Sweet. My old boxing coaches, Bernard and Tommy at Felling Victoria, would have been proud.

I love a good joke, and am lucky that I can laugh at myself. At one stage Legends was renowned for its drug using customers and, as I spent most of my time there on the front door, I would have to carry out spot searches. I must admit that I hated searching people as, having experimented with drugs myself when I was younger, I felt hypocritical. It wouldn't have been too bad if all we had to do was knock these people back, but no, the police wanted us to detain and arrest people. Anyway, I had to be seen to be doing the job and this particular night I had decided to wear my new suit. As I bent down to check the customer's legs I heard a loud rip my new pants had given way and a cool draught was evident at the rear. That is the only time in my life that I can say that I well and truly had my back to the wall! Still, it gave everyone a good laugh that night.

The night Robbie Williams came to my club was one of the most interesting nights on the doors. Graham Hancock, the owner of the security company that had the contract at Sea nightclub, knew that I had looked after a few people in London in my time, so he had designated me to look after any VIPs that came into Sea. Looking after a celebrity is the easy bit, it's keeping the public at bay that tests your patience. With Robbie Williams we weren't sure whether he would be turning up at all, then out of the blue he arrived with an entourage of about 30 people in tow. We had a VIP bar and had to ask ordinary punters to leave their seats and make room for him. Needless to say, there were a lot of people with their noses out of joint. "Why should we move for him? Has he paid to get in? Will he be here next week?" I agreed, but I was just doing what I was told, mate! Once the area was cleared, Robbie appeared and the drinks started to flow. Bottle after bottle of the finest champagne was downed as more and more people flocked upstairs to get a view of their idol. He was a lot smaller than I'd imagined and was jumping all over the place. If he had been anybody else he would have been chucked out! I was on the door of the VIP lounge and a lot of girls were trying to get past me to get to Robbie, some even offering their services if only I would just let them past. Not a chance! Even people who should have known better started to say that they would report me to the owner if I didn't let them in! (I just couldn't understand why someone would want to embarrass themselves like that.) Just as we had things under control, Robbie jumped up again and started singing his number one hit 'Angels'. Well, the place went mental as his fans sang back to him. I wasn't impressed; I was just glad I wasn't his personal security because they really had their work cut out. The paper next day reported that Robbie had bought everyone in the club a drink. Well, we didn't get one! There was also talk of an alleged £3,000 bar bill outstanding. That's rock and roll.

My Top Ten Tips for staying safe on the doors are:

Talk first and foremost and assess any situation.

Socialise with your door team. It builds morale.

Get to know every local face, inside out.

Be as respectful as you can be to everyone you deal with.

Don't get involved in backstabbing; causes problems in all lines of work and sinks morale.

Get to know the bar staff and glass collectors. They could help you inside your venue when you least expect it.

Do each shift as if it's your first and avoid complacency.

Try to avoid choking people out; nine times out of ten a walk out is achievable.

Make sure your back is covered before you go steaming in.

Make a note of any ejections. You never know what's going to happen next and that write-up might be vital.

Lastly, there are many great doormen and friends who have influenced me over the years and for whom I have the greatest respect, including Geoff Oughton, great guy, hard man and bloody good gaffer; Alan Scott, a man's man and an old hand that you would want in the trenches with you when things got nasty; Graham Hancock, who showed me how to do the job simply and effectively; and many others. I will always have your back.

Do You Know Who I Am?

By Robin Barratt & others

It was my first night on the doors in Manchester city centre. I had quickly learned the word 'scrote' and I already knew what a 'knobhead' was, and these two black guys approaching my door certainly looked like both. I looked across at my colleague, Steve, who nodded to me knowingly, and we instinctively moved closer together to block the entrance. It seems that all scrotes and knobheads are the same the world over; they have a kind of walk that lends itself to severe constipation and they flap their hands and fingers about in various poses that remind me of the mentally retarded in a psychiatric hospital (no offence to the mentally challenged!) They also have this vacant look in their eyes, as there is little brain matter in their tiny skulls and even the most basic skills and actions for most scrotes and knobheads are complicated; they understand little and communicating with them is almost impossible. "Sorry, lads, you can't come in," I said as plainly and simply as I could as they approached the door. "You're 'avin a laff int ya?" the taller of the two mumbled. Now I know I'm not the most educated of doormen, but I'd previously worked the doors for many years in many towns and cities across the UK and I really didn't understand one word of what he'd just said. They were obviously alien scrotes and knobheads as well, and I was sure that they'd just arrived from the planet Zob they looked as though they had. I looked at my colleague, who smiled and shrugged. "Sorry?" I said to them, confused. "A laff, you're 'avin a laff." I turned again to Steve and quietly asked, "What is a laff, as I'm supposed to be having one soon?" He smiled and shrugged again. Steve was not a man of many words. I turned back to the alien scrotes from the planet Zob and said, again as simply as I could, "Sorry, buddy, I don't know what a laff is and I'm sure I don't really want one anyway, but you're not coming in tonight." "Do you know ooiam?" the taller scrote replied. "Do I know Ooiam? No, never heard of him. Does he work the doors too?" I asked. There were many Asians in Manchester and I knew a few of them, but I'd never heard of Ooiam.

Steve laughed.

"Listen, lads," I said, "I don't know who Ooiam is and I don't want a laff, whatever that is."

I knew they were obviously not of this world and I simply didn't speak their strange language, so I thought I wouldn't try to communicate with them any longer. I was tempted to try sign language, or perhaps a few musical notes from Close Encounters, but decided against it.

So I said, "Just fuck off."

Amazingly, they must have had the very same word on the planet Zob, as they started screaming, waving their hands around and shouting in some strange language.

Steve looked at me and laughed and then responded, "We're going to have to teach you a little Mancunian."

When I was on the doors, if I stopped someone coming into my venue and they said to me, "Do you know who I am?" I normally replied, "Yes, you are a cunt, now fuck off." Now, I have to admit that this wasn't always the best of replies, and I wouldn't recommend that you say the same thing. And I will be honest with you and own up by saying that it did often cause me quite a few problems. Surprisingly, wannabe gangsters never really liked being called a cunt, not to mention being told to fuck off! But people saying to me, "Do you know who I am?" was a real pet hate of mine. If you wanted to piss me off, then that was definitely the way to go.

Over the years I've met and made friends with some real hard men. I'm not talking about local gangsters who are big fish in their small pond, but real hard bastards who would take on just about anyone, in any situation, anywhere in the world; mercenaries, bareknuckle champions, Special Forces soldiers and, of course, some really fucking hard doormen. And I mean 'for fuck's sake' hard! And yet very, very few had an attitude. These hard men know who they are and what they are capable, and they don't have to prove it with arrogance and a bad attitude. Cross them and you're fucked, but otherwise they look and act fairly normally, and generally real hard men have immense respect for those around them.

I remember working one night at a pub on the outskirts of Manchester. It was full and there was a queue waiting to come in, so we were operating a one in, one out policy. Walking down the queue I noticed a 'face' with a couple of friends. He was a local well-known Macclesfield hard man. I recognised him immediately, said hello, shook his hand and ushered him and his friends in. He knew who he was, and everyone around him knew who he was, but he was still willing to queue up. He didn't walk past the queue saying, "Do you know who I am?" as many scrotes seem to do, nor did people think he was a knob for queuing either; he respected those around him and, because of that, people around him respected him as well. And the fact that I recognised him and let him in then made him a friend, whom I later came to rely on in a rather difficult situation a few months later. Show respect and you get respect. Disrespect people and you get that too. How many times have you heard of a so-called local hard man being floored by someone half his size? Wannabes saying, "Do you know who I am?" will only ever be wannabes.

Geoff Carter is currently 'inside', but he has written a very good, brief account of his experience of reputation and how you can really come unstuck if you think you're someone you're not. The main point of this story is not about violence – for admittedly it is a violent tale – but the fact that for everyone, no matter who you are, or who you think you are, there will always be someone out there much better than you and if you have an attitude and think you're above everyone and can handle anyone, you're eventually going to get the hiding of your life. I'm sure that on the doors, and in life, most of us have met similar people to those in Geoff's story.

I've often wondered how reputations are built and how respect is earned and how both can literally be shattered in an instant. Back in the '90s I remember a local nightclub whose doormen had a terrible reputation – although I'm not saying that all doormen were like that back then! My sister currently works on the door and the majority of her colleagues, whom I have met, are as good as gold, but things were very different then than they are today and this bunch were horrible, bullying cunts. You can ask anyone in Stechford if they remember the bouncers at the Gary Owen and most would likely agree with me and say the same thing: bullies who would stamp on women as well as men. I remember one particular doorman called Verne, who looked a bit like the boxer Jack Johnson. Sixteen stone of muscle, Verne had a mean reputation. He wore black leather gloves and would knock out just about everyone he hit, and that was quite a few! Most people were scared of Verne; his reputation stretched far and wide.

The one thing about the Gary Owen club was that it was the place to pull a bird, and so most of the local lads ended up there on a weekend, and Verne would keep on sparking them out and his pals would be stamping on them in the car park. And so it went, on and on, week in, week out, Verne this, Verne that, don't fuck with Verne. Then one night a lad called Piggy turned up. Piggy worked the door at my local and he was well liked and, more importantly, well respected. He arrived at the Gary Owen on a night off from the door, letting his hair down, having a few beers. What Verne didn't know was that Piggy had just turned pro boxer light welterweight, I think. Verne started mouthing off at Piggy, who responded by throwing one right hook, flooring Verne immediately. After that people were queuing up to bang Verne – his reputation has disappeared in an instant. I'm not sure what happened to Verne, but the club eventually closed down. Apparently Piggy went on to become quite a prolific fighter, but he always remained polite and respectful. Another fella from that time springs to mind. From 1989 onwards I kept hearing of Benny, the bareknuckle boxer; his name and exploits seemed to crop up in many conversations in the Blakesley pub I frequented. I was only 18 years old, and many of the older lads I hung around with seemed to look up to him and speak about him in awe. I copped a 30-month jail term for crossbow robbery and on my release in 1991 I finally met this Benny fella. Actually, it was funny how I got talking to him. I pulled up outside my uncle's house in my spanking new XR3i, bounced out of the car, all full of myself, and swaggered down the path when I heard someone calmly say, "You wanna put the handbrake on that, mate." I turned to see my car rolling slowly down the street. I felt a right lemon running after it. The voice belonged to Benny and we hit it off after that and became earning partners. Although he had close cropped hair, stood 6 ft 4 in and weighed a good 16 stone of solid muscle, from the start I realised that he was far from the 'monster' he was made out to be. With his piercing blue eyes he looked awesome and he was brilliant company. He was seven years older than me and was constantly trying to educate me to save my money and not take any crap from anyone. To many of the older lads in the pub he was hard and a bully and I was constantly being told to watch my back as he would switch on me whenever we had a big earner so that he could keep all the money. All this talk pissed me off because to his face the lads acted as if they loved him. I was brought up to speak my mind, and always have done, and I told things exactly as they were. Benny told me that I was the only one he respected out of all of that lot in the pub, simply because I was direct with him. One thing I discovered about Benny was his total lack of showing any fear. Sure, we all have fear, but Benny never showed it. He once opened up to me that he'd once lost someone very close to him and it had turned him to stone; since then he showed no fear, no emotion. One time, in a really rough pub in town, I had some fella purposely stand on my toes. I had no doubt that I could chin this prick, but it was his boozer with his lads barring their teeth at me. My mouth was dry with fright, but Benny said he had my back this was against maybe ten geezers, but I knew he wouldn't let anyone else steam in, so I ended up kicking the geezer senseless and not even his brothers tried to help. The next day Benny called and told me that the fella's mates were wanting to pay us a visit, tooled up and with shooters. "Come on, let's go to them," he said, and we went to the pub and had a pint and a good laugh while everyone looked on, yet still no one did anything. Another time in another boozer (yes, I went to pubs a lot before being banged up!) a big lad tried to have it with Benny. He was a recently turned pro boxer and really full of himself, embarrassing Benny in front of everyone with his remarks and taunts. In all my life I can honestly say I've never seen any better performance of knocking the fight, the hope and the pride out of someone. Benny just knocked this arsehole senseless, and he actually ended up kissing Benny's feet for forgiveness. Some may say that this was bad taste, but this fella was a bully and had little respect for anyone, so he had his comeuppance. Benny's lack of fear has sometimes been his undoing, however. We eventually went our separate ways, but I did get firsthand info on a severe beating that Benny took a few years back. He'd chinned a fella in a nightclub who was from a premier league firm I mean a real heavy firm. The next day while Benny was in his local a team entered and gave Benny a really severe beating. They came at him from all angles, dragging him outside into the car park and jumping off the cars onto his face and body. There were seven to eight of them and it went on for about 20 minutes. Apparently, you could hear shouts of, "Shoot the cunt." Somehow he survived and staggered away in a terrible state. It wasn't long before he was back to normal. He'd heard that a particular 'head' was boasting to everyone how Benny was too drunk to fight back, so one evening Benny knocked on his door. When the head answered he asked, "Do I look drunk now?" and knocked him flat out before he even had chance to reply. Benny had a reputation; that's without doubt. But he also had respect, for himself and for others. In fact, I have met many 'heads' over the years and Benny is the one I have the most respect for. At the time of writing this I'm serving eight years in jail, but I still have an ear to the ground on the out and the impression I get is that the youth of today try to build a reputation in the wrong way. For some reason they think a tacky ten grand motor gives them the authority to mug other people off and when it comes on top they won't have a fair go, simply because they can't. They can't fight anymore. Most so-called 'gangsters' are scared. They don't know how to fight and they don't know how to take the occasional beating we all get in this game. They now run in packs, mobhanded, and pull out knives or guns. They think that a Lacoste tracksuit and a Tag watch make them something special. It's all bollocks. It's sad to accept but the 'old school' ways are gone; respect is no longer earned, it's bought and sold to the highest bidder! It's a real shame that it isn't like it used to be, as the world would be a much better place.

"Are you disrespecting me?" As door supervisors you've probably heard these four pathetic words time and time again when turning someone away or asking someone to leave. They come from the mouths of scrotes and scumbags who want to be someone and who want to be recognised in their own tiny, pathetic little world, because in normal life they're nothing. They somehow think that they can suddenly command 'respect' by the way they walk, by the clothes they wear, by displaying their bling or by the car they drive. It's strange that people can openly disrespect door supervisors on the door as well as other customers and people around them by causing trouble or behaving badly, or by being bad-mouthed and unreasonable, but they're suddenly the first to brandish the word 'disrespect' when you attempt to do something about it. They're pathetic, narrow-minded cunts in my opinion.

Out of all the places and doors I have worked, for me Manchester was the most notorious for people coming to the doors and saying, "Do you know who I am?" Maybe it's the fact that there are a huge amount of gangs running different areas of the city, e.g., Salford, Cheetham Hill, Moss Side, Wythenshawe, etc., and in all of these areas there are tons of soldiers, all fighting their way up the social ladder and all thinking that they are 'hard'. I have met many of the 'heads' of these areas and know quite a few personally, and I have never once heard a 'head' say, "Do you know who I am?" even to a novice doorman who really doesn't know who they are! But it's their soldiers that say it time and time again, using their 'head' as a threat.

I was once on the door of a posh wine bar in Manchester when three scrotes approached the door wanting in. I turned them away, as they really were scrotes and they would have stuck out a mile in that particular venue. I'm not sure why they wanted in anyway, but they didn't like being turned away and became abusive, giving me the "Do you know who I am?" line. You would have been proud of me, as on this occasion I didn't actually call them cunts, but I stood my ground nevertheless. One of them said that they were Mickey's Crew. Now Mickey Francis was a big 'head' at the time and well known and respected, and it just so happened that I knew Mickey very well and had worked with him on many occasions. So I got out my mobile, showed them Mickey's number on the screen and told them I was calling him to check that it was okay for them to be abusive to me using

Mickey's name. They almost shit themselves and disappeared fairly quickly.

Of course, it can be a big problem when a new door supervisor doesn't really know who is who in a particular area, especially when a 'head' wants to enter a club and the new doorman just hasn't got a clue who he is and tries to stop him. And this can be even worse if the doorman is an arrogant cunt with an attitude who is trying to prove himself, and many door careers have been cut short for people with this type of attitude. Whoever you're dealing with always be polite and respectful, because sometimes you just don't know who it is that you're dealing with! Thankfully, real conflict with 'heads' doesn't happen too often, as novice doormen either don't work the front door of the venues that attract the gang 'heads' or they're teamed up with someone who does knows who's who. Fortunately, most 'heads' tend to stick to the places they are known and recognised, or they send someone in advance to sort things out with the head doorman and clear the way, thus reducing any embarrassment for either the 'head' or the door team.

There are tons of scumbags on the streets wanting to cause trouble and, of course, even with vetting, licensing and training there are tons of door supervisors that still fall into the category too. There are still those doormen that intimidate and threaten, those that look 'hard', not because it's just the way they look, but because it's the way they want to look. I've been there. I've pretended to be hard, to be someone that I'm not, and I admit over the years I've done things that I shouldn't have done and have behaved badly and have treated people badly. I know what it's like and I know this is not the route to take. Arrogance means an offensive display of superiority or self-importance; overbearing pride. Don't be an arrogant door supervisor. Be good to people and good will follow you; be bad and it will follow you too.

Real Training for The Doors

By John Brawn

John Brawn is one of Southern Ireland's leading self-defense instructors and is recognised as an expert in both self-defense and security. Under the banner of his security company, JB Security, John works full-time teaching, lecturing and running doors, and he has trained with experts like Marcus Wynne and Geoff Thompson. Born in 1961, John grew up in Westport, Co. Mayo in the Irish Republic, where he still lives. In 1989 John became a coach with the Irish Amateur Boxing Association, in 1992 he became a Black Belt in Karate Kyokushinkai and in 1993 he became an instructor with the Association and Register of Self Protection Instructors. In 1996 he also earned his Certificate of Completion in Advanced Learning Technologies for Close Combat and became an instructor with the US-based Rape Awareness and Prevention Organisation. John is now the Irish director for several of the world's most advanced self-defense and protection techniques, such as the Blue Max and Bullet Man, and he is undeniably one of the most experienced doormen and instructors around. Both the novice and the experienced should listen carefully to what John says, as his words on training for door supervision are wise and make complete sense.

Would you ever go to a brain surgeon who had never done an operation? Of course not. So why put the safety of yourself, your clientele or your establishment in the hands of untrained personnel? Just as important: why do a job that you aren't sufficiently trained for? The outdated image of 'the bouncer' looming in the doorway or tossing out unwanted customers is now being replaced by the politically correct, licensed doorman who is expected to be a combination of diplomat, legal expert, fire safety officer and first aider, not to mention proficient in filling in the correct forms (in triplicate, of course!) Legislation has been introduced in the UK, and also now in Southern Ireland, to regulate the private security industry, which has been generally welcomed by the sector. Accredited courses for door supervisors may cover all the rules and regulations, but nowhere, it seems, is the actual physical fitness to do the job included in the accredited training programmes! In the UK, the Security Industry Authority (SIA) only requires door supervisors to complete a four day, classroom based course to become licensed. While knowing the theory of any subject is a vital part of being properly trained for any job, it is not the same as being able to do it! I've worked as a doorman for 17 years, and from my experience in the security industry I know that there are people out there who have their door supervisor's licence but are likely to be seriously injured because they don't know how to handle themselves on the job. Door supervisors need, as much as the whys and wherefores, the actual physical skills they may have to use, the level of fitness to apply them and, most importantly, the knowledge of when it is appropriate to use them. The doorman's primary role – or, as I should say, door supervisor's in this politically correct era is to keep underage, drunk, aggressive and otherwise unwelcome individuals from entering an establishment. They generally also have to monitor crowd behaviour, resolve conflict within the venue or ensure that troublemakers leave before anything untoward happens. Although this is now changing, from the initial course content approved by the SIA it is clear that these licensing authorities do not think that training in either self-defense or control and restraint are necessary skills for door supervisors. What happens when all the talking finishes and you have to get physical? For a tiny minority of the population, the only thing they can understand is physical force, and if you can't physically put them out of a premises what options do you have? Experience has taught me the best methods of training for the job, and the course for doormen that I instigated a few years ago certainly shows the difference it can make. A realistic form of self-defense, such as full contact karate, boxing, kick boxing or other combative training, is vitally important. Also important is realistic, scenario based training and disciplines such as Bullet Man or Blue Max, which teach you what it is like to take a punch, self-control and confidence in your own ability – something that you can't get if you don't train in a combative art. Self-defense training programmes are suitable for both sexes. Male and female door supervisors do the same job, so it is essential that the training is the same for both. Female supervisors are now a very important part of most door teams, particularly as violence between members of the so-called 'fairer sex' is becoming increasingly common and can be extremely vicious. The current theoretical training to obtain a licence is generally broken down into two fundamental areas: (a) the role and responsibilities of door supervisors, which includes knowledge of regulations, the law, health and safety, first aid, record keeping skills, and so on; and (b) conflict management, a module that covers communications skills, and recognising, defusing and resolving conflict. Some of the courses provide practical training or work experience as well. All these are very necessary but not nearly sufficient in either depth or breadth of skills. So if 30 hours isn't enough, how much training is needed to provide the basic skills necessary for someone to work as a door supervisor? First of all, you need to have the right kind of trainer, and in my opinion that should be someone with a minimum of five years' experience on the doors. Secondly, it is important to identify the basic skills needed. Strange as it may seem, the first thing I look for in a new team member is appearance. Door supervisors must project the right image and demeanour. You wouldn't turn up at any job looking unkempt, with shoes not polished, etc., so grooming skills should be an important part of training. The most important skill is to be able to talk; to communicate clearly under stress. If communication fails you then have to be able to fall back on your control and restraint skills. You need to know the law, civil and criminal, particularly the use of 'reasonable force' and where you stand as a door supervisor in conflict situations. The theory taught in the government accredited courses is important but definitely not enough to prepare you for a job on the doors. The self-defense and fitness course that I teach to door supervisors in the Irish Republic is 80 hours in total (in addition to the theoretical course), and following that I recommend an 'apprenticeship' with an experienced doorman on a straightforward job the last thing you need is to start out on a difficult situation and be out of your depth. Once you have these skills they need to be put into effective practice on the doors and the best way to do that is as part of a team: men and women working together, each of them having a defined role to play. Regular monthly training as a team is also important to maintain effectiveness and improve your skills. Also, it is extremely important for door supervisors to be fit and healthy. Once you have learned the basic skills you need to maintain a training programme in order to be able to cope with the demands and pressures of the job. I recommend heavy weight training two or three times a week. Anaerobic hill sprinting or 400m sprints, Tabates, kettlebells and hardcore bag and pad work will help to keep you in training for real life situations. Diet plays an important part in any fitness programme. The food you eat is the fuel for your body's activities, and the quantities and types of foods need to be tailored to suit the body's needs. A low carbohydrate diet is best, except on days when you are doing heavy bag work or sprint work, for which a high carb diet is needed. Supplements are essential to give energy and to help maintain the metabolism at optimum level. The high amounts of stress that go with the job, both physical and mental, mean that your body is burning energy more and you need to take extra dietary supplements. Most important are branchedchain amino acids (BCCAs) and vitamin C, along with glutamine to help strengthen the immune system. The types of self-defense training that I provide for door supervisors include pressure point control and restraint, knife defence, Kubaton training, Maglight training and, very importantly, scenario based training. Do I hear you say, "Now that's more like it"? But along with the ability to defend yourself, protect others or simply forcibly remove a customer from a premises, you need to know how not to use your skills to be able to assess a situation from a risk management point of view, control a situation and calm it down, prevent or minimise the risk of violence and, if all this isn't enough, to be able to identify and deal with troublemakers before they get out of hand. Here is where the self-discipline from training in the combative arts comes into play; your posture, your control, your whole approach should be one that will not increase tensions, backed by the clear message that if things get ugly you will deal with them. Basically, the training is a solid preparation for working the doors and gives everyone an overview of the job they're going to be doing and a taste of the pressures that they'll be under as they work nightly on the doors. The best door supervisors are pleasant and friendly and can talk to patrons without appearing threatening or intimidating while at the same time giving off an aura of controlled self-confidence. The right training gives you the skills you need to do the job and the necessary level of physical fitness; it also gives you the self-confidence that brings with it a recognition by others of your abilities, which can be enough in itself to prevent trouble before it starts. And, if there does happen to be that small percentage who are just out for trouble, then you have the ability to deal with it appropriately, effectively and legally.

Thoughts On Respect

By Robert MacGowen

Respect, to those who receive it, induces a frame of mind that is valued, particularly by men who come by it later in life as opposed to the fortunate individuals amongst us who nonchalantly accept it as a right during childhood. Statutory respect as a member of the human race is not gifted or presented as a matter of course to all members of the population, especially in Western societies. This early dearth of respect often leads to a lack of self value, which in turn leads to problematic behaviour.

Respect is a societal reward for position, status and, ultimately, power. During mankind's early evolution this would simply be physical power, and, although many people now hate to acknowledge the fact, physical power and prowess still command respect from others because the human mind-set is still largely that of the evolving animal fighting for its place in the overstretched food chain.

The vast majority of men do not possess exceptional power or strength because it is not now necessary in our organised world of plenty, but in many situations they still instinctively adopt a secondary position to those who do. In the modern world it is possible to claim power in other ways, particularly by becoming wealthy. Having lots of money to hand enables a person to command and claim power over those around him, possibly employees or those excluded from his select circle because they earn less than he does. Low earners, though many may be physically strong, are seen as poor providers and therefore less powerful than their often fat and inactive bosses.

Others claim power over peoples' minds because they are more intelligent or cunning than their contemporaries, and indeed this asset enabled *Homo sapiens* to reach and dominate the very head of the Earth's food chain, despite being much smaller and weaker than many of their competitors. They were even able to change the very environment around them for their benefit and relegate the physically powerful to a much lower position in the hierarchy.

But for those still lingering at the edge of today's society, bereft of superintelligence or great wealth, herded like cattle into schools, jobs, conformities and drudgery by those in command, their innate yearning for respect as an individual is stifled, strangled, and this often leads to difficulties in coping with life's demands.

Those who inherit the genetics of physical power and dominance from their forefathers, those very few who could be 'alpha males' before the invention of money, are now told from an early age that displaying their power in an aggressive manner is a bad thing to be shunned and made illegal by a society based on who can grab or inherit the most wealth. These alphas soon discover that, often without any other means of gaining respect for themselves, displaying their physical power in an aggressive, violent manner commands an awed and instant respect from even those who belittle and deride their actions. Though often eliciting screams of horror and protest, the open admiration, envy and respect show clearly on the faces of both men and women when a physically capable person takes instant control of a violent situation by meting out superior violence in an otherwise equal contest. Displaying violence in a non equal contest is simply bullying and does not earn respect; it rightly reinforces society's revulsion of bullies.

The true alpha is never a bully, tyrant or braggart self pride in his physical ability and manly superiority would not allow it, and he is often quite shy and self effacing. Dominating those that are less able does not earn him the respect he needs; in fact, it achieves exactly the opposite and he is soon despised for his behaviour. The true alpha male carries himself with dignity and an air of approachability – his power and confidence are such that he need not worry about minor challenges or irritations that he knows to be ineffectual, and he is able to rise above such petty situations and the people who cause them. The alpha does not have to seek or work hard for respect; he is given it freely, along with praise and often adulation, because he functions easily as a person and a fully accepted member of society who carries his power discreetly, like a sidearm to be used only when strictly necessary in a fair and non cruel manner. He is, in fact, a man worthy of respect from the whole of a society that acknowledges his qualities, and not just from fellow warriors who recognise his fighting ability.

There are, however, those amongst us who, for one reason or another, are unable to participate and mingle freely in society but who eventually manage to earn respect by facing up manfully to their often insurmountable adversities, taking squarely on the chin everything that life has to throw at them, knowing that resistance is futile but still maintaining the true alpha male's courage, dignity and readiness for repeated battles against massively overwhelming odds. Perhaps it is these individuals who as in the case of fellow author Charles Bronson, incarcerated, demoralised, hidden away from public view and at the mercy of his captors for many years – are often most worthy of our respect and admiration as men of bravery?

Unfortunately, reputation does not work or accrue in an equally simple way, and the possessor of a violent reputation should be extremely careful that it is not built on false reports of their actions. This false reporting, sensationalising and overdramatisation of Mr Bronson's actions, in particular, are undoubtedly the cause of his being locked up for far more years than is just, appropriate or morally acceptable. Charlie poses far less of a threat to society or any individual than the average bent copper or greedy bank manager, and he is certainly a nicer, more humorous, interesting and honest person. We, as members of the society that holds him captive, should demand his release as soon as possible, as history is already showing that we have been extremely unfair to him and, because of that and many other similar cases, that ours is a very faulty society.

Girls On The Doors

By Robin Barratt & others

What is it like being a girl on the doors? These are the observations of doorman Chris Houghton:

I don't think female door staff are given much respect, not just by the punter but by other male door staff. I have worked with many female door staff over the years and in most cases they are definitely a great asset to a door team, especially where female customers and situations with women are involved. Actually, they can also deal with many other problems and can sometimes shut men up quicker and far more easily than male door supervisors too. Men just don't like to argue with women, period, and even more so on the doors. Women are much better than men at calming potential aggressive situations before they turn nasty. But to a drunk, aggressive punter it sometimes doesn't matter if you're a female. At one venue I worked with a female member of my door crew who nearly got bottled by a bloke. Luckily for her I was alert and got to him before the bottle got smashed over her head. As for the bloke, he got dragged out the back and was given the kicking of his life, but the next week he came up to the front door on crutches and apologised to the doorwoman, and ever since that day he has never played up again.

Being a female door supervisor in a still predominantly tough male environment can be pretty difficult and many female door supervisors I have spoken to mirror Chris's sentiments. And almost every male door supervisor has said that when it kicks off big time they would prefer the female door supervisor to disappear somewhere until it's all over – but preferably on the front door rather than hiding in the toilets!

Grandmother Donna Stanley, at just 5 ft 1 in, has been working the doors for over 15 years. She tried to retire when she was 45, but that was almost four years ago and she is still on the doors, and she adds an interesting perspective to the discussion:

As a grandmother, gaining respect as a female door supervisor was a real struggle in a still predominately male-dominated and fairly aggressive industry. My journey started with first gaining the respect of my fellow doormen, and then later some of the more scrotey punters. When I started the doors, over 15 years ago, I was seen as a novelty, kind of fairground attraction. As a female door supervisor, it goes without saying that at first the majority of doormen saw me more as a hindrance and a pain in the neck. And to the punters I was a pushover. So I found myself having to be much harder than most men, which was quite unlike my real personality, being a bit of a softie at heart. My real baptism of fire came at a pub in Twickenham, London, which was filled with the usual gathering of Feltham and Hounslow pedigree scrotes. I had some of the biggest doormen I had ever seen working with me, and so I knew I had to really prove myself and gain their respect. And that opportunity came within 15 minutes of my shift when some little treasure decided to help himself from the bar. As my colleague said, after seeing a man being dragged backwards through the bar by a five-foot-nothing woman, it was a sight you wouldn't forget in a hurry! That evening continued very much in the same vein, with little ol' me, along with what was later to become known as 'the dream team', clearing the pub of undesirables! But I am not just a toughie, and on many occasions I have had to use the feminine touch as well. So after five years of working in that particular area, the respect I got from both customers and door staff alike was amazing, to the point that if I did ever have to use real force the police were usually more concerned about me and my welfare rather than the punters I had ejected. And, amazingly, for the four years I did a one man door I was only in any serious trouble just the once, and that was from a stag party that should never have been admitted in the first place, but was allowed in despite my advice to the manager. As usual, managers think more about money than they do about the security of either their punters or their door staff. But it's true, being a female door supervisor is not always an easy job. However, despite the SIA's attempt to ruin the industry, I will probably be around for another few years yet, and after all these years on the doors it is still great to hear the older 'old school' doormen say, "Wicked! We've got Donna working with us tonight." It's also funny to see the young doormen's faces when I rock up to the door to work. After the shift I either get a "You're bloody mad," or "Hope we get to work together again soon." Now that is what I call respect!

Zarah is another female door supervisor and she works for AS1 Security (formerly SPS) at Mardis in Braintree, Essex, which is a local town centre pub with music, live bands and a pool table. It's a two man door for a 240 capacity venue, although it never gets that full. As there are only two of them, they frequently switch roles, so sometimes Zarah could be front of house, meeting and greeting, and at other times she could be inside the premises, walking round, checking the toilets and the outside smoking area, talking to customers and generally making sure that everyone is having a great, safe night. She loves her job, Here's her story:

I've pretty much always been a big, strong girly and drawn to the idea of a role in security of some kind. As a young girl I wanted to go into either the Navy as a Wren or Army as Military Police, but when it came time to make that decision I had found a boyfriend and decided, in my stupidity, not to do it. A little later I was offered the chance to do some security work, which I thoroughly enjoyed, but it wasn't until last year, after my 33rd birthday and a stint working on a reality TV programme called Jade's PA, that I decided to put myself through the SIA course and get my door licence, so that I could do more of what I seemed to have a talent and passion for. My first door was The Ship in Chelmsford, a busy two man door local pub. I was working with a lovely bloke called Ashley, who had to stop working just a few weeks after we teamed up due to a bad motorbike accident. He taught me lots, as he had been working the doors for over ten years and had tons of experience. My tasks were manning the front door, toilet checks, walk a rounds, customer relations, evictions; in fact, pretty much everything a door supervisor is expected to do I was doing virtually from my very first night. I loved it – and still do. I still get a real buzz from getting ready to go to work early in the evening to actually being there working on the doors, and I love being a female in this environment. So far I've not had any major objections. For the most part the guys see me as a welcome addition to their team and know it makes sense to have a female on the staff to deal with female related incidents. Also, with my outgoing, bubbly personality, I can often defuse aggressive male situations before they get testosterone fuelled and out of control. I think my warped sense of humour goes down well with the guys as well I can talk to them on a kind of 'guy level', which makes for some interesting conversations during the quieter times! Also, being a big, strong girl, I have no problem backing up my team in the occasionally aggressive side of our work, which I'm sure helps the guys see past any preconceived ideas they may have about girls in the job. I enjoy welcoming clients and making them laugh and I always try to be happy as they walk through the front doors. I think that girls feel more comfortable with a female on the doors and that guys initially don't see you as a threat. I think that being female and not looking intimidating puts most people immediately at ease. But it is not just a female thing I think what makes things easier is having a great sense of humour: make customers laugh and the job's half done. I'd have to say honestly that standing on the door watching the general throng of drunken idiots walking by makes me giggle the most. For instance, once a guy came out of another pub nearby and proceeded to try to untie his push bike from its stand. The local police were soon having a word, obviously telling him that he was too drunk to ride home and that he should start walking. So he did and they left. Five minutes later he was back trying to untie his bike and it just so happened that the police were doing the rounds and saw him again, so they had another word. And again he left only to come back again, and this time he got on his bike and rode off! It was just like some Carry On film! Another thing that makes me giggle, and is a trait that we all have, is when we do something embarrassing we pretend it didn't happen and we don't admit it for fear of people laughing at us. For example, some guy pulled up to the parking area in front of my venue in his new, shiny, posh, black Hummer, thinking he was the 'bee's knees' with everyone looking at him. He then proceeded to hit a bollard with his huge bumper and smashed up his (I'm very sure expensive) front bumper and grille! How we winced and then laughed as he hurried out of the vehicle, setting off the alarm, and stomped off up the road without even looking to see what he had done! The police, who had heard the crunching, grinding noise, came to investigate and waited for him to return, as he had damaged public property! One of the most worrying times was a suspected bomb scare in a crowded nightclub. It had been phoned in anonymously and, although it ended up being a false alarm, these situations need to be approached with extreme caution. The thought of possibly dislodging something and ending up being blown to bits did make me a little nervous. But we ended up doing a full sweep of the premises without having to evacuate the building it was not a good time, but it was very satisfying as it was handled professionally and in an orderly way.

Karen's first ever door was back in 2004 as part of a team at a Student Union with a capacity of 400. She had just turned 22 years old and the week that she decided to start working the doors she had been offered a place to start training as a volunteer Special Constable with the police force.

I was down my local pub and chatting to one of the door staff there. We were talking about the SIA course and they told me that the course was actually free at that time there was local funding to run it. At the end of that night I got the details and decided to give the security company a call. I was asked in for an interview and, shortly after, was booked onto the next available course. I decided it would be more interesting and exciting working the doors than being a Special Constable, plus of course I got paid for it and could work alongside my day job. My very first task for the first three hours of my first night was working the front door with the head doorman! I helped with the checking of student IDs, signing in guests, and making sure that customers queued up and were not too intoxicated. I was also keeping an eye on the tills so no one sneaked passed and kept an eye on the numbers so we didn't go over capacity. I was then placed inside the venue, generally making sure that people where behaving on the dance floor and not sneaking in via the fire exits as well as checking the female toilets. My initial impressions of being a door supervisor were mainly very good, although sometimes it was hard work, as certain students seemed to think that they ruled the world! However, I enjoyed building up a good rapport with them and found that having a friendly approach, but firm when need, worked well. The head doorman was actually in his last year at that university and had worked the venue for quite a while, so he sort of knew everyone and told me who were the troublemakers, who liked to be a bit boisterous and who we could rely on if things became difficult, which they never really did with students. Overall, the most important first impression I got was the need to work as a team if you have trust in your team and respect them for the work they do it makes life so much easier. I'm now working at a bar called Babylon. It's a '90s themed bar playing '90s music in a funky environment. The capacity is 300 and I am working within a team of four. The three other guys I work with are classed as 'old school' doormen who between them have 67 years of experience and have built an awesome reputation. With the head doorman I check IDs, conduct female searches and deal with crowd control on the front door, while the other two doormen make sure all is okay inside the venue. By having a firm but friendly approach, our customers have an enjoyable and pleasant experience; they can have fun in a safe environment and therefore come back week after week. That's the real key to good door supervision; be firm but fair and make customers feel safe so they come back time and time again. I think many door supervisors forget this and wonder why they find themselves out of a job. Overall, I don't find being a female much of a problem in this industry, I suppose mainly because I work with a good team who accept me. It's definitely a case of everyone there doing a professional job and you work as a team to the best of your abilities, whether male or female. I have also found that if there is a confrontation between groups of men I have often been able to calm the situation down easier than the male door supervisors. When faced with a female on the door rather than a male, most of the time the aggression and tension will lessen and you can sort the situation out a lot more easily. However, there are always situations that just don't calm down with the feminine touch, which is when you need a good male team to deal with it. The funniest thing that I find being a female on the doors is when male customers believe they can chat me up and get my phone number almost instantaneously. But when I say 'no' and they are embarrassed in front of their mates, I am called every name under the sun. I have now taken to adopting the lads I work with as husbands, for the cases when 'no' just isn't good enough or for some of our occasionally overly eager male customers. Saying that a fellow doorman is your husband works wonders!

How The SIA Fucked Up The Industry

By Robin Barratt & others

At a door supervisors network meeting attended by the chairman of the SIA and a couple of his top executives (none of whom, by the way, had any security experience or background, nor I doubt had ever done a day's work in security in their lives), I asked the member of the SIA panel in charge of training a very simple and straightforward question: if the objective of the SIA is to implement professionalism in the industry, why is the exam to be a door supervisor so very simple and the pass grade so low that virtually anyone (who could speak English) could pass. Also, I questioned why door supervisor courses could be run by instructors that have never set foot on a nightclub door. Even with my limited intellect and understanding, I could see that this is a complete contradiction. Surely, if you want to upgrade and professionalise the industry and you want a higher calibre of professionals looking after the safety and well being of the public in high-risk, alcohol-fuelled environments, you should make the profession of door supervisor much tougher to get into and would also make the training more difficult and the exam pass level much higher. The SIA promised me a reply to my questions, but to date I have not heard back from them, despite sending a number of emails directly to the chairman himself.

Since its inception I have spoken to a lot of people about the SIA and have continued to be one of only a handful of outspoken critics of the organisation. From individuals to directors of large security companies, many people agree with many (but, of course, not all) of the things I believe, but quite frankly it seems that the security industry in general has been scared to stand up to the Authority, firstly because security companies need the SIA to trade, and secondly because individuals need the SIA to work. So nothing much is said and the line is towed, even though almost everyone I have spoken to has said how the SIA have completely fucked up the security industry and not just the people on the doors either. For example, British bodyguards are now the laughing stock of the world. You can be an 18-year-old Tesco shelf filler, attend a course, pass and get your UK government approved licence to work as a bodyguard (no offence to Tesco shelf fillers, just an example). Bodyguard training is now available to absolutely anyone without any form of vetting and testing whatsoever, and apart from having to undergo a criminal record check literally anyone, no matter who they are or what their background, can get a government licence for Close Protection. All you need to do is pay your money. And, unbelievably you don't even need to have worked as a bodyguard in order to become a course instructor you just need a teaching qualification. What a farce!

And, of course, the same is true with door supervision. Aberdeen's Scott Taylor makes some very pertinent points about the job:

Many of us doormen are still portrayed as the mindless, knuckledragging thugs of yesteryear. But things have moved on since those days and now a lot of the time doing the doors is not about the violence or abuse, it's about building friendships with our customers, having a laugh with our work mates and, at the end of the day, having respect for our jobs. The job has certainly changed over the past ten years, some of it for the better and, of course, some of it for the worse. It's because of the bad things that have happened to the industry that I shall shortly be leaving the doors for good, as I have had enough and just do not agree with some of the changes; for example, one man doors. Managers' greed and saving an extra 50 quid a night have meant that they really don't care any more for both the sole doorman appointed to the door or their customers' safety. I think there are now more one man doors than I have ever seen before. And over the past few years I have even had to reluctantly work a few one man doors myself! But every time I have, I've made a point of telling the manager that, should the proverbial hit the fan, I'm there as a witness only and won't be jumping in solo to tear people out of the venue. This is what being a door supervisor on a one man door means now: if it kicks off, just watch! Sadly, we've followed in the Americans' footsteps and have become a very litigious nation. The TV channels are flooded with adverts for 'no win, no fee' companies, which will sue all and sundry if you have the misfortune to stub a toe on a door frame or slip on a wet floor and bruise your arse. I wonder how many door supervisors can tell a story about how they've unfairly been charged or stuck in the cuffs and a cell because some drunken idiot has taken umbrage to being politely escorted off the premises and has gone on to tell the police a dramatic tale about having seven bells knocked out of them? This rarely happened in the past. Let's face it, now the risks are too great not to have an independent, sober witness working beside you in order to defend you against these false claims! Only recently a friend of mine was jumped by four guys while working a solo door, and they knocked seven bells of merry hell out of him before leaving him in a heap. However, whilst trying to defend himself he bloodied one of their noses, so the guy went straight to the cops and made an assault allegation against him. Since he had no witness himself, the door supervisor was charged with assault; the lad with the bloody nose had three witnesses with perfectly contrived stories in place. Because of this my friend lost his SIA badge and, of course, the job he loved. So if I'm requested to work a one man venue, I'm there to act as a visual deterrent only. Even the training required for door supervisors can be a joke, and many trainers have never done a day's, or rather a night's work on the doors themselves. This is another thing that the SIA have done: legitimising and legalising door supervision training by people with no experience of the job other than a teaching qualification. I'm a firm believer that the people who are showing us how to do the job should have some on-the-job experience themselves, but this is not always the case. I and my team were lucky that the instructor we had was a time served doorman, and he had little difficulty in not only gaining the respect of his class but also putting across the coursework as it should have been taught. To give you an idea of how important this is, back in the day when the local councils in Scotland issued their own badges we had an awful, mismanaged course set up in Aberdeen by the city council. A lot of the customer care portions of the course were based on the model used by the fast-food chain McDonalds, and the legal aspects of the coursework covered not one issue that we would face in our line of work as door supervisors! Although we approached the council and asked them if they could please consult the door community about the coursework, even with us bringing examples of well run courses from other councils, they dug in their heels deeper and kept the course as it was. It was an absolute disgrace. At least now we're all being taught one course all across the UK (despite the odd difference due to variations in Scottish and English law), and that is definitely the good side of current door supervisor training. However, like the much maligned courses set up by the Scottish local authorities of the past, I can't help but feel that the current syllabus put forward by the SIA is still woefully inadequate. As much as they hope to improve things, I still feel that long term the SIA are causing more damage than good. We're losing time served stewards who can't get badges, sometimes losing their jobs for things they've done in the distant past or that are in no way related to their employment! Now, young men, foreign students and immigrant workers are being put through the course and being launched onto the doors with very little training or experience, and because we've lost the older, experienced lads there's nobody there to help these young bucks get through their 'apprenticeship' and learn how to do the job properly! I've seen many doors in my city where agencies have thrown together six or seven young lads or girls with badges with nobody there to lead or guide them. What happens in such circumstances is that they then all compete to be the 'alpha male' of the pack and inevitably fall into the old 'bouncer' stereotype as they battle to be the leader. That's not to say that I have anything against foreign workers coming into our trade, but as there's nobody there to show them how to work properly, can you expect them to do any different than to become generic thugs? Sure as hell, the SIA in their infinite wisdom have given them little or no guidance due to their overpriced and under researched courses. Thankfully, many years after the first SIA course was introduced, control and restraint training should soon become a part of all door training and every door supervisor will need his or her certificate. This is one of the most important aspects of our job, yet amazingly it is also one of the most neglected when it comes to training! It baffles me that the whole 'stop, stop, stop' philosophy taught by the SIA isn't absolutely laughed out of the building! I'm sure if I tried that when some 20+ stone rugby team were laying out folk in the middle of the bar, I'd probably wake up two days later with a tube down my throat and a foreign object rammed unceremoniously into my anus. Sadly, with the loss of a lot of our older and more experienced stewards, newer stewards aren't getting the guidance that would have been available to them a few short years ago. During my first few years working the doors, I was lucky enough to work with a team of lads that not only showed me how to develop my confidence and conquer my fears, but also showed me the safest ways to restrain people and to defend myself. This doesn't happen much anymore, because there is no one around with this experience. As I mentioned, sadly the licensing debacle with the SIA has forced many of the widely experienced guys to call it quits either because of previous convictions or through refusing to pay for new training and a licence to do a job that they've done well for a number of years. So what we're seeing now are teams of young door staff being thrown together with no guidance, and without the guidance of an experienced, mature doorman I can only see more and more of these young guys and girls with the wee blue badge becoming bouncers again rather than professional door staff, and, despite the SIA's best efforts to professionalise our industry, it will start stepping backwards into the pit that we've all worked hard to dig ourselves out of. Another thing missing in the training for door supervisors is first aid training. The first person anyone goes to in a medical emergency is always the door supervisor, and yet the SIA have still not made First Aid a compulsory qualification! Here in Aberdeen we're in the middle of talks with a large, offshore training company to set up a first aid course that will be targeted towards those of us who work in the nighttime industry. This will hopefully work out at a very low cost, and it will be aimed at training us to deal with events that we may face, ranging from stab wounds to drug and alcohol abuse. I think it's very important that we have at least some grasp of first aid in our work, and sadly this has been an area largely neglected. I think more door companies should ensure that at least one of the venue's team is trained in first aid that would be a great start.

I completely agree with everything Scott has said.

Over the years I have literally received thousands of calls, emails and letters about the industry from door staff around the country. (In 2008 I also tried setting up a Door Supervisors' Association, which sadly stalled before it really got off the ground due to lack of support.) However, as time passed and as I spent longer and longer away from actually working the doors, I found I couldn't really reply to all these comments and questions effectively or with any real knowledge and sincerity, because I just wasn't up to speed with what was going on in this rapidly changing world. Although I had held various licences, including Manchester and Westminster (London), my experience was pre SIA and 'old school' and so I decided to attend an SIA accredited door supervisor training course in order to experience the level and standard of training that door supervisors were getting today and to try to understand the 'new school' philosophy.

As pointed out earlier by Scott, many door supervision courses around the country are taught by people that have never actually worked the door and whose only objective is to pass as many students as possible. The only qualification you need to teach door supervision is a teaching certificate! This I consider foolish, dangerous and downright arrogant. When I was researching for this book one course provider actually boasted that their instructor was a retired college teacher who had not been in a nightclub himself for almost 30 years! "But our quality of instruction is first-class," they told me. Maybe the quality of instruction was 100 per cent, but the knowledge of the subject taught was less than zero.

The first door supervisors course I ever attended was with the Ealing Council, in west London. Run by the then Metropolitan policeman Andy Walker, it was excellent and pioneering and one of the very first door supervisor courses for the industry in the UK. Even now, many years later, I remember the course well and the venue, a nightclub/theatre in Northfields, near Ealing Broadway. And then for a security contract I had in the centre of London I attended the Westminster course. After that, as a career doorman, I attended a number of other courses all over the UK, including Manchester and Macclesfield. Although some of the core skills were the same as those taught on door supervisors courses now, the style of training back then was very different and, in my opinion, the training we did in terms of relevance and connection to the actual job on the doors was infinitely better. Back then we were taught also about fundamental first aid, which I still absolutely believe should be a key requirement of training for the door supervisor today. In my opinion every professional door supervisor should have his or her First Aid at Work certificate, and until that happens *every* door team, whether two man or a team of twenty, should by law have at least one qualified first aider on hand *every* night of operation. I have worked the doors for almost 20 years, and every single time a customer has suffered a physical injury he or she has always sought assistance from the door staff. Always. They don't fight their way to the bar and ask a barman, or stop a glass collector, or wait around for the management to turn up; the first people they head for are the door supervisors. However, according to the SIA, door staff do not need to be qualified in first aid, and therefore the very people appointed to look after the general public in times of danger or difficulty are not qualified to do the job!

Back in Ealing and Westminster we were also taught control and restraint techniques. I also fervently believe that all door supervisors (and close protection officers) should have some form of self-defense and control and restraint training. At the time of writing, the SIA still do not see this as a requirement, however. As a member of the British Bodyguard Association I speak to many, many close protection officers (CPOs) worldwide, and when I mention the fact that CPOs in the UK do not need to undergo any self-defense training they literally roll about in laughter. As with close protection, I think that all door supervisors should be able to defend themselves, for if they can't because they do not have the knowledge and power to do so, how can they defend the people they are employed to protect? I agree that in most cases verbal communication can, and will, defuse most potentially violent situations, but not all of them! Without even the basics of self-defense, door staff and their customers are clearly being put in harm's way, even though courses clearly state that if the situation escalates then the door staff should stand back and call the police and not ever put themselves in danger. What a load of bollocks! In my opinion, this attitude of retreat when the going gets tough is what is fuelling this downward spiral of disrespect. On every course I attended back in the '80s and '90s we were taught restraint techniques and they really did work when out working on the doors. We learned the basic skills and practised them time and time again within our team, and then we used them when we really needed to and when other nonviolent solutions just weren't an option. Security guards working at hospitals are taught these techniques, and so are many nursing staff, especially in psychiatric wards, so why aren't door supervisors? The SIA want to professionalise the industry and get rid of thugs and bullies and yet, by not including these techniques as part of the training, they are still treating us as though we are all thugs and bullies. Even with their licensing and criminal records checks, it seems that the SIA still don't trust their license holders and so they won't offer proper training relevant to the job.

So I decided to attend the Level II course in door supervision and I have to say that I was both appalled and dismayed at the standard of the people now entering this industry. I simply couldn't believe that some of the people on the course actually wanted to work the doors. If I wasn't a polite person (and, of course, respectful, ahem!) I would've asked them if they were actually in the right training room and suggested that perhaps they should be on the needlework and crochet course next door. In particular, two of the students were only there because the 'dole' sent them (otherwise their benefit would be suspended), and they thought it might be a bit of a laugh to work as doormen. They turned up late almost every day (which showed a complete lack of respect for both their fellow students and the instructor) and failed to show any real interest in what was being taught. They were complete knobs but passed the exam nevertheless, and a few weeks later I heard that one was actually working as a door supervisor!

Fuck me, what is this industry turning into?

Twenty years ago I would say that 80 per cent of those attending a course looked as though they could handle difficult situations, such as violent and aggressive punters and real emergencies, and could quell most potential unpleasantness with just their physical presence. Now 80 per cent of the candidates on the course look as if they would run a mile at an angry voice! For example, on the course I attended there was a 55-year-old frail looking woman, the two 'dole' scrotes, numerous timid looking 18/19-year-old university students needing a little extra cash to pay off their loans, and an assortment of other characters who would never make it past the first group of irate rugby players intending to storm the door. Whilst I understand that in many ways the doors are very different now, the actual environment in which door supervisors work hasn't changed, or at least not for the better. I'm sure everyone would agree that there is now more violence on the streets than ever before: more stabbings, more conflict, more disrespect and more attitude. Why, then, are door supervisors not trained with this in mind? Or do people think that it will never happen to them and they will have a trouble free, stress free career on the door? Or perhaps they think that the police will always be there for them if things get a little too tough? What, then, is the point of qualifying and licensing door staff if they have then to rely on the police?

In April 2009 I read a shocking story in a Nottingham newspaper about jobless youngsters being trained as door supervisors for city pubs and clubs in the Nottingham area. The Unity project has apparently already helped more than 40 youngsters to train for the job.

How in God's name is this professionalising the security industry?

Have any of the senior managers at the SIA ever been around the roughest pubs and clubs in Greater Manchester and chatted about the job to actual door staff? Have they ever worked the doors themselves in order to gain complete understanding of the nature of the people that door staff have to deal with on a nightly basis? Have they ever had to turn away a group of scrotes determined to wreak havoc?

I understand that while originally researching the licensing system for the security industry the SIA spoke to and consulted with many well respected, well-known and well regarded individuals, so why did they not, as a result, introduce real and relevant training tailored to a real and relevant environment rather than an environment that the chairman and his cronies know nothing about?

Another question: why, if the SIA want to professionalise the security industry and raise the standards of both security training and operations – objectives that I and everyone else in the industry fully support – are they so unprofessional themselves? For the first few years of trading, the SIA rarely answered their phone and almost never replied to emails, and when they first started they took months to process applications (my own application form took almost three months to arrive after an online request!) And they still continue to lose documents and application forms and treat most people with complete contempt. The SIA want to get rid of arrogance and incompetence in the security industry, and yet for a long time they led the way in terms of arrogance and incompetence. Ask anyone what they think of the SIA and most will be of roughly the same opinion. How can an organisation that runs an industry be so detested within that industry and continue running it? If that happened in any other environment the organisation would be immediately closed and the directors brought to account but not the SIA.

However, having said all that, undeniably the SIA have done some really good things for the industry as well, and they have definitely paved the way for accountability and responsibility, which everyone will agree is a good thing.

But they have also completely fucked it up too, and they have not, in any way whatsoever, professionalised the industry.

One day something really bad will happen on the doors and it will demonstrate the lack of relevant training for door supervisors. Sadly, only then will society start to question the sanity of an organisation that accredits and approves door staff who are unable to deal with medical emergencies or even restrain someone adequately.

Showing Disrespect

By Paul Knight

Respect: *A feeling of appreciative, often deferential regard; esteem. The state of being regarded with honour or esteem. Willingness to show consideration or appreciation.*

Back in my day, when Greater London was all fields before there were loads of hospitals built that Thatcher's government closed and eventually tore down to make way for... fields the word respect had meaning. You were brought up to respect your elders, the police and other people's property, and you were well aware that almost anyone could clip you round the ear if you were out of line! Being an East End lad, respect ruled for those dark, shadowy characters that spent their time frequenting the boxing gyms, local boozers, West End clubs and, more often than not, the police cells. These were the dangerous men that your mother would want you to stay well away from but that your dad would be proud to see you grow up like. If there had been such a thing as reality TV back then, these guys would have stolen the show (quite literally). Just having their names connected to your establishment kept trouble to a minimum if there was any at all. These were the warriors of the streets, the minders of the clubs and pubs; these were doormen of reputation, and they were 'old school'.

Today, 'respect' is just a throwaway word that no longer has any meaning. Kids seem to add it to the end of every sentence (along with such other favourites as 'yeah', 'ya get me' and the ever popular 'right'), and the plastic gangsters, wannabes and hangerson seem to feel that it boosts their own existence if it said to them (usually in writing on such social networks as Facebook or MySpace, so everyone on their friends list can see it, click the 'like' button and comment with a series of parrot like words). And the regard that was once shown to your elders, the police and other people's property has vanished in the night, along with manners, accountability and that unhealthy fear of having your parents know what you have been up to. We have become an island (after all, we are no longer a nation or empire) of people that feel that it is right to demand respect rather than earn it. When you mix this attitude with a dash of alcohol, an intake of drugs and an easily obtainable weapon (like a knife or gun), what chance does the 'new school' doorman/woman of today's society stand when their tied hands and regulated code of practice prevents them from ever achieving the same level of esteem that was once shown to their predecessors in the gladiatorial world of security?

Reputation and respect are the foundations of an effective door team in clubland, no matter in what part of the country. Each town has its own collection of venues that are guaranteed to generate their fair share of trouble, from binge drinking revellers to confrontation seeking punters and drug dealing parasites. Nothing has really changed over the years other than the terminology and the selection of venues that are targeted. The clubs of yesteryear (and I'm talking about the '60s, '70s and early '80s) had known 'faces' working the doors, all with a street reputation that discouraged certain people from wanting to peddle their wares or cause any trouble within those particular walls. Granted, reputation was generally earned through a string of publicly prominent displays of violence and whispered connections to the most notable criminal organisation that operated within that area, but it did serve its purpose of being a deterrent. A proverbial 'blind eye' could be turned to these people and their extreme ways of upholding that reputation mainly because most venues were owned by individuals' who operated in accordance with their own needs. But in the late '80s the corporate world took over, chains of nightclubs emerged and the profitable bottom line became all important. The same happened with security companies and the expensive blind eye could no longer be entertained. It boiled down to who could supply the cheapest price for the necessary 'evil' that was the door team; after all, they were a cost that had no real benefit to the establishments. Every member of staff has a function that should generate a return that is greater than their cost: the cashiers take the money, the bar staff sell the drinks, the cleaners make the place presentable to encourage return visits. Every member has a function except the door team, who are an expense that brings little return; in fact, if they are a good team they actually cost the venue money because as part of their job they turn away paying customers to prevent trouble. Prevention, rather than cure, saves time, effort and, of course, money, so when the nightclub trade became all about the 'bottom line' the manager had to take control of the door once more. No longer was a blind eye turned, no longer were door staff the actual people that controlled the club, no longer was a dip in profits due to cash in hand deals to the door team. This was a business and so whenever there were cuts to be made it was the door team that generally suffered.

Most insurance policies for licensed venues stipulate that there should be one security operative to every 100 customers. However, say a venue holds 2,000 people, the new manager's attitude is, "Sod that, there's no way I'm paying for 20 door staff! Give me eight and a couple of lower paid stewards to stand near the fire exits, and I'll guestimate that we'll only have 1,000 punters in on Christmas Eve."

Heard that before?

Respect for the door team went out of the window a long time ago when profits became all important. Where there is no respect, there is no trust. Where there is no trust, there is no commitment, and eventually door work becomes just a job rather than an adventure.

By the early nineties the government had realised that there were 48,000 police officers operating in the UK compared with 120,000 security guards (including door staff) and the latter were going unchecked and mostly getting paid cash in hand. Moreover security, specifically door security, was the one field that almost anyone from any background could walk into without fear of rejection. The government was missing out.

Allow us to introduce the original Door Supervisor's Badge. You are told that you need one to work and to obtain one you need to spend at least £100 on a two day course that will teach you how to do the job that you've been doing (successfully) for the last decade or more. Once that course is completed and you have scored at least 50 per cent in the exam, you then have to pay another £25 to the Council for your badge. Oh, and you also have to wait for a police check and be given the okay before you can go back to work at the venue you have been working for over the past decade or more.

This was the government's way of legitimising the door industry and weeding out those with a criminal history of violence or known notoriety (you know, the type of people you wanted and needed working your doors). The councils want to cash in big time on the security industry because you now have to pay to earn. The only other industry where you have to pay to earn is the 'work from home' scams of stuffing envelopes, but, with 120,000 people out there that needed to fall into line in order to carry on supporting their families, it was kind of guaranteed that this was going to make a lot of money for the councils. So, naturally, it wasn't long before other councils around the country introduced their own badge. It wasn't about professionalising the industry; it was all about money. And it was even worse in London, with each borough having its own badge. I remember back in those days, if you floated around taking work as and where you were needed, you literally had to wear a £500 Rolodex of door supervisor badges around your neck just so that you could be sent to any venue to get a night's wage.

So the venue managers shows you little respect by cutting down the hours and the number of men to squeeze out an extra few quid in profits, and then the government shows you little respect because if you work security you have to pay to work. And then it comes to pass that your own teammates no longer show you any respect because of the constant changes in the people actually working the doors.

What's a person gotta do to get a bit of fucking respect around 'ere?

With the introduction of local council and London borough badges, and the weeding out of the more 'dangerous' door staff, who had done time in prison or had a more 'colourful' police record, the new school of door supervisor became your plain, run-of-the-mill student out to earn a bit of beer money. (This is from my own observations when working the doors around London and its outskirts during this time.) Many door teams had no consistency and it seemed as if there were new additions to the teams each and every week; people would start and never come back once they'd got a taste of what working the door of a busy club was really like.

So, amongst the established teams, doubt and distrust were given to the new 'green as grass' operatives with their fresh door badge around their necks, who thought it was great that they were now the big, tough men turning drunks and the like away. And with this came a lack of respect for fellow teammates.

As with any group, a door team is very wary of new members, and new people have to prove themselves before being accepted into the clique of a good door team. In 'door' terms, that means holding your own when it kicks off, standing your ground when turning people away and having your teammates back you, no matter what. And until that happens you are on the outside looking in. If you don't prove yourself quickly, you'll find yourself on your own: the conversations will be limited, the camaraderie won't be shared and, although the team will still be there to bail you out if there is trouble, you'll be seen as a hindrance rather than an asset. I've seen a colleague physically turn on another at the end of a shift because they were seen as a liability. So the building of a strong team is paramount if a security company wishes to retain a contract. Naturally, once a full team has bonded and everyone works well together, each member's capabilities having been proven, it becomes a well oiled working machine and in the past that team then rarely changed.

Once you have created that 'perfect door team', you would think that respect would be shown to all its members, wouldn't you? Respect for the door supervisor who knows the customers' names; respect for the one who remembers the troublemakers and drug dealers and effectively keeps them out; respect for the one who welcomes new customers and deals with trouble professionally, discreetly and with precision. Respect for the perfect door supervisor and door team would seem a natural reaction, wouldn't it? Admittedly, for many it is: regular customers do feel safe; new customers do want to come back time and time again because they had a good time; bar staff and the box office staff do know that they are protected and safe; and the members of the door team know that they will be there for each other, watching backs and not disappearing at the first sign of a confrontation. This works fine before you take into account the overzealous, business minded, profit-driven managers (or owners). Then it all comes back to the bottom line, and they would rather replace their perfect door team with a team that costs half the price! After all, there are now no more problems; drugs are no longer an issue and the establishment has a good, friendly clientele, so why waste money paying for the old team?

Bang! And then it happens. The fragmented team, or one that comprises those on a minimum wage, no longer goes that extra mile for the venue or its management and trouble creeps back in. With new, cheaper faces on the door, novice and unprofessional, the club slowly gets a bad name again, the customers stay away and finally the club is either sold or closed for a refurbishment and relaunch.

I saw this happen many, many times when I was doing the doors. Businesspeople never understand the benefit of a good door team and why they are worth the extra expense. Respect is lost to those who truly deserve it and who have put in all the hard work to earn it.

The following is a true account that illustrates, firstly, the level of disrespect given to door staff by a venue manager and, secondly, the lengths you have to go to in order to earn respect amongst door staff!

Disrespect at the Mean Fiddler

I had been doing the doors on and off for a couple of years before signing up full-time with Scorpion Security in North London. My personal life at the time was not in a good place; mentally, my thoughts were dark I was sinking fast and I didn't know it. It just seemed as if I had nothing left to lose. I'm not setting the scene for some reckless moment, or trying to make excuses for my actions or outlook, I'm just trying to point out that if I'd been thinking straight during this particular period of my life there is no way in hell I would have put myself in the situations I did, let alone been crazy enough to have survived them!

I signed up on Scorpion's books in November 1992. I worked the door at Sam's bar (owned by Samantha Fox – model, singer and then British icon) in Tottenham as well as at Enfield Palladium, Burger King in Leicester Square, World's End in Camden and on and off at other venues. For my first six months with Scorpion I didn't have a permanent venue and just floated around for them, covering absences and holiday time. I didn't mind, as it made the job varied and I got to know many of the door teams pretty quickly too. It also allowed me to take one off jobs that occasionally came up, like the one I was offered on 13th March 1993, St Patrick's weekend.

My boss, Steve Gordon, chuckled as he handed me the details and an invoice for the venue. Scorpion had been asked to supply two additional doormen for a music venue that was holding an early St Patrick's Day celebration. My partner for this gig was my kid brother, Vaughan. Now, I know the term 'kid brother' conjures up all sorts of images of a small, weedy looking, snotty nosed brat that annoys their older siblings by tagging along behind them everywhere they go, but that certainly wasn't the case with Vaughan. He was a month shy of his nineteenth birthday, stood at 6 ft 1 in and weighed in at around 260 lbs. He had signed up to Scorpion a month or so after me (probably because he was tagging behind me, everywhere I went!)

Now it wasn't unusual for an outside security company to be hired to make up the numbers at a venue with an established inhouse door team. Big club promoters did it all the time, so I didn't understand why Steve had a sly look on his face and was chuckling about the assignment until he told me it was at The Mean Fiddler in Harlesden.

Harlesden was renowned for being a rough, tough and 'lucky to get out alive' place. It was populated by a large Irish community, who would be partying all that weekend because St Paddy's Day was on the Monday. The biggest, Irish owned venue large enough to house such party animals was The Mean Fiddler, and anyone thinking that this was going to be an easy night obviously lived in a cotton wool world. I finally got the joke.

Steve had handed me the assignment on the Thursday afternoon prior to that weekend, and by Thursday night my mobile phone was ringing off the hook. Word had got out that I would be doing the door at The Mean Fiddler and all and sundry were calling me to relay the horror stories of the year before, including the fact that one of the six doormen hired the previous year had been put out of commission with a near fatal stab wound.

Now, I know how much doormen can gossip and, yes, we can sometimes be like a bunch of old women when talking door stories and can occasionally exaggerate a story to make it a tad more exciting, so I was taking all these warnings with a pinch of salt. My reasoning was, if it had been so dangerous previously, why would Scorpion accept the job again? Also, if six guys were hired before and it had been so mental, why were only two being provided this time? In my mind none of it made much sense and I reckoned that the stories had been blown out of proportion, mainly by those who wouldn't be in a fight if the lives of their loved ones depended on it! Over the years I have met a lot of big built, 'I'm hard' doormen who would chat nonstop about the fights they'd had, all talking the talk but actually only walking the walk in the opposite direction when it really did kick off. I had no time for them, and I didn't have time for all these bedtime horror stories about The Mean Fiddler either.

Saturday evening came and Vaughan and I wandered up to Harlesden. As we didn't know the area, it made sense for us to get there early, find the venue and park the car in a good position, i.e., in the light and facing the way out – just in case! We grabbed something to eat from the local burger joint and passed the time by swapping all the scary stories we had been told about this door and the stabbed doorman.

The Ronald McDonald clock was showing it had just gone 7.30 and the doors were opening at 8.00, so we slowly made our way up to the entrance of The Mean Fiddler. The moment we reached the outside of the venue we both looked at each other and decided that perhaps there could have been some truth to the stories after all.

To get into the club you have to walk down an unlit alley, four foot wide by about twenty foot long. It had a kind of 'muggers' paradise' feel about it, which was amplified somewhat by the refreshing smell of stale urine and mounds of litter interrupting each and every step. And at the end of this yellow brick road stood the inhouse security team all two of them. I can't remember their names, so we'll call them Bert and Ernie.

Bert was the first one to speak: "Alright fellas, you with Scorpion?"

Me: "Yeah, that's right, I'm Paul and this is Vaughan. What's the coo for tonight?"

Bert: "I'm Bert and this 'ere is Ernie. Where's the rest of ya team?"

Vaughan: "What team?"

Me: "It's just the two of us tonight. How many in the inhouse team?"

Bert: "Just us two... That cheapskate bitch has done it to us again!"

Ernie: "Fucking slag! I got a good mind to walk off right now. What d'ya say?"

Bert: "Could be the way to go."

Me: (cough, cough) "Excuse me, guys, but what the fuck is going on?"

Bert: "Sorry, mate, the bird who runs this gaff is as tight as they come. You'd think she was Scottish not Irish, cos a penny's a pound to her. We used to have a six man team 'ere, but because numbers dropped for a spate she got rid of four of them , and when the numbers went back up she never replaced them. This ain't right."

Vaughan: "You think... what happened last year... we've heard some stories."

Ernie: "Yeah, one of your guys got stabbed. It was a full on night there were 12 of us on, and we took lumps and gave 'em. But I don't know if I'm gonna stick around if there's only four of us."

Me: "But if you go, then there's only three of us! It can't be that bad. How about a quick tour?"

Bert: "Come on then, I'll show ya around."

We went inside with Bert, who gave us the guided tour: the fire exits, the back stairs and things we should be looking out for. The Mean Fiddler was a two-storey venue, the top floor overlooking the dance floor and stage area, with an open balcony around the middle. It was a large place that could easily hold 1,000-plus punters at any given time and it didn't take a genius to work out the maths: 1,000 pissed up Irish punters, well known for fighting (even the women), to four doormen, i.e., 250 punters each! Christ, what happened to the one doorman for every 100 punters? Things didn't seem so funny to me at that point and I would be talking to Steve about it on the Monday if we survived!

We were then greeted by the manageress. I can't remember her name either it was something Irish sounding and started with a C so I'll refer to her as Cat. Cat told us what the law was in 'her' place, given the type of clientele there. What we needed to stamp on quickly was fighting and punters trying to steal the tills, and no one was allowed on the stage area whilst the band's equipment was there. All ejected punters had to be taken through the front door rather than a side exit, as she only had one CCTV camera, whilst trying not to disturb the other punters. She then said that she wanted one of us on the top floor and the other on ground level all night while her inhouse team handled the door and box office, and if we had any problems then we should go and find her first. We said, "Okay, but if it's only two of us inside and on different floors do we get radios?" Cat laughed. "If you wanted radios you should have brought them with you," was her reply as she walked off laughing to herself.

With the two inhouse guys allocated to the front door, the ratio figures suddenly doubled; now it was 500 pissed up Irish punters each! I pulled Vaughan to one side and asked him if he was up for all this. His response was that as long as I was there he was there.

We decided to knock that 'one upstairs, one downstairs' crap on the head and do a continual walkround instead. We reckoned that constant motion was the best approach in such a situation, and the punters would keep seeing a different face passing by every few minutes.

It sounded like a plan.

The doors opened and people started to trickle in; no long queues and no mad rush, just nice and easy. Perhaps this wasn't going to be such a bad night after all.

By 9.30, as the band did their first set, there were only about 300 revellers in the venue, around 90 percent of whom were on the ground floor cheering and dancing. So, with most of them centralised, we stopped our walkrounds for a while; Vaughan stayed upstairs and leaned on the balcony overlooking the dance floor while still keeping an eye on the top floor, and I stood on a raised drinking area so that I could see over the heads as well as having the bar in plain sight.

The band played for about 45 minutes and then the DJ came back on, starting his new set with House of Pain's 'Jump Around'. The crowd went wild, raising their arms in the air and jumping up and down. Things started to become a tad boisterous. Then, as the Irish national anthem bellowed out, it suddenly dawned on us that admissions had almost doubled, with people still coming in through the front door.

With the influx of additional punters, all jumping around, I lost my visual on Vaughan and no longer had a plain view of the bar either. The crowd were also getting more and more aggressive, because everyone wanted to be on the dance floor but there wasn't enough room for them all. Jumping quickly turned to shoving and, in a blink of an eye, it kicked off.

Instantly I was off my perch and cutting through the crowd at speed to reach the group that had started that evening's first fisticuffs experience. I had no backup, no radio and no idea if Vaughan had seen what was going on. All I knew was that I was alone and had to break up this group of drunk Irish revellers directly in front of me. The music was loud and I was greatly outnumbered. There were just too many for me to try to separate them and I had neither the room nor the time for diplomacy, so I went in swinging.

I clocked the two main combatants with swift shots to their noses, growled at those trying to defend their friends and started throwing out some wild lefts and rights to create some room before grabbing the collars of the main two and pushing them through the crowd towards the front door. Bert and Ernie were no help. I could see Ernie leaning up against the box office, seeming like he didn't have a care in the world, and it was obvious that he wasn't going to be doing much more than that for the rest of the evening either. Bert was still controlling the incoming punters, but he at least moved to lend a hand with ejecting my troublemakers.

Just as I turned to go back inside, Vaughan threw a geezer, who had tried to whisk a round of drinks away without paying for them, down the stairs. His friends weren't happy and were attacking Vaughan from behind. I rushed up the stairs to help my brother whilst Bert threw the non payer out.

Business had well and truly started to pick up. Vaughan and I went back upstairs, where yet another fight had broken out, this one involving broken beer bottles and an attempt to throw some bloke over the balcony and down onto the dance floor. In we went again, dodging jagged glass whilst putting those involved down on their arses before any further damage could be done. It felt like it was nonstop; the adrenaline was pumping around our system and had consumed us. Both Vaughan and I were excited and tense, and because of the place I was in personally at that time this night couldn't have been any better!

There was no real malice in the fights that were erupting. The Irish are a tough people who love to have a drink and let off steam by having a 'row', but you can bet your life that by the next morning they'll all be the best of friends again. So it wasn't real nasty fights I was stopping; I was just trying to ensure that situations didn't get too out of control and go any further than necessary, so that friendships could still be resumed. You could throw someone off the balcony or slice them up with a broken bottle, but then things between them, and for us, would have been much harder.

The band came back on stage for the second set and the venue settled down again, just as though nothing had happened. We knew we had another 45 minutes or so of relative peace and quiet before it all started again, so we thought it was time we grabbed ourselves a much needed lemonade from the bar before the next innings began. Can you believe we were charged for the soft drinks? What kind of shitty, money grabbing venue charges their staff for soft drinks? The complete greed and tightness of the manageress were ringing loud and clear in our ears, and I was really going to let Steve at Scorpion have an earful on Monday if we survived the rest of the night!

The band finished their set, the DJ came back on and 'fight club' started up again, and this is how the evening carried on until about 1.00 a.m. Then things seemed to mellow out; the anger had gone and the atmosphere was a bit calmer. The end of the evening was looking as though it would be less fraught and good note to end on. Friends of those we had thrown out came up to us, laughing and joking, and thanking us for a great night and for not going too overboard when throwing out their mates. The punters slowly started to peter out, so Vaughan and I resumed our continuous patrol routine with a smile on our faces along with a bloody mouth for me and a cut eye for Vaughan.

And that's when it happened.

The dance floor was still fairly busy and the DJ was putting on all the right records for the younger ones in the crowd to suddenly go into 'prat mode'. One youth jumped onto the stage and started kicking the band's drum kit, so I cut through the crowd to reach the front of the stage and beckoned the idiot over. When he arrived I motioned for him to bend down so that I could say something to him over the loud music, his friends' cheers also still egging him on in the background. As he dipped down a little I grabbed his tie and pulled him closer. The sudden movement made him lose his footing and he lunged forward. I reached out to catch him. I was able to support the top of his chest with the hand that was already on his tie, while my other hand went for his belt. I couldn't stop his fall but managed to control it so that he didn't hurt himself, and he landed on his back on the floor, with his friends cheering loudly around us. Surprisingly, he got up, dusted himself off and then happily allowed me to escort him off the premises.

When I reentered the venue after depositing the perpetrator outside the front doors, Cat was waiting to speak to me. She had already summoned Vaughan and beckoned me over to the stage behind the curtain. It was 1.30 a.m. and the venue was due to close at 2.00, so I figured that she was going to settle her invoice so that there was no hanging around for additional business when the place had emptied. But I was wrong! It was then that I realised that C didn't stand for Cat, it stood for Cunt.

"You're the kind of animal we try to keep out of this place. You're a disgrace and I won't be paying for you tonight. I want you out of my club."

Was she shitting me? I was standing there bruised and bleeding from the night's activities, her bar takings had been protected and her troublemakers had been thrown out, despite being understaffed, under equipped and overwhelmed, with little help from her own security team. She turned to Vaughan and instructed him to eject me from the premises. He took a step back and said, "No".

She then called for her own security team, who hadn't been inside the club all night, to throw me out. I was being ejected by the other members of the door team for being too aggressive for The Mean Fiddler! That must've been a first for a doorman!

She then threatened not to pay Vaughan either if he didn't work the last 20 minutes, so I told him I would wait outside in the car for him. Ernie then grabbed me by my arm. I was half tempted to kick off there and then with the both of them, but I figured they were scared, not just of me but also of losing their jobs, so I went quietly.

Vaughan finally emerged and proceeded to tease me all the way home about being kicked out of a venue I was working in! By the time I got in I was pissed off, hurting and tired, but I was determined to have eight hours straight of sleep before I worried about it again.

The next morning I lay awake thinking about the previous night's events and hankering after a salt beef bagel. I was living in Walthamstow, which was a stone's throw from Tottenham and the Jewish quarter of north London. So I got up, washed and changed and jumped into my motor to go and get my bagel, not realising that there were several missed calls on my phone. I reached the bakery in Finsbury Park and had just placed my order for two salt beef and mustard bagels with a couple of side orders when my mobile started to ring. It was my boss, Steve Gordon.

"Geezer, what the fuck happened last night? I got a call to say you went off the deep end and now we're not getting paid. I want to see you in the office Monday morning. We're gonna have this out."

I snapped and laid it on the line to him, about how he seemed to find it funny sending just two guys into a place where only the year before they had six and one of the team had been stabbed, and how we had no radios either and were understaffed in an Irish club on St Paddy's weekend. And now he was busting my balls over a night's wage? He certainly didn't appreciate being told how it was and still insisted that I attend a meeting with him on the Monday. I agreed and hung up.

I left the bakery with my hot treats, and my stomach was growling with anticipation as the smell of the beef and mustard wafted from the bag. I'd just get round the corner when my phone went again.

"Geezer, we've got a situation at the World's End and I'm phoning round to get a team over there ASAP. Can you make your way there?"

And this was from exactly the same bloke who'd just chewed me out! But, as I said earlier, I was in a dark place in my life and turning down a 'tearup' just wasn't going to happen.

"I'm in. Which World's End Camden or Finsbury Park cos I'm in Finsbury Park now?"

The line went quiet for a few seconds. "Shit, geezer, yeah the Finsbury Park one. You're the first one to ask which one. Shit." And then he hung up.

I quickly jumped back in the car and drove up the road to the World's End pub in Finsbury Park (not Camden). I had no idea what the situation was, but I walked straight in anyway and then it all became apparent: the pub was playing host to swastika sporting, onesyllablespeaking skinheads. Now I hate racists with a passion and saw that this was definitely time to vent that passion! I rushed over to the bar where the bar manager, Simon Bird, was doing his very best to stop the place from being smashed up. His unwanted patrons with their neoNazi intentions had scared off his regular customers after all, this was north London and not exactly known for its Caucasian persuasion. And let's face it, that many skinheads don't just turn up in the area for a quiet drink and a spot of Sunday lunch.

"Rest easy, mate, Scorpion is here," I said casually.

Simon must've thought I'd lost it! Just me against this mob and I'm telling him to rest easy! What was I, Superman? Or just plain suicidal?

I took a seat and began to take out my now not so hot bagels. The aroma started to fill the room and the skinheads looked like a bunch of meerkats as their heads up, reacting to the smell of Jewish cuisine. At least I'd got their attention.

"Oi, Jew boy, take your foreign crap and get out of here while you can!"

Now, just for the record, I'm not Jewish, but I do enjoy salt beef bagels and I didn't see why I had to put up with these knuckledraggers.

I stood up from my seat, approached them and said, "Okay, fellas, I'm the security here and I think it's time for you to leave."

They started to crowd round me, with the same look in their eyes as Simon had when I told him to rest easy. Superman? Or just plain suicidal?

"Or what?" Now there was the question that is always asked before the make, or break, of a physical confrontation.

"Or I'm gonna smack you all the colours that you don't like. Now get out!"

The thought that this was going to be a one-sided fight against me suddenly left my head as the rest of the Scorpion crew, who had all mistakenly gone to the Camden pub, came flying in through the doors. And all of them were triple B's Big, Black Bastards who loved nothing more that beating up on racist white boys. They dragged the skinheads outside, and the rest of the story is for them to tell. All I wanted to do was sit in the bar eating my almost cold bagels.

After the boys had finished their business outside and the skinheads had retreated to where they came from, Steve Gordon came in to check that bar manager Simon was okay and that no damage had been suffered. Simon regaled him with the story of how impressed he was that a lone representative of Scorpion had turned up and was willing to take them all on. It showed exactly why Scorpion had the reputation it had, and Simon said that he would definitely suggest to the brewery that Scorpion be hired for more of their venues.

That was the first time I'd ever met Simon, but they say first impressions count, and when our paths crossed years later he was still retelling his version of that Sunday afternoon only the number of skinheads had risen!

Steve sat down at my table as I wiped mustard from the side of my mouth. He looked at me and I looked back at him.

"Geezer, don't worry about our meeting on Monday," he said, and then he left. That was Steve all over: quick to blame but slow to say well done.

I was given permanent work after that weekend, but I never worked at The Mean Fiddler again. My reputation certainly grew as the gossip mongers told their own versions of my story. I think the last I heard I was up against the IRA at The Mean Fiddler and almost all the members of the British National Party at the World's End!

But then doormen do like to gossip like old women, don't they… ?

As we all know, some managers and employers are great; others not so good. Some will back the door staff whatever the situation, whereas others would sack a door supervisor in the blink of an eye. Some venue managers are egotistical knobs on a power trip, while others are friendly, caring and immensely respectful. During the past 20 or so years I have met them all! However, no matter who they are, at the end of the day (rightly or wrongly) they are the ones in charge and, whether we like it or not, we should respect their authority. If we respect them, they are more likely to respect us in return. The strength of a professional is to try to respect others regardless of whether they deserve that respect or not.

Stories From The Doors About Respect and Reputation

Me and Lenny McLean, By Paul Knight

This is a tale that I (not so) cleverly disguised in my novel *Coding of a Concrete Animal* about my first night working with Lenny McLean, at the Hippodrome in Leicester Square, London, back in the very late '80s.

For those of you that have not heard of Lenny McLean, he was a renowned bareknuckle fighter whose life was the told in the bestselling book, *The Guv'nor*, written by Peter Gerrard.

The 'setup' was the same as on other nightclub doors: after a certain hour you are always guaranteed to have to deal with those that chose to get drunk in the pub before having the brainwave of going clubbing. On this particular night a couple of 'suits' started shooting their mouths off because they were refused entry for being too inebriated. They were being abusive towards Lenny, who had taken it upon himself to deal with the situation. I truly thought it was only a matter of time before Lenny smacked them silly. I stood there watching how Lenny positioned himself while his fellow teammates moved with grace to watch his back and move in to inflict damage when the time came. I just kept thinking, any minute now, but nothing happened. Eventually these suits got bored with arguing and staggered off, still shouting insults and threats towards Lenny. Once the two drunks were out of sight and off bothering another doorman at another club, Lenny turned towards me and leant right into my face.

"I bet you would've hit 'em both, wouldn't you son?" Lenny's gravelly voice was enough to make you tell the truth better than any polygraph on the market.

"Well, you definitely showed more patience than I would've."

Lenny eased his face back a bit. Changing the tone from enquiry to wisdom, while looking me square in the eyes, he waxed lyrical with a piece of philosophy that would've toppled Socrates.

"If you learn anything from me during your time here, it should be this: 'It's nice to be important, but it's important to be nice.' You should always remember that."

And I always have…

When you think of Lenny, you think of him as the hard man he was: over 3,000 fights, 3,000 wins and a thousand lifetimes of stories whether or not they were all true, or at least semi fictional, is a different matter. In my eyes, this god could stand toe to toe with Godzilla and hold his own; he was a man's man and didn't have to take shit from anybody. Nevertheless, there he was, listening to those two supposedly intellectually superior beings insult him and his chosen profession, besmirching his capabilities to do anything other than stand on a door like a trained gorilla, turning people away just because he didn't like them. Yet he let them walk away, unharmed and feeling as if they were better than him because of the line of work he did. For all the stories out there about Lenny being a bully (and I'll admit I did see some things that didn't sit right with me regarding Len), it was times like this that made you realise in whose presence you were standing. I will never forget what Lenny said to me that night:

Not everyone knows who I am, not everyone walks our path, and therefore those who are insecure about their own inadequacies will always try to put you down. What's important to me is that I know who I am; my family knows I am a loving father and husband and my friends know I can be relied on. Along the path I have chosen, I am known for many things, but no matter what reasons it all comes down to one thing: I am known. I am a somebody to somebody else, and whether it is out of fear, respect or loyalty, certain people will always listen to what I have to say. It is a good feeling knowing you can hold court whenever you want; most people will never experience that, yet it is something they wish for. By not hitting them two prats, I have given them their moment; it's now something they will talk about for years. They will wake up tomorrow and feel big about themselves for putting a bouncer in his place; they'll feel even more special if they ever realise who I am. It has cost me nothing. I am still the hardest bastard you will ever meet, it has taken nothing away from me, and so I have nothing to prove. Never feel you have to prove something to someone whose opinion will never count; know inside what you are capable of. As long as your nearest and dearest know of your importance, 24/7, then any chance you get let someone else have a brief moment of importance. It could be the only moment they will ever have. You won't be thanked, and it could take years before they realise what you did, but you'll know and that's all that matters.

By Lenny standing there telling me this, I understood that he was giving me, a young fresh faced newbie to the security game, my moment. Lenny was letting me feel important by giving me his fullest attention. I knew I would never be an equal with Lenny, but from that point on I didn't feel so insignificant next to him either. I can only hope that you can take something from this story and apply it to yourself in life.

Michael Jackson's Monkey, By Mick Lyons

I could tell you more stories than the *Arabian Nights*, but mine will be true! Here are a couple of funny ones.

Way back in 1971 I was working at Wigan Casino with one of my mentors, Bert Green, on the Palais door, from which a passage ran for about 60 metres to the street. A certain individual called Roberts, who had been serving even years for shooting at police officers, had just been released and had somehow got access to the club. He was already inside when we were told. Obviously, by shooting at policemen he had gained a reputation as a dangerous man. Anyway, we had the idea that if he behaved we would leave him to his own devices, but if he didn't behave he would have to leave like everyone else. And, of course, he didn't behave! Bert got to Roberts first and proceeded to knock him all around the club and down the 60-metre passage. When Roberts left the building, horizontal of course, he shouted, "You're all dead! I'm coming back with a gun!" We made our way back up the passage and left a guy called Ray on the front door.

Thirty minutes later Ray came flying up the Palais passage shouting, "Bert! Mick! Roberts is back and he's got a gun! What steps should we take?"

Bert shouted back, "Fucking big ones! Follow me!" obviously in the opposite direction.

Another story dates back to the Michael Jackson concert at Aintree in 1988. There were about 170,000 people and it was absolute mayhem. I was in charge of the mixing tower, and about a hundred of my best lads were all working really hard carrying out people who had fainted or been crushed. We had just had a major altercation with Jackson's black bodyguards, who were from the Bronx and were working with us. They were bad bullies, these guys, and had tried it on with us by pulling out blades. Big mistake. We were on them like a rash and fucked them right off, much to the delight and admiration of the American promoters, who said that they had been waiting for that moment for years and couldn't wait to get back to the States to tell the story.

Just after this, when Michael Jackson was in full flight on stage, Gary Spiers, a famous martial artist and my business partner at the time, said to me, "Listen, Mike, I've got an idea. Jackson's monkey, Bubbles, is behind the stage. If we can have that monkey off, he'll give us a million dollars to get it back!"

I thought carefully for a minute and replied, "Gary, do you not think we've got enough foreign monkeys working with us?!"

We never did nick Jackson's monkey.

Professionally Handled, By Jim Myers

I remember one night when the landlord asked me to tell a stag do to drink up! My colleague was outside and out of eye contact and so I walked over to the group of rowdy lads and told them that the management had requested that they drink up and leave. When the gobby little fucker, who was also the local village idiot, started taking the piss, I thought this was about to go 'Pete Tong'. He was the first to go and, as he went out of the door, my colleague suddenly realised what was going on. He told the rest of them that they'd had their chance to drink up and that their mate outside had spoilt it for them and they had to leave too. Surprisingly, as they left they all shook my hand, and at that point I realised that there were some real big fuckers among them and I could have been in some serious shit. A week later another mate and I were out having a few beers when we bumped into a couple of the same blokes. He knew them! They were a couple of 'old school' doormen and they told him the story of how they'd all had to leave my bar the previous week. They said that they were impressed that I'd actually stood up to them all. They also said that I was 'really professional' in my actions and the way I conducted myself. I shook their hands again and thought to myself, thank fuck for that!

New to the Doors, By Jim Thompson

This is the story of my first ever night at work.

I had a call from someone called Kurt from the Mercy nightclub in Norwich and he told me to be at the club for 9 p.m. I was excited and happy, as I was finally getting my foot in the door, so to speak, and would be working my first ever shift as a doorman. Finding my first job after getting my licence had been hard. Norwich was a small place and established door supervisors tended to stay where they were, so there were very few positions available. I got my uniform nice and neatly ironed, polished my boots and made sure that I was looking smart and ready for my first shift. I would be working at Rocco's Bar, part of the Mercy nightclub. I got there just before 8.30 so that I could meet the team that I would be working with and could be shown around. Being new, they didn't put me on the doors, but I didn't care; I just followed orders and did as I was told.

I was alone inside, with two men on the doors. I was asked to stand next to the DJ box, which overlooked the nightclub dance floor. I was given a radio and instructed to radio in if I saw any trouble at all. A 'code green' indicated possible trouble and a 'code red' meant that a fight had actually broken out.

I was standing there alert when suddenly I saw someone landing a punch on someone else. There was no argument beforehand, which I thought strange, just a flying punch. I called in a code red and then went in to deal with it. When I got there the lad on the floor was being picked up by his mates. I escorted the lad that had thrown the punch over to the corner of the nightclub without the need for further violence. I told him to calm down, which he did. By that time the other door staff had arrived and asked me what I'd seen. When I explained what had happened they then took him out of the club, as you can't allow someone that has punched someone else to remain inside. The rest of the night was quiet and I finished my shift at 3 a.m. The first night was great. I had chatted to people and made acquaintances with the door team and I couldn't wait to get started the following week. However, for a few days after my first night I kept asking myself if I could have done anything more during the incident. Did I behave correctly? Did I do the right thing? Even though it was only my first night and I knew I had a lot to learn, I desperately wanted to be a good door supervisor and I wanted other door supervisors to think I was good too.

Because I was only working at Mercy and Rocco's now and then, covering shifts, I moved to another security company and started working at Squares on a permanent contract involving more nights. I would also help cover Henry's and Po Na Na. One night, when I was working at Squares, I had a real urge to knock someone out, but decided simply to remove him from the building calmly. It made me wish that we were bouncers from the '80s, because the shit and abuse we have to deal with now would not have been tolerated back then. Respect for door supervisors has definitely disappeared. I was working the back door and the policy of the club was 'no drinks outside in the smoking area'. It's the policy of many clubs – you can smoke outside in a designated area, but can't take drinks with you. So I told this 'chav' politely that he couldn't take his pint outside, so he said, "You can fucking watch my pint then." I told him that unfortunately I couldn't do that and suggested that he could perhaps leave it with some friends. He then told me to listen carefully, telling me that we were not bouncers anymore but just "a fucking bunch of door attendants, and no different and no better than toilet attendants," followed by, "Now watch my fucking pint!" I wanted to kick the fuck out of him, but it wasn't worth it as I'd lose my licence. This is what the SIA have done to us and the industry. I had him removed instead and he probably spent the night being abusive to other door staff in another venue.

Lastly, a funny thing happened to me with a woman when I was working the door at Henry's nightclub. I have nicknamed her 'the carpet lady', because she was probably in her sixties and was wrapped up in a huge pink blanket, which looked like a carpet. It was gone 2 a.m. and she was in the women's toilet and had apparently been in there for over half an hour. One of the bouncers asked if I could try to get her out, as we needed to lock up. So I went in and saw her over near the sinks doing nothing, just standing there. I told her that we all wanted to go home and had to lock up and close. She asked if I could walk her to the outside gate and I said sure, no problem, as I was now going home anyway. Unfortunately, what I didn't know was that this crazy woman had suddenly taken a fancy to me, and as we got to the outside gate she wanted to kiss me and just wouldn't take no for an answer. I told her I wasn't interested, but every time I struggled free she tried to kiss me again. So I decided that the best thing to do was run away! But no matter how fast I tried to run up the road away from the club she managed to keep up! I could hear the other door staff laughing their arses off as they watched this mad woman chase me home!

Giant and an Axe, By Ryan Hucker

I have been a door supervisor for seven years and during that time have gained much experience in the security industry.

One particular evening back in March 2002 I had managed to get a Saturday night off (which was very rare). I had arranged for my friends and family to pick me up before heading out to Portsmouth for a few drinks and decided I would wait for them at The London Arms in Woolston, Southampton – the venue that I looked after every weekend.

It was around 6.30/6.45 p.m. and there were no door staff working at that time. I had just sat down with a nice cold pint when I heard the manageress screaming, "Ryan! Ryan! Quick! QUICK!!!"

Jokingly, I shouted back, "S'pose I'm working then?"

"Yes, you fucking are!" came the reply.

I got up from my position around the corner of the bar and headed towards the pool table area, which was on the opposite side of the pub. As I was making my way there, I noticed the 'local crew' rushing out of the pub's main door, as though gripped by the fear of God. I remember thinking that this reaction was strange, as they were all supposed to be 'hard men' – or that's how they always acted. They had certainly wanted to be perceived as hard by all and sundry around them, so I had obviously entertained that impression up until that point.

As I approached the pool area, standing directly in front of me was a towering burly character that wouldn't really go amiss as a relative of *Harry Potter*'s Hagrid. In his hand was an axe, which looked distinctly like a tomahawk.

My initial reaction was to take things extremely carefully, so I inched slowly towards the guy while constantly trying to explain to him what sort of position he was in and that he would not be doing himself (or me) any favours by chopping me into tiny pieces.

Luckily for me, the guy listened and laid the axe down on the pool table, but evidently he was still after blood and quickly tried to barge past me and exit the main door. With all my might I struggled to hold this guy on the pub doorstep, at which point I noticed he had a big gash in his lip, presumably from an encounter at some point with his own axe blade.

While the incident was progressing the manageress had called the police. In the meantime, I was on the doorstep holding onto the 'man mountain' – several inches taller than me and twice the size. I breathed a sigh of relief when I noticed a police van approaching the set of traffic lights across the road at speed, heading for the venue. My relief was short-lived, however, as the van drove straight by. After slowing down to take a good look, they seemed to opt for driving around the block rather than stopping to help.

Once the police finally did arrive on the scene, I handed the guy over to them. It took five police officers with pepper spray to subdue the poor sod, and they had to call an ambulance to take a look at his slit lip.

Now, while I was dealing with this situation my friends and family turned up to collect me for our night out. They couldn't believe what had happened. I tried my best to clean off the splatters of blood on my shirt and told them that this was normal for the work we do, and then continued to go out and have a good night.

The following week I popped into the venue and asked about the guy. It turned out that the giant had come into the pub looking for a group of lads in order to confront them over an incident in which they were supposed to have cracked his son (who was half their age) around the head. Unfortunately, though, the giant had got the wrong pub altogether and had started on the wrong crowd.

After that day I was welcomed into that pub with open arms, as prior to that incident the management and staff had become a bit weary of door staff. You could say that I gained a lot of respect that day, and personally I gained an important lesson from that experience – to always think twice about confronting a giant madman holding an axe.

The Week Before Christmas, By Ryan Hucker

'Twas the week before Christmas And all through the club There were 20 or so people All up for a ruck... ... Oh, and how they did ruck!

The night started well. We had been drafted in on the anticipation that the club would be busy. The mood of the team wasn't at an all-time high, but it was jolly enough nevertheless and the evening was relatively pleasant.

... Well, at least for the first three hours.

As usual, we were expressing our concern to each other about the calibre of punters normally allowed into the club (typical chavs; Burberry, Argos gold jewellery and lots of attitude). In fact, it wasn't at all busy and we, the door staff, were politely requesting an early close. However, as expected, management in their infinite wisdom – were claiming that their hands were tied and we had to open for the whole hog.

Anyway, after much boredom and thumb twiddling we suddenly got a call over the radio that there was a scuffle going on at one of the bars. As I attended, I noticed a colleague struggling with someone; then, all of a sudden, hell broke loose. Things went from a two man 'bitch slap' to an all-out 20-plus man brawl. We call this situation a 'code black', as the door staff were severely outnumbered (6 against around 25!) A 'code black' means anything goes!

Whilst grabbing a couple of scrotes and trying to get them towards the door I was punched twice in the back of the head (cheap shots) and bottled. However, I think the highlight for me was when I grabbed another bloke: he and his mate overpowered me and I fell to the floor, with a long haired, ugly freak on top of me! As I grabbed his arm to stop him lashing out, the bugger decided to bite me in the chest. I responded by grabbing the yeti's hair, but the next thing I saw was this guy floating up and away from me. I then quickly realised that another doorman, with the help of a regular customer, was dragging him off me. Thanks to the Good Samaritan would you believe they still exist? As the yeti was being dragged away, I still had a tight hold on the ugly freak's hair and heard tearing sounds as a great wad came away in my hands. I suffered dramatic carpet burn for my trouble, too!

All in all, it was only about ten minutes of rucking, but it seemed to last forever. I would say it was most definitely a team building experience and I personally would like to thank a doorman nicknamed 'Frisky' – he knows why (but that's another story). The guy had only been in the game for a short while, but he sure saved me from a few kickings that night!

We all handled ourselves pretty well and as a result we came out on top. No one found out what it was all about and why they all suddenly turned on us. Out of approximately fifteen people that definitely needed to be arrested the police saw fit to arrest just two of them.

Oh well, all in a night's work, I suppose.

Tragedy at Tiger Tiger, By Anonymous

One of the main tragic episodes, which I can remember as clear as day, happened while I was working at Tiger Tiger in Manchester. I hadn't been working the doors for long and, although this incident happened many years ago, it still feels like only yesterday.

Tiger Tiger is a big club with many levels and a grand staircase running from the ground floor to the top floor. As doormen, we constantly had to make sure that no one attempted to get onto the balustrade or got too near the top floor balcony. This was fine at the beginning of the evening when everyone was sober, but as the evening progressed and people drank more and more, the task become harder and harder – the alcohol inside people gave them a stupidity rarely seen in a normal world!

One of the inebriated customers decided to slide down the balcony from the top floor. Needless to say, this didn't work out as planned and he fell about 70 feet into the basement, with the place packed with around 2,000 people.

At the time of the incident I was inside the front door and just saw this blurred figure falling at speed down the centre of the stairwell, clipping the walls and banging into every protrusion as he fell. We later saw claw marks down the walls where he had frantically tried to grab hold of something to stop his fall. I, together with a colleague, ran down the stairs to the basement, to find this poor bloke just a mess on the floor.

It was a very emotional time as we tried to revive him. We managed to keep his heart going, but his brains were scattered all over the floor underneath him and blood was pissing from every orifice. He seemed alive, though, and had an expression on his face that seemed to indicate that he was thinking and trying to say something.

When the paramedics finally arrived and he was lifted onto the stretcher, parts of his back were falling on the floor (gruesome), and they were trying to keep him together as best they could.

Because this was taking place in the cloakroom downstairs, nobody was aware of it. There were still approximately 2,000 people dancing to the music, unaware that a tragedy had occurred just below them.

At the end of that night all those that had been involved gathered together and sat down with the manager, all devastated. In our heart of hearts we all knew that there was no way he could have survived, yet we were clinging onto the hope that we had done just enough for the professionals to perform a miracle and keep him alive. It was then that we found out that he had passed away.

The Luckiest Doormen Alive, By Robin Barratt

I was working on the front door of a bar and nightclub on Deansgate Locks, Manchester. The Locks had been redeveloped into a row of trendy bars, restaurants, cafés and clubs, all situated under the old railway arches and along a wooden causeway overlooking the canal. The venue opened at midday seven days a week and closed at midnight except for Thursday, Friday and Saturday, when the nightclub was open and it closed at 3 a.m. Most of us started work between 8 and 9 p.m., and the only other times they needed doormen outside these hours was on match days.

On this particular day Arsenal were playing at Man City and we expected trouble. A team of four of us were due to start at noon; it was going to be a long day, as we were to stay on duty and on the doors until the venue closed at 3 a.m. – a 15-hour shift! However, it was going to be a good earner and we would all take advantage of the free food offered to us.

The day passed relatively peacefully. We had a few football knobheads trying to get in before the match started, but they were generally in small groups of two and three and were turned away without much trouble. There was also a heavy police presence on the roads, with regular flashing lights and sounds of sirens rushing past us to other clubs and pubs where the fans were probably causing trouble, but thankfully not to our venue.

It was late afternoon, the match had finished and four of us were standing outside the closed doors of the venue chatting casually. We had very strict instructions to vet all our customers carefully, and only when we were absolutely sure they were okay would one of us then open the doors and let them pass by us and into the unit. Admittedly, it was quite an aggressive way of running the door, but on that particular day we couldn't take any chances; both Arsenal and Man City fans were known to be extremely aggressive and violent and both the police and we doormen expected a lot of trouble.

As we were standing chatting we suddenly heard a rumble. It was quiet at first but quickly grew louder and louder as a horde of Arsenal fans rapidly and thunderously made their way towards our unit. It seemed to happen so fast and, before we could get inside and close the doors, we had our backs to the glass and were surrounded by what must have been over a hundred screaming, ugly, shaven headed football thugs.

There was nothing we could do; we were all expecting to be slaughtered. They were spitting and flicking cigarette ends at us and, with their fists clenched, were ready to have a go. They were just waiting for someone to make the first move. Once the first punch had been thrown we knew the rest of the pack would quickly move in and we would likely be murdered.

As I was wiping their spit off my face I admit that I have never been so scared in my life. I knew I could take two or three down with me, but then we would all be very quickly overpowered and would have been beaten and kicked beyond recognition.

On that afternoon in central Manchester we were all going to die.

At the very moment that one of the yobs stepped in to throw the first punch, the screaming sirens of the police surrounded us, and riot clad officers with batons at the ready spewed from the back of their wagons, causing the thugs to disperse in every direction. Without a second thought or a moment's hesitation, the four of us scrambled over ourselves to get into the unit and to the safely of being behind closed and locked doors.

We must have been the luckiest doormen in Manchester that day.

A Walk on the Wild Side, By Rob MacGowen

The English Lake District in summer was a wild place during the 1960s, and not just with regard to its abundant flora and fauna. Many young Liverpudlians traditionally migrated north from the work derelict streets of home to the richer pickings and catering industry jobs created by the flourishing tourism of South Lakeland. Glaswegians invaded the area in pursuit of a lively and easily reached holiday destination, in addition to the millions of other annual visitors and fellwalkers from all corners of the world.

The hostelries and entertainment centres were packed to capacity nightly, and at weekends additional hordes of locals headed in from the surrounding localities to swell the already volatile mix. Top this off with a motley crew of workers from the nearby M6, which was under construction at the time, and things invariably got lively as the pubs emptied and dance halls filled.

The Embassy Ballroom, sited on a strip of real estate stretching down the centre of Windermere's Main Street, was also home to the local and successful amateur boxing club, having produced several national champions. One of them, Mick Byard, ran a barber's shop next door to the hall. Chief coach at the club, Ian Irwin, was a joiner by day and also worked weekends as a doorman at the Embassy dances, along with an ex boxer colleague, Archie, who had not been the best exponent of the noble art but was big, rough, tough and could give or take solid blows all night. Ian, on the other hand, had been an excellent boxer and had beaten his closest competitor for a place on Great Britain's 1964 Olympic training squad twice in a fortnight. Ian, from the north, didn't get the nod for the Tokyo trip, but his oftdefeated foe from the south, Alan Tottoh, did. No British boxer won a medal of any hue that year.

In 1969 I was training at the club thrice weekly as a 17 year old and usually made it up to the weekend shindig as well. On entering the nearby Elleray Hotel with a few friends one balmy Saturday evening, a terrified girl ran out screaming, bumped into a passerby and fell on the pavement. I was helping her up just as a 6 ft 4 in leather clad biker lumbered out, shouting at her. She hid behind me and I held up two open palms to the biker in a peace gesture. He, though, lurched forward and let loose a mighty swing in my direction. It was easily evaded and I replied sharply and venomously, as I did in those times of my unenlightenment, by knocking him to the ground. The girl ran off across the street, which disappointed me somewhat as she was quite attractive, even with black mascara streaked across her pale face. I joined my friends at the bar.

Later, in the Embassy, I was smooching with a girl to 'Whiter Shade of Pale' when I discovered that the biker was not in town alone. I was surrounded by six of his pals and quickly danced my way towards the exit, trying not to alarm my partner. The leather jackets followed us, however, and moved in closer as we reached the doorway. I told the girl to go into the ladies cloakroom for safety, stepped through the open double doors into the better light of the corridor, and turned to face the 'Angels' with my back against the wall.

As I prepared to go down fighting but take at least two of them with me, I saw Ian and Archie appear in the doorway.

"What's the problem, boys?" asked Ian.

The bikers' heads twisted towards him in unison. "We're about to tear this bastard to shreds," snarled the apparent leader.

"That's what the fuckin' problem is."

Archie glowered at them through his knotted eyebrows, his lower jaw protruding and big hands curled into fists. "Not in this fuckin' place yer not," he warned.

The bikers turned around to confront the doormen and I considered kicking off proceedings by KO'ing the one nearest to me.

"Hold on now, hold on," said Ian, walking over and standing right in front of them. Archie stood by his side and I positioned myself on Ian's other flank. The odds were only two to one now almost in our favour, I thought.

"We can't let you do that, I'm afraid," said Ian to the sextet of cyclists.

"An' how the fuck ya gonna stop us?" asked the leader.

"Believe me, lads," Archie promised, "we'll stop ya."

The gang looked at Archie's battlescarred countenance and probably saw in his eyes a different kind of humanity that did not know how to be intimidated. In Ian they could see a quiet, efficient confidence that was actually more menacing, to those in the know, than his colleague's demeanour, and in me they probably saw an eager youth too stupid to be afraid of them.

There was a distinct deceleration in their joint aggression.

"As I was saying," continued Ian, "we can't let you do that because it's our job to prevent you, and because young Rob here's a friend of ours."

"Yeah," growled Archie.

I smiled confidently, knowing that we were taking control of the situation, though the smirk was probably provocative.

"Of course, if one of you and I mean only one wanted to go outside with Rob and settle your differences there, we could possibly turn a blind eye to that… " Ian paused for a moment. "… But, on the other hand, we could all show each other some mutual respect and shake hands."

The leader pointed to me. "Him and his mates just did my brother over outside the pub, and they've fucked up his eye."

All eyes looked at me, but I never took mine off the speaker. I pointed back at him. "No, only I hit him and only once, and that was because he was chasing a girl and took a swing at me for helping her."

The bikers looked at each other. "What girl?" one of them asked.

"Long blonde hair and short leather skirt," I said. "Pretty face, screaming her little head off in terror."

Looks of recognition and understanding passed between the gang members.

"Look, lads," said Ian, "if there's been some misunderstanding here that's okay, but I can guarantee you that Rob doesn't get involved in gang fights. He's a member of our boxing club."

The boys eyed me in reassessment.

"Nobody's broken any rules yet," he continued. "You've paid to come in, so why don't you go back in there and enjoy the night?"

After some mumbling and nodding to each other, the group shuffled back into the dance hall. The leader stopped in front of Ian and shook his hand.

"Sounds like his girlfriend," he offered. "They're always fallin' out over somethin' or other."

He then shook Archie's hand, and even mine.

In later years a gang of six half drunk bikers probably would not be allowed into many venues, but in those days most were presumed innocent until proven guilty and it was a distinct policy to relieve all potential customers of their entrance fees before possibly ejecting them later. On this occasion, however, the party caused no trouble. They were shown a measure of respect and returned it in similar spirit. They were from Carnforth, about 20 miles south, just over the Lancashire border, and revisited the Embassy nightclub several times that summer, sometimes in increased numbers and often with the injured brother in tow. He was reported to be getting along a lot better with his girlfriend. No trouble ever ensued from their being allowed entry and they did, in fact, become quite friendly with the door staff, even assisting them one torrid night against a Glaswegian onslaught.

The original situation had been handled well by the doormen. They had forcefully stood their ground but provided a peaceful way out of the deadlock for the bikers, which did not cause any loss of face or respect to either side. Violence had been avoided and their status as paying customers had been preserved. They even passed on good reports about the Embassy staff to other Lancastrians, who also visited and spent money there. Obviously, though, this approach might be different at venues where no admission fee is charged.

Ian and Archie are both long retired now. Ian went on to become senior national coach of the British boxing team, guiding its members through major competitions such as the Olympic Games, and he steered heavyweight Audley Harrison to his one notable victory.

Archie eventually started a separate boxing club in his home town of Flookburgh, looking south over Morecambe Bay directly towards Fleetwood, home of the first ever licensed female boxer in Britain Jane Couch MBE, winner of five world titles, who retired in December 2008. I wonder if she's interested in a job on the doors?

A Fighter is a Fighter, By Paul Knight

A fighter is a fighter is a fighter, no matter what their arena. The boxer prevails in his controlled and disciplined training; you have the ref that steps in, the timed rounds, the standing count and the judge's decision. The same can be said for the unlicensed fighter, but they are a little less controlled, a little less trained and have a ref who lets that extra bit of blood get spilt for all to savour. The savage bareknuckle fighter, now that is the true brawler; no gloves, very few rules, any time, any place, anywhere this street fighter wins with heart, aggression and pure fury to feel the pride and respect that they receive from their peers. All very different, yet all the same; a fighter is a fighter is a fighter.

But then there is the bully, the chancer, the vulture of the fight game; those who will fight if they know their opponent is weaker, smaller or already down for the count. They terrorise in packs, use weapons and have little respect for the code that a true fighter would honour. This category of person is a gnat's cock above the lowest of the low on the fighters' ladder the verbal fighter, the one who talks a good fight but cowers in the shadows when it's time to put the theory into practice.

You will find many like this in industries and circles where violence is the only language, and never more so than in the world of doormen.

Back in 1993, when I was 25 years old, I used to work the door of a pub called Hamilton Hall, situated in London's Liverpool Street station. I only worked Saturdays, from 11 a.m. to 7 p.m., because that was the only day that doormen were needed. Saturdays brought the football crowds, the club colours, the supporters and the hooligans to that spot, as Liverpool Street station offers a vast array of train and underground connections to London based football grounds. Hamilton Hall was a preferred meeting point for most out-of-town fans, who would converge on the pub from 11 a.m. until 2.30 p.m. The place would then empty as the patrons went off to the match, only for them to return again from about 5 p.m. to catch their home bound trains, or to meet up as a starting point for their night out in London.

Every week it was guaranteed that there would be at least one big 'tearup' between large groups of people, either boisterous before the game or let down after it. It was not a venue for the fainthearted; you had to be confident, diplomatic and eager to have a row. Everyone knew what working this venue meant it meant trouble.

The manager of the pub was a decent enough person but he would only spring for two doormen, so I saw a wide variety of colleagues come and go week after week, but the most regular was my good friend, Derek Hart, out of north London.

Like me, Derek was a trained boxer. His skills far outweighed mine, but each of us knew that the other had our back when it kicked off. You can tell a lot about a person when you fight side by side, especially on a regular basis.

The biggest problem about being 'security' is that the fight rarely starts with you. You're only involved because you're trying to break up someone else's squabble and it's from there that it really becomes your problem. Eight times out of ten you can get away with a bit of diplomacy when breaking these things up; if you're experienced you can get in there and prevent the fight from actually starting. It's normally the mouthy ones that catch your attention; the big, bold ones that can't hold their alcohol intake or are of a particular build that visually intimidates. These are also the ones who normally cannot fight their way out of a paper bag. These are the ones that you approach because you know, deep down, that they're hoping for that one excuse to walk away unharmed but will give the big 'I am' routine to impress their followers. Rarely have I found the loud ones to be the danger; it's mainly the quiet ones the ones that are standing back from the crowd, observing everyone involved, or the ones that shifts their weight from one foot to the other as they respond to the situation and position themselves accordingly. This is what an experienced doorman looks for: the telltale signs that highlight who the real fighter is out of the group the one you know you have to put down first if it all goes 'Pete Tong'.

A fighter knows how to identify a fellow fighter. Most will say that you can tell by the fact that they're the ones that are punching and kicking the crap out of everyone else around them! I agree that that is one good telltale sign, but I liked to avoid a situation going that far. I would get paid the same whether I worked a shift with no violence or I was fighting nonstop for eight hours, and I know which of those two options I prefer.

I'd been working at Hamilton Hall every week for about four months. It was great fun and did wonders for my reputation with the company I worked for Scorpion Security out of Finsbury Park. When I was assigned to work at other venues I didn't have to go through all that 'rites of passage, proving yourself' bullshit with each new door team; I just said my name and people connected me with the trouble pub in Liverpool Street station. I was known as being okay, for stepping up when needed, and others knew that I had their backs. That is one of the main rules in door work: no matter what, you have to be able to hold your own and protect the backs of your team members; it's a given.

Being known and accepted was ideal for me. I've never been big on the whole 'bragging' side of things; to me a fight was a fight and wasn't something to be talked about all night. I didn't feel I had to prove myself and was able simply to get on and do my job, and working alongside like-minded people was a godsend; there was no need for falsities or finding excuses to walk away from a babbling colleague.

So imagine my horror when on Christmas Eve I was asked to work Hamilton Hall with some new faces to Scorpion.

Working from midday to midnight meant that this would be a long shift. Christmas Eve that year fell on a Friday, so the pub goers were mainly city types, last minute shoppers and those out for long liquid lunches (give me a football crowd any day). Entry was free, but the doors were closed at 5 p.m., so all those already inside got a sort of lockin; if you were in, then you were in, and the doors only got opened to let people out and there was no reentry that was the price you paid that particular night. However, a good way to guarantee that punters spent their money in just one place also meant a pub full of drunken people contained in a confined environment for seven hours.

We were working a fourman team: the two new faces, Derek and myself. Hamilton Hall has two entrances: a main one at the main entrance to the station; and a side door in the station area that was left open as it allowed direct access to the toilets and the upstairs restaurant areas without people cutting through the pub.

The plan was simple: all four of us would mingle around until 5 p.m., and then the two new faces would go and man the side door while Derek and I handled the main entrance. The side door was about ten feet from the bar and, although it gave no direct vantage point to the whole area, you were nevertheless close enough to hear any commotion or to be the first point of call by the bar staff if something was wrong. The main entrance was about 20 feet away from the bar. As it was open plan, you could see most of the inside from the entrance, but when that space was filled with punters the front of the bar was blocked from view.

The first few hours of the shift were uncomfortable because the two new guys for argument's sake, I'll call them Bill and Ben were yakking in our ear holes nonstop about the fights they'd been in and the incidents that went down at a club they'd worked at previously. Bill and Ben were visual doormen: they looked the part. They both stood at around 5 ft 10 in and obviously knew what the inside of a gym looked like, as they were big, strong, stocky types. Bill was from up north and had come down to London to earn a decent wage, and Ben was from Hertford. Both had started with Scorpion at the same time and therefore got partnered on a regular basis, but they were obviously green to the industry. Far too many conversations started with, "I fucked this geezer up the other night" or "I banged him cos he didn't want to leave."

Just how many times do you need to listen to the same old boring record? Yes, we get it: if it goes off you two will clean house, you'll put everyone in hospital, you're both wrecking machines and you are what other doormen aspire to be like!

Derek and I were a little older, and a little wiser. We both knew what kinds of scrapes we got into week in, week out, and we certainly weren't into the whole blow-by-blow retelling of minor incidents, especially when told in a way that made them out to be more than what they were. Both of us were wishing for 5 p.m. to come round so that Bill and Ben would go off to their door for the rest of the evening and leave us in peace.

On a couple of occasions people were asked to leave, but there was nothing that a friendly grip on their arm didn't solve. After all, no one really wanted to wake up on Christmas morning with a black eye, bruised ego and blood traces in their urine.

Finally 5 p.m. came around, the manager made the announcement and we proceeded to lock the doors. Late arrivals were banging on the glass wanting entry and when we refused we were called every name under the sun. Some people just can't take rejection very easily. Someone should point out to disgruntled punters that they're not the first to utter the phrases: "You're having a laugh, ain't ya?", "But my mates are in there", "Go on, mate, there's a drink in it for ya", or my personal favourite, "Do you know who I am?"

All I have to say to them is: "If I was having a laugh I'd come out with something funnier than 'You're not coming in'", "If you didn't turn up on time to meet your mates, then stop being the unreliable one of the group", "Letting you in could cost me my job but you're right a £2 drink would make it all worthwhile and cover my bills whilst unemployed", and my favourite, "if you were someone I should know, you wouldn't then be outside not getting in."

By 7 p.m. the mood in the pub was set. Most were on the verge of leaving as they'd reached their limit, but there was one group that just got louder with every sip they took. There must've been around nine of them, mixed ages, and if I had to guess their profession I would go with window cleaners all looked handy, but with a few too many fried breakfasts. This was the crowd that Derek and I were used to dealing with on a Saturday afternoon.

Derek walked over to Bill and Ben and told them to keep an eye on this group and, as he walked back, he stopped and in a friendly, almost laughing voice he asked the crowd to quieten it down a touch. They apologised and did just that.

Five minutes later a bloke, probably in his early thirties, tapped on the door to ask if he could get in. I opened the door to explain that it was a 'closed' night, no entry, and that we were sorry. He said okay and asked if there was anywhere else that he and his mate could go to get a drink. I suggested some alternatives and off they went. However, ten minutes later they returned, explaining that they had just travelled down from Scotland (although the accents didn't support that story) to meet friends but had lost them along the way. Nowhere else would let them in and those that would were charging silly money for admission. It was a heart tugging story but the answer was still the same: no entry. But that didn't stop these two guys from standing there having a joke with us. They seemed to be all right about it all.

They were there for 40 minutes; polite, no sarcastic comments, no insults just two understanding people out for a drink but with no drink to have. Derek took pity on them and said that when the next person left he'd let them in; no bribes, no need for drinks to be bought on our behalf. He reckoned they'd earned a squeeze having been patient and courteous for 40 minutes. On saying that, a couple of people left so Derek let the two 'Scottish' guys in.

The bar was 20 feet away and realistically, even with a crowd, it should only take ten seconds to walk from the entrance to the bar – what could go wrong in ten seconds?

No sooner had we closed the entrance door than we heard the sound of a bottle smashing. We both spun round to see the group of 'window cleaners' smashing bottles and glasses on the heads of the two Scottish guys. However, the Scottish guys were not going down and, as the blood poured down their faces, they started laying into the nine blokes. The onlookers had two reactions: screaming and running for the entrance doors, or standing in bewilderment as they watched the violence in front of them.

Naturally, Derek and I had to enter into the fray: our job was to stop everyone doing any more damage. We were both trained fighters but without the protection of the 'rules of the ring'. We represented the unlicensed fighters we had training but the protection in this bout was limited. The two Scottish guys were the bareknuckle fighters – the ones that fight with passion and for survival. The group of 'window cleaners' were the pack fighters individually they were nothing special, but put a weapon in their hands and they act as though they are gods. It was a tense and, I'll admit, scary confrontation. With the loss of blood and the vicious nature of it all, anything could happen and the odds were greatly in the favour of the pack fighters.

We went in.

I was prising people off each other whilst trying to avoid being cut up. I was kicking out knees and throwing nose shots while Derek, who had a stronger knockout punch than me, was throwing the big haymakers – as one went down he would soften up the next one with a quick elbow and then the hefty right. We were good but not unbeatable, and the focus changed from the pack fighter against the bareknuckle fighter to both of them against the unlicensed fighter. I threw out a wild left and caught one of them in the mouth, resulting in one of their teeth embedding itself in my index finger. As the punch followed through, the tooth stayed with the finger, coming straight out of the guy's mouth (I still have a tooth shaped scar) and flying across the bar. We started lashing out, not relying on just one punch to stop each individual but making continuous shots to the face. The ground was covered in spilt beer, broken glass and blood. Our fists were swelling up but the adrenaline was blocking out the pain. It was two against eleven not the best odds but not the worst.

We were coming out on top when the doors flew open and the police came pouring in the manager had called them and they responded with some very heavy-handed tactics. They were pulling everyone out and into a van anyone with blood on them, whether they were involved in the fight or just a bystander.

I had no intention of being stuck in a cell on Christmas Eve, so I slipped into the kitchen, threw on some chefs' whites and plunged my hands into a sink to hide their bloodied appearance. Derek managed to make his way up the side stairs to the restaurant area and to the waiters' galley at the back of the pub.

Once all the suspects had been bundled into the van to be whisked away to the station for processing, the police urged the manager to call it a night the pub was now empty anyway. When we came out of our hiding places the manager thanked us and paid us up until the end of the night, even though the place was being closed down before it had turned 8.15 p.m. We were told that we could stay on and have a drink, but then Bill and Ben showed their puzzled faces.

"What the hell happened here?" they asked.

What the fuck!!!" I screamed.

These were the two bulky doormen who had bent our ears for four hours about fighting. These were the same two doormen that had been told to watch the group and that had been standing ten feet away from the bar where the fight started. And yet these same two doormen apparently didn't see or hear it kicking off even though 11 people were involved, they missed their colleagues doing their job, and they didn't even realise that the police had come in and emptied the pub out!

Do you know what they said once they were told that they were getting any early night? They asked if Derek and I wanted to join them on a night out uptown. They thought it would be fun and, you never know, we might even get to have a row!

We were fuming and just wanted to lay these two cowards out, but we left it and told our boss at Scorpion what had gone down. Bill and Ben never worked a Scorpion door again.

I am by no means a fighting legend, but I know what true violence is and have experienced my fair share of close calls. A man is measured by his ability to protect himself without relying on others or resorting to using any weapons other than his fists. The reality, however, is that I have frequently got lucky against impossible odds. On any given day, no matter what the odds, you can be the winner or the loser, but it is how you carry on that reveals what kind of fighter you are, and that is something that should always be remembered.

Earning Respect by Facing a Man With A Reputation

By Robert MacGowen

Despite his troubled and violent childhood, Alan Fletcher grew tall and joined the British Army as soon as he could, where he filled out further on the ample, if simple, food available.

He was trained up and shipped out to help police in the reopening of the Suez Canal, following agreements between British Prime Minister Anthony Eden and Egyptian President Gamal Abdul Nasser. He was stationed at a tented encampment close to the east bank of the Nile, not far from the Nubian Desert in Sudan.

As part of international accord, American and Italian troops were stationed further north to protect their economic interests in the area, in particular the major trade route through Port Said and the canal itself. However, they did not have to live in bell tents as the British soldiers did, but were housed in rigid structures with modern facilities.

As Alan walked around the camp early one morning, before the scorching sun had fully ascended to its zenith, he heard a voice that he recognised shout his name.

"Awreyt Al?"

He turned in the direction of the speaker.

"'Ow's it goin', mate?"

"Bloody hell, Scouse, how long have you been over here?"

"Oh, a good few months now. It's a right doss."

"Thought you were still at Donnington. Are you still with the REME?"

"Well, I am officially like, but I'm on secondment to the Logistics Corps over here, attached to the officers' mess."

"Christ, the officers' mess? You haven't packed the tools in and become a cook, have you?"

"Naw, I'm still a blacksmith, but I'm workin' full time as a farrier here."

"A farrier? We haven't dragged the bloody cavalry out of retirement, have we? I'd have thought camels would be better."

"No, I just look after the officers' polo horses. It's a doddle. And anyway, they reckon camels are shite at polo."

"Polo in the desert?!"

"Different world, Al. I've seen 'ow the other 'alf live with this job. It's a different friggin' world, mate. By the way, this lieutenant I've got pally with 'as given me a coupla invitations to see a picture bein' made if ya wanna go? It's s'posed to be officers only like, but we can say we're drivers if anybody asks."

"A picture show? We're in the bloody desert, aren't we?"

"We are, mate, we are, but this is at the American base near Cairo, an' it's not a show it's a movie bein' made, with Sophia Loren in it! They've a bloody viewing gallery and drinkies an' all that, like a big party."

"Sophia Loren?"

"Yeah, an' some geezer by the name of Anthony Steel. *The Black Tent*, it's called, an' anybody who's not American Forces personnel needs an invitation to get anywhere near it."

"See what you mean about different worlds."

"Yeah, but don't forget we're talkin' about the bloody Yanks here!"

The following Saturday they drove to the film set in a spare jeep, on the pretext of collecting blacksmith's supplies from their main depot at the docks.

"Ya know, there's a bloke in our billet who ties 'imself up on the tent pole at night if it's rainin'," mused the muscular Liverpudlian as they bumped along the desert road.

"What the hell for? Is he a sleepwalker?"

"No, 'e's terrified of the sand spiders. They shelter in the tents when it's rainin' 'ard. Mind you, the bastards are about a foot wide."

"They're harmless though, aren't they?"

"Yeah, he knows that, but it makes no difference."

"Mmm, we've got a guy who takes a teddy bear to bed with him."

"Never!"

"Straight up. They reckon he's from a wealthy family who lost a fortune on war bonds. He seems pretty normal in most ways, apart from his little bear."

"Must be the army full of weirdos."

They arrived at the Giza camp and parked the jeep at the side of the road, so they could get out and seek directions. When they returned a few minutes later, an American soldier was rifling through their jackets on the back seat.

"Hey!" shouted Scouse as he and Alan ran over.

The GI pulled a switchblade knife and shouted to a group of Marines, who came running. "These Limey bastards just pulled over and tried to rob me," he cried.

The Americans scowled at the two Brits.

"You lyin' bastard!" snarled Scouse, lunging forward and grabbing the GI by the throat.

The Marines were on him like a pack of wolves. Scouse, though, after years of lifting iron and swinging hammers, was no ordinary prey and withstood the attack. After a brief struggle, during which it appeared that the Liverpudlian was carrying the six Americans about his person in some kind of acrobatic routine, he finally threw the half strangled knife wielder to the floor.

Alan looked on, mesmerised. He was frozen to the spot because his childhood conditioning did not allow him to fight if he hadn't been attacked first. As his stepfather's brutal indoctrination did battle with his free will, the American thief staggered to his feet and retrieved his knife from the ground.

The glint of the metal flicked a switch in Alan's brain and he moved forward. The knife fighter noticed and turned to face him, but as he did so his head was knocked back by a punch of such force that a bone in his already mangled neck was damaged. He was unconscious before he hit the ground, and Alan turned to help his friend.

The melee now resembled a rugby scrum as the Americans struggled to bring the powerful blacksmith, who was at last beginning to weaken, to his knees. Suddenly, there was a scream of agony as one of his assailants reeled away clutching two broken ribs. Another one was knocked flat on his back by Alan's next ramrod punch, and Scouse, realising that the odds against him were diminishing fast, roared like a lion and erupted in a frenzy of power and aggression. He shook the remaining three attackers from him like cowboys from a rodeo horse. As they scrambled away, hurling obscenities as they went, Alan and Scouse looked at each other and the latter wiped sweat from his brow.

"Tell ya what, Al," he gasped.

"What, mate?"

"Think I'll give ol' Sophia a miss tonight"

"Yeah, I was thinkin' that. Better get out of here before they order an airstrike against us."

"They'd probably miss anyway. They usually do."

The friends walked back to the jeep laughing, but another American voice called out from behind them, "Just a minute there, boys."

They looked back to see a big, lantern jawed sergeant walking towards them with two armed guards at his elbows. A patch emblazoned across his chest proclaimed the name Kilroy.

"That's a helluva right hand you got there, soldier," drawled the Marine sergeant, standing with feet apart and hands on his hips like a gunslinger waiting for the call.

Alan and Scouse stopped but said nothing, fearing the worst. The sergeant ambled over to the groaning thief on the floor and dragged him to an upright position by his collar. "You wanna press charges against this piece of shit?" he asked them.

"No, he didn't get away with anything, and who needs the hassle?" answered Alan.

"I'll catch up with you later," the sergeant promised his groggy countryman, helping him on his way with a size twelve boot to the rear.

"You musta done some boxin'?" he asked Alan.

"Me, no, not really. Maybe a little bit in the cadets."

"Well, I think you got a talent for it, boy, an' I got just the outlet for your talents. What are ya, 'bout six three, two forty pounds?"

"Six two and a half two thirty."

"You're just what I'm lookin' for, son. Know what it is I'm lookin' for?"

"Nope."

"Hell, son, you could be the next Great White Hope."

Alan laughed. "Don't think so, sergeant. I'm no Rocky Marciano."

"No, not yet, son, not yet, but lookey here. We got a goddam nigger challengin' the all American army champion for the right to represent the good ol' US of A, in the Olympics. You whup him and you'd be a hero in the States overnight."

"I'm no boxer," protested Alan. "I couldn't beat an army champion, it'd be suicide."

"We can train you up, son. What's yer name, by the way?"

"Alan," volunteered Scouse.

"Well now, see here Al, we can train you, get you outta the army and you could be on your way to a world title. How'd that be?"

Alan laughed again and shook his head. "I don't think so," he said, turning back to the jeep.

"Okay, son, ok, let's just take it one step at a time here. How's about fightin' this arrogant nigger for us to start with anyhow. I gotta put somebody up against the son-of-a-bitch or we all gonna look pretty damn bad as an efficient fightin' force, if ya know what I mean."

Alan looked at the sergeant and shook his head. "Well, it's not going to be me," he stated, climbing into the jeep.

"How 'bout a hundred bucks to make the prospect a little more attractive?"

Alan laughed.

"Two hundred?"

"Make it five 'undred," suggested Scouse enthusiastically.

"That's one helluva sum of money, soldier," said the sergeant, as his two guards guffawed.

"Shut the fuck up, boys," snapped the sergeant. "Okay, Al, we'll make it five hundred bucks if you beat the punk, two hundred if you last three rounds. How's that sound, huh?"

"I said no," replied Alan flatly. "Drive the bloody jeep, Scouse."

"Well, here's my office number," offered the sergeant, stuffing a piece of paper into Scouse's breast pocket, "Just in case you change your mind," he winked.

"Lorra money, Al," reasoned Scouse as they drove off.

"You bloody well fight him then! You're the one with the muscles."

"Yeah, I got the muscles, but why d'ya think he asked you? It's cos you got the height and the punch."

Two days later the company sergeant major marched into Alan's tent as he laid reading on his bed.

"On your feet, soldier," he ordered.

Alan jumped up and stood to attention.

"You been in some trouble over at the American base, private?"

"Trouble, sergeant?"

"Yes, fucking trouble. What the hell were you doing there in the first place?"

"We went to see Sophia Loren."

"You went to see So Fear fucking what?"

"Loren, sergeant. She's a… "

"Shut the hell up, sonny, before you talk yourself into a load more trouble that you do not want."

"Yes, sergeant."

"The major's had a call from the Yanks' top brass. You are now our official boxing team and will commence training tomorrow morning at six hundred hours. Fall out!"

He had three weeks to prepare, and Scouse was appointed as his official coach.

"I got word down at the stables," confided the Liverpudlian. "This black bloke is shit hot but they 'ave to put somebody up against 'im for the newsreels and politicians back in the States. They don't wanna risk the champion though, cos 'e's white an' the Olympics are only a few months away. They want somebody that's not well known over there, so the public won't realise it's a setup, and if 'e's not even American they won't give a shit if 'e gets hammered anyway, which 'e probably will."

"You're not doing much to cheer me up, Scouse."

"No, but you should know what's goin' on. This black and white thing is a very hot potato in the States at the moment. The blacks are marchin' up an' down the streets shoutin' about equal rights and the whites are stringin' 'em up from trees an' lamp posts. We've walked right into the middle of a very political situation an' they reckon even Joe Kennedy's involved."

"Who's he?"

"American ambassador accordin' to the lieutenant. They've even threatened us with legal action for assaulting American soldiers on their own base. Could end up in a court martial."

"Fuck, but they attacked us."

"We know that, an' they know that, but four of 'em were injured an' we weren't. They've got nine eyewitnesses, includin' a sergeant, against us two, an' we shouldn't 'ave been there in the first place. They've got us right over a barrel backwards, Al."

"Bastards. What's he called?"

"Who?"

"This bloke I'm supposed to fight."

"Get this. His name's Solomon McTier. Solomon 'Jackhammer' McTier, as he's known in the ring, an' he's already beaten Rademacher."

"Who the hell is Rademacher?"

"Well, he ain't no ham an' eggs fighter, Al, he's the reigning American All Army and Combined Services Heavyweight Champion, that's who the hell he is."

"And McTier's already beaten him?"

"Yep, an' not too long ago either. But the good news is, we're flyin' a pro over to give you a few tips before the fight, somebody called Bygraves."

"Bloody hell, not Max?"

"No, it's Jim or Jack or somethin' like that. They reckon he's from Liverpool but I've never 'eard of 'im."

The day of the fight arrived all too soon and Scouse told Alan to have a late morning in bed until 7 a.m. He then walked him over to the NAAFI canteen for a big cooked breakfast, after which he was not allowed any more food until tea and toast two hours before the bout.

Joe Bygraves flew over in a military plane and sparred a few rounds with Alan, gave him some advice, a little hope in the fact that a 'puncher' always has a chance, and an old pair of his boxing boots.

Joe had emigrated to the UK from Jamaica as a youth and, although he became a registered British citizen, he was never allowed to fight for a national title. He settled in Liverpool in 1957 and during a chequered though high-level career he managed to beat Henry Cooper, the future European champion and world contender who floored Cassius Clay (later Muhammad Ali) in 1966, but went on to lose the fight with a bad cut. (At least we won the football World Cup that year!) And Walter McGowan from Scotland won the World Flyweight title. Bygraves, though, eventually tired of internal politics and racial prejudice and left the country.

Alan rested up most of the day, trying not to think of what was to come and listening to Scouse's advice on how to avoid being maimed for life. At 5 p.m. he showered under a bucket with holes punched in the bottom and changed as if in a dream, before going out to join Scouse in the same jeep that had landed him in his present predicament. To his surprise, there were several more jeeps lined up behind it, and a six wheeler truck behind them. They were full of jubilant squaddies, and a big cheer went up when Alan appeared. A Union Jack waved from the lead vehicle and shouts of encouragement filled the early evening air. Alan smiled, waved, shook his head, and sat in the jeep next to a beaming Scouse.

Although the American base operated from masonry buildings, none were thought big enough to house the expected numbers of spectators and so the contest was to be held outdoors. There were concerns about the possible affects on the boxers of the desert heat, but the politicians were keen to stage a sporting spectacle for their overseas troops and, in doing so, provide some good preelection radio and TV coverage in their home states and also distract attention from the fact that the current army champion, currently stationed on American soil, was not one of the participants. The public were unaware of any behind the scenes politics and the hopeful candidates for state governorship were anxious to preserve that situation.

McTier was glad of any opportunity to display his considerable skills in pursuit of an Olympic team placement, or to attract an offer of a professional contract.

A large canvas camouflage sheet was rigged up above the ring, and as the blistering sun began to dip towards the western dunes Alan was led out to the cheers of the small British contingent, in comparison to the hundreds of GIs clustered around the roped square. They, too, cheered because they were very happy – if, as seemed very probable, McTier won, then he was an American beating a Limey, and if he lost, he was a black being beaten by a white. They cheered and clapped politely. The officers smiled and the politicians laughed as they puffed on their cigars and sipped bourbon.

"Hope everybody's not going to be too disappointed," said Alan.

"Well, they've been told you're an experienced boxer, Al, but even the best have off nights, don't they?"

Once up in the ring, under the shade of the overhead canopy, Alan found the air cooler than he'd expected. A slight breeze blew in from the desert as it cooled towards the bitter cold of night. He shuffled around awkwardly as Scouse pulled the borrowed airforce blue towelling dressing gown from his shoulders and pushed the dental paste, guttapercha gum shield into his mouth with shaking fingers. Alan seemed surprisingly calm. In his mind he was thousands of miles away from the desert, walking through a lush, verdant park with a beautiful dark haired girl.

Sergeant Kilroy appeared at the ringside with a flock of photographers, leaned through the ropes to slap Alan encouragingly on the back and motioned, with an aggressive example of his own, for him to strike a boxing pose for the cameras, so that the folks back home could see what a fine looking opponent they'd found to stand in for the champion. Alan obliged halfheartedly as Scouse attempted to renegotiate a payment. "We're goin' down in the first round if the money's not back on the table."

"It's irrelevant which round he goes down in now, boy, and the only thing that's on the table is gonna be him an operating table."

Suddenly, the crowd hushed to an expectant murmur as the door to the nearby toilet block, which was being used as an impromptu changing room, swung open. Out into the fading sunlight shuffled a little entourage led by a stocky trainer in a white cotton jacket. Behind, with his gloved hands on the trainer's shoulders, came 6 ft 2 in of taut, battle hardened muscle in the shape of Solomon 'Jackhammer' McTier. His head, covered by the hood of a white satin gown, was bowed between massive shoulders, and the balls of his feet touched the dusty ground with short, measured steps in time to the rhythm already pounding in his brain. Following him came an assistant carrying a water bucket, towels, Vaseline and a cuts repair kit.

All eyes followed the group as it made its way through the throng of spectators, most of whom were standing and stretching or clambering onto the jeeps and trucks or machinery scattered about, in order to see the famous fighter. Some even climbed onto the ring apron, completely ignoring Alan, who also watched the approach of his adversary with fascination, and more than a little trepidation.

Scouse looked at Alan through his eyebrows whilst checking the lacing of the leather gloves. "We could just call it off, ya know. Just walk away, get in the jeep and live to fight another day."

Alan gazed across at the Union Jack fluttering in the strengthening breeze, and the cluster of pink faces beneath it. "No, we couldn't," he said softly.

McTier's presence in the ring was awesome, and as the Italian referee brought the two combatants together to hear his instructions in broken Eengleesh he looked at Alan with a chilling, expressionless stare.

The fighters walked back to their respective corners as cheering from outside the ropes reached a crescendo, heard the final instructions from their trainers "Crack 'im in the teeth soon as you can, Al," Scouse advised then turned to face each other as the bell sounded from ringside.

The first thing that Alan noticed as he brought his gloves up to a defensive position in front of his face was that his opponent was a southpaw. He remembered now that Scouse had attempted to drum that fact into his preoccupied brain, but he'd since forgotten until now.

McTier glided effortlessly forward behind a long right-hand lead and, as Alan peered over the top of his gloves, he popped a lazy, range finder jab off his forehead. It was a scoring shot, though not troublesome, and Alan moved to his left as he now rapidly recalled being instructed by his trainer, away from McTier's powerful left. With a neat shuffle of the feet, however, the American changed direction and whipped a right hook to the side of Alan's head. It was a stunning blow and the recipient stumbled a few steps, drawing a roar of excitement from the crowd. But, as McTier moved in for the kill, Alan grabbed his outstretched hand and pulled him into a clinch. The referee parted them and, as they resumed combat, McTier pivoted quickly on his right foot whilst pushing off his left to deliver another vicious right hook. Alan fell into the ropes and went down on one knee. The crowd went wild. He stayed where he was, breathing deeply until he heard the referee count 'eight', and then rose to his feet. McTier moved in again, knowing his man was hurt, but as he came into range Alan swung his own right in from the side, out of the line of vision, and caught him high on the jaw. A look of astonishment flashed across the American's face as he rode the blow and took a step sideways to maintain his balance. In his excitement, Alan charged forward and threw another right instead of advancing behind his lead, and McTier easily avoided it. He did so, though, by moving backwards. Alan pursued him as a stunned silence descended over the spectators, except for the little band beneath the Union Jack flag, who cheered loudly. The American pulled Alan up short with a series of stiff jabs and again took control of the fight. Alan retreated behind his peek a boo defence and saw out the first round without further drama.

At the start of the second round McTier moved more cautiously, probably aware by now that Alan was not much of a boxer, but that he did possess a powerful and potentially dangerous punch. He could not risk being suckered by a loose haymaker, so he moved forward behind his own, now tighter, defence. Within range again, he used his rapier right lead, picking up points and demoralising his opponent, until Alan suddenly pulled his head sideways, avoiding one of the punches, and charged forward again. He surprised McTier and they fell into a clinch, but this time Alan was expertly turned and thrown into the ropes. As he rebounded with his gloves in position, the American dug a ramrod right into his solar plexus, which brought down his defence, and then cracked a straight left onto the point of his chin. This time Alan staggered a step and collapsed onto his back. McTier turned and walked to his corner with one arm held aloft, assuming that the fight was over.

Alan lay on the canvas, watching the fluttering camouflage sheet above him and wondering where he was. He could hear distant voices and see a finger waving in front of his face, and he thought, in his confused and concussed condition, that it was his stepfather threatening him. His well-honed survival instinct kicked into action and he raised his head a few inches. The surrounding noise grew louder as he heard the word "Six" shouted above the background tumult.

He began to move.

"Seven."

He scrambled to his knees.

"Eight."

He grabbed the ropes and pulled himself upright.

"Nine," said the referee, looking deeply into Alan's eyes.

Alan nodded and tried to smile in an effort to show the referee that he was willing and, more importantly, able to continue. The referee wiped Alan's gloves on the front of his own white shirt, knocking his black bow tie askew, and shoved the gum shield back into place as McTier slowly turned from the corner to look at his opponent. He shook his head in dismay and disbelief and prepared for battle once more.

"Box," instructed the referee as the fighter moved forward, banging his gloves together. Alan leaned back against the ropes for support as his adversary came into range, and covered up. McTier prodded the defence with a right glove, but Alan grabbed him around the waist and pulled him close again, so that he couldn't release his devastating left, and they milled around unattractively until the bell ended the round.

The sweat of exhaustion streamed from every pore on Alan's body and his breath came in great, rasping draughts as he stumbled to the corner. Scouse pushed him onto the stool and positioned himself between the boxer and the referee, who peered in closely.

"He's fine," said Scouse over his shoulder, flapping wildly with a bloodstained towel.

Alan again produced a lopsided smile.

"Do you wanna pack it in, Al?" stammered the trainer. "Yer gerrin' fuckin' killed out there."

The question seemed to come to Alan from afar, through a foggy haze. He shook his head slowly and spat blood into the water bucket.

At the start of round three McTier strode across the ring and blasted a left straight through Alan's now feeble guard. He slumped into his own corner and McTier hooked several right and left body shots into his ribs. Alan gasped and tried to cover up as the referee moved in and Scouse screamed hysterically through the ropes. The previous cheering and baying for blood of the crowd, though, had now subsided to a hushed murmur, and some spectators even began to drift away. Gasps of horror accompanied every blow. The boxing match had become a slaughter.

McTier stood back and threw a long left at Alan's stationary head. He went down to one knee but got up immediately. McTier breathed hard from the exertion of beating him up and leaned in close. "Stay down, man. Ah'm gonna have to kill you if you don't stay the fuck down," he advised.

Alan squinted at him through swollen eyes and poked out a hand in token aggression. McTier put in a few more flurries between rests.

"Thank fuckin' God!" exclaimed Scouse, grabbing his fighter as the third round ended. More people walked away, shaking their heads in disgust.

The bell for the fourth and final round rang and both contestants trudged to the centre of the ring, touched gloves and threw jabs at each other. They boxed at long range for several minutes until McTier feinted with a right and brought over his left, which sent Alan staggering back into the ropes once more on rubbery legs. The ringsiders behind, some spattered with Alan's blood, looked away. The American pursued his advantage, but Alan came to meet him and shot out the right hand that had KO'd the American thief. It hit McTier in the middle of his face and rocked his head back. The British supporters exploded in applause as Alan attacked and forced the American back. He launched another big right, but his timing was gone along with his energy, and McTier slipped it as he turned him sideways. Alan swivelled, still trying to attack, but as he came on he was clipped with another vicious right hook and fell onto the seat of his white army issue shorts, with one arm hooked up in the ropes. He looked to his trainer with an expression of waning hope as his opponent strode to a neutral corner. A few boos could be heard from the British supporters.

Alan struggled to his feet, the referee waved the fighters together, and McTier again shook his head in disappointment as his cornermen shouted for the kill. Alan lunged with another desperate right, but McTier slipped it easily and covered up, and they clinched again.

"Stay down. You don't gotta be no fuckin' hero, man. Just stay down so I don't gotta hurt you no more," the American shouted into Alan's swollen ear.

Alan smiled, revealing bloodstained teeth.

McTier looked at him as though he were a madman.

The referee pulled them apart and again, as they parted and the ref stood back, McTier hit Alan with a fast left. Once more Alan landed flat on his back with a deep expiration of breath. More boos rang out, floating on the still, sultry air. This time they were louder and from the American contingent. He was not as dazed this time, the punch having caught him high up on the temple, and he began to get up almost immediately. McTier turned away in genuine despair and started to climb through the ropes, but his trainer pushed him back. "Da fight's just about over," he screamed in panic.

"Jeez, man, I ain't hittin' this cracker no more. He gonna die on me in there if I hit him some more." Alan tottered forward on legs that did not appear to be under his control. "Shit, man, this boy ain't right in the head," protested McTier, as he realised the fight was still not over.

"Box," demanded the referee, bringing his hands together after wiping Alan's gloves once more and checking he was fully conscious.

The fighters came together in renewed conflict, with both men trading punches, but a few seconds later the bell sounded to end the round and the fight. Alan was still on his feet, just, and fell back against the ropes with a puffy, distorted smile on his battered face. The spectators that were still watching, both British and American, erupted in rapturous applause.

McTier put a glove on Alan's shoulder. "You a good fighter, man, fo' a white boy," he said as a sincere compliment. "You're not too bad yourself," gasped Alan through bloodied, swollen lips. It took Alan six weeks to recover fully from the injuries he received in the fight, which included cuts, bruises and abrasions to his face, a broken tooth, heavy contusion to his torso and a dislocated finger, but no serious damage.

Solomon McTier went on to win the North American Golden Gloves Tournament that year but was not selected for the US Olympic team. Instead he turned professional, ran up a respectable record but then retired early to become a trainer. After 12 years, when in his early forties, he returned to the ring as a combatant and won ten out of ten comeback fights. He finally retired for good at the age of 45.

Pete Rademacher, totally unaware of any political infighting, represented the USA at Heavyweight in the Melbourne Olympics. He won the gold medal and subsequently became the only boxer in history who fought for a world title in his professional debut. Despite flooring champion Floyd Patterson in the second round, he was himself knocked out in the sixth and never won a professional world title.

A War I Could Never Win

By Robin Barratt

I don't consider myself a violent person, although I have lived in a violent world for much of my adult life. Violence has never disturbed me; in fact, the thrill of it often enthralled and excited me and I have, on many occasions, thoroughly enjoyed the buzz of battle. But the consequences of living in this violent world have also worried me and, more importantly, have worried my family. And I don't mean just the consequences of what might happen to me in combat, but the consequences of what would occur following a wrong punch or a bad fall. It was one thing having a good scrap, but another putting myself or indeed someone else three feet under because of a simple mistake, and in battle mistakes can easily happen.

I suppose I was (and still am in my philosophies and attitude) an 'old school' doorman, having racked up over 20 years' door experience in a whole range of venues all over the UK, from bikers' bars to gangland clubs. I have always fervently believed in teaching scumbags and scrotes a lesson. Sadly, the world now is in violent turmoil because as a nation we are too frightened of teaching people a lesson; we are too frightened of being stabbed or attacked, as well as the worry of being sued or arrested. In my day there were no knives; if you caused trouble you got a kicking, so you could either cause trouble again and get another kicking or you could behave. And no one sued anyone! Thankfully, most punters in the clubs I worked eventually behaved.

In between working the doors I also worked within the close protection (bodyguarding) field in some of the worst environments in the world, including a stint in the Congo, a couple of years in Bosnia during the conflict, and in Moscow during the economic crisis when it was a virtual free fall – assassinations were a daily occurrence. For me, close protection (CP) wasn't always a permanent occupation, so working the doors frequently filled the gaps and gave me and my family the choice of either a good meal or bread and water!

From around 1998 to 2003 I lived in Wilmslow, Cheshire, and over those five years I worked off and on in close protection as well as running a nightclub called Equivino and working the doors at various venues in and around Manchester.

I knew a local pub called The Rectory, where the same door team had worked for quite a number of years – they often came into Equivino after they'd finished their shift. I knew The Rectory was a nice venue for the older, more respectable crowd and so I thought without too many problems. I eventually left Equivino, which finally closed because of gang problems, and went back to working the doors off and on in between CP contracts.

Tony Hill, managing director of a north Manchester door company, had just taken over the door at The Rectory and he approached me to run the door. He told me that they needed a new, strong team, and because of my impressions of the place I had to ask why. Wilmslow, although a well-to-do area of Cheshire and an affluent suburb of Greater Manchester, was only a 15-minutes drive from Moss Side, and even less from Wythenshawe, two notorious trouble spots. This meant that Wilmslow attracted more than its fair share of opportunist crime, such as robbery, theft and burglary, as well as attracting quite a number of scrotes from Manchester city centre at the weekend. My impression was that almost anyone could work the door there; it just didn't seem like a challenging door. As far as I knew there were rarely problems inside the venue and only occasionally on the door itself when out-of-town scrotes were trying to get in. Wilmslow on a weekend night was a strange mixture of Cheshire yuppies and city scrotes, which did occasionally cause problems. But The Rectory, although directly in the centre of the town and fairly high profile, had a reputation for being an older person's venue with a strict dress code and tight entry regulations.

Doors are gained and lost all the time and no one likes it. Losing a door contract to a rival company in Manchester can cause big problems. It can become personal. Not only is there a loss of revenue but also there's an infringement of territory and a battering of egos. "It used to be someone else's door," Tony explained, "and they are a bit pissed off that we have it."

It wasn't the fact that the previous door team at The Rectory were doing a bad job. On the contrary, they had all been there a long time and were generally good lads who did their job well. The problem was political. The brewery's new area manager wanted Tony Hill's National Security Network to be the preferred security supplier for all their venues around the UK.

So the previous door firm one of the most notorious door firms not only in the northwest but throughout the UK were told that they no longer had the door at The Rectory. They were not happy bunnies.

I knew the previous door firm very well; in fact, they had sorted out some real big issues for me while I was running Equivino. However, I was sure that our previous history wouldn't cause difficulties and they wouldn't just turn up one evening en masse and give us all a real battering. The Rectory was a nice venue and, yes, I wanted to work it. I lived just ten minutes away and it closed at 1 a.m., which meant no more late nights. The music was more mainstream and it attracted a decent client base. I'd done my time in high risk venues and just wanted a quiet life. I didn't need the money so badly that I was prepared to get into any door war. I was too old for all that. I didn't want to be fighting or wearing my bulletproof vest and being constantly on my guard not for a measly £50 a night. I just wanted to do my job and go home safely at the end of the night.

Out of respect for the old door team, I called the boss of the company at his office and asked what he thought about the situation and about me working there. He was certainly extremely pissed off that Tony Hill had taken over the door. At first he strongly recommended that I didn't work there, but he called me again a few days later. After calming down a bit he told me that was hoping to be able to take back the door at a later date. He had most of the other doors in Wilmslow and the surrounding area and causing trouble might have brought him unwanted attention from both the police and the licensing department at the council. So he told me that he didn't mind me working there and promised me that neither he nor any of his team would ever cause us problems. And he was true to his word.

However, we did have big problems with AK, a local hard man. He was a hood and a thug who had made some money and had recently moved to Wilmslow, and he was trying to stamp out his territory. I suppose, in some twisted way, AK thought he could fit in with the Cheshire set. He had decided that The Rectory was going to be his personal venue, a place where he could do what he wanted, act as he pleased and cause whatever trouble he desired without anyone daring to lift a finger against him.

I came across AK on the first Thursday night I worked at The Rectory. It wasn't busy and I was on my own, standing just inside the front door; winter was creeping in and it was getting cold, and I didn't have a decent outdoor jacket.

AK walked in with his brother (I learned his identity later) and a couple of pretty girls. At around 17 stone he was a big guy, a bodybuilder, not tall but broad, with the usual shaved head and quite menacing to look at. He obviously took steroids, which would have made him quite strong as well. It was rumoured that he was also once a semiprofessional boxer. He looked the part, with scars on his head and a face that had obviously seen some battles.

As he entered The Rectory he stopped briefly at the door, said hello to me and shook my hand. He said he recognised me from a gym in Altrincham, but I didn't recognise him. I knew he was going to be a problem, as he was immediately sarcastic and rude. He had attitude, and lots of it. I could see he was marking his territory, fronting me and showing me that he was not someone to be messed with. In his eyes he was now the law at my venue. It was the same old story narrow-minded, ignorant, pathetic scrotes trying to prove themselves. I would've had so much more respect for the guy if he'd been polite and civil, if he'd taken a little time out to have a chat or perhaps offer a drink. But, no, he decided to walk in with a high and mighty attitude, believing that in the absence of the previously respected door team The Rectory was going to be his. He held up his girlfriend's coat, whistled to me from the bar and beckoned for me to come over and take it. Of course I ignored him, and starting thinking about what would be the best way to deal with this cunt.

After that first encounter, I knew he was going to be a big problem. I was certain that I would be battling with him in the near future, and I was under no illusion that he would be a hard man to fight; I would have to pool all my resources and destroy him as quickly as I could. I had hoped that The Rectory was going to be a quiet, calm place, but it was looking as though it would be just the opposite. So much for my retirement plans. As Tony Hill had rightly said, we definitely did need a good, strong team on the door. This narrow-minded cunt would quite simply walk all over anyone weak, and then it wouldn't be too long before he'd be taxing the bar (drinking without paying) and running drugs. This is typically how many wannabe 'gangsters' get their slimy fingers into venues.

The following night I discovered that I would be working The Rectory with a guy named Dave Power. Dave used to work with me at the Loaf bar in central Manchester, but unfortunately we fell out big time when I got him the sack for being really abusive to a female customer and friend of mine. I suppose, in hindsight, I should've sorted it out with him myself and probably would've done if the manageress hadn't been nearby and heard what had gone on. Backing up door staff is one thing, but not when it compromises one's own morals and ethics of behaviour, and since that day we had hated each other. However, we 'respected' each other enough not resort to sorting things out in a violent way, although I'm sure we both wondered whether it might end in some sort of physical confrontation. Wisely, the office didn't tell either of us beforehand that we would be working with the other, and we only found out when we turned up to work. We met while standing at the bar and realised that we would either have to bury the hatchet there and then or one of us would have to turn around and swiftly move on to another venue. We walked outside to settle things. Although it would've looked awful for two of the venue's doormen to be fighting outside, our dislike for each other was so intense that I genuinely believed that this was going to happen.

After about 15 minutes of mild argument we did eventually sort out our differences in a fairly mature and sensible way. We let bygones be bygones. I told him exactly what I thought, and he told me what he thought. We basically agreed to disagree, and as time passed on the door of The Rectory we actually became good friends, worked extremely well together and ended up being a good, strong and efficient door team. And if it hadn't been for Dave's intervention and diplomacy we would've received a severe battering a few weeks later when AK and his gang eventually arrived in force.

The standard of dress was no real reason to stop AK from entering the premises again. He had money, drove a BMW M5 and was normally very well dressed. However, I didn't like his attitude and I didn't want him in. People such as him like to menace and threaten and rule their territory with fear, and I knew it would soon become personal between him and me. On his next visit I intended to make it clear that he was welcome in the venue if he dispensed with the bad attitude and respected the staff, otherwise I would have no choice but to bar him. However, I knew that barring him would cause a problem and we would probably end up fighting. I had been in the business too long to expect anything else from these sorts of scumbags.

He looked menacing, he had a 'reputation' and, truthfully, I didn't want to fight him. I knew that if I couldn't beat him in the conventional way (which I admit would've been extremely difficult) I would have to resort to some of the nastier tactics I had learned in some of the worst environments around the world, and I didn't really want to go down that road again. It's not hard to kill someone one quick twist of the neck, or one hard punch into the spinal column at the base of the neck. Killing is easy, but the fear of killing haunted me. What frightened me the most was not the actual act of brawling but rather going too far. I had constantly lived with the fear that one day something would snap inside me, that I would lose all self-control and that I would end up looking through the bars of a jail for the rest of my life (although I was sure that no one would actually give a flying fuck if AK was killed!)

It was a Saturday night at about 11 p.m., The Rectory was full and we already had a long queue and so we were operating a 'one in, one out' policy. There is a long drive leading up to the entrance of The Rectory and, standing on the front step of the front doors, it was possible to look down the drive and see everyone walking towards the club, which gave us a little time to assess the people approaching before they got too close. You can tell a scumbag a mile away; they have a walk and posture that are quite distinctive and, of course, there's the way they dress. I think there's a particular 'scrote' dress style – you can easily identify other like-minded scrotes just from their clothes.

Standing on the front door that evening I could see AK walking up the driveway with his brother, another even bigger bodybuilder, and about ten other scumbag kids all scruffy in T-shirts, hooded tops, trainers and tracksuit bottoms. This wasn't looking too good there were 13 of them, far more than David and I could handle on our own.

Dave was standing behind me, and we both knew that we were going to have a big problem. AK and his scrotey looking crew walked straight past the queue up to the front of the door. They didn't even pause to stop and acknowledge me; they just started to barge straight past. There were just too many of them, but I tried to block their path.

"Are you all together?" I asked fairly casually.

I was nervous. No matter how good we were, we were totally outnumbered.

"Yeah, they're alright, they're with me," AK replied, and he started to usher them all in.

"Sorry," I said abruptly, holding out my arm, "you three are fine, of course, but your friends are dressed too casual and are all a bit too young. Sorry, they can't come in."

Now was the crunch. We were going to see his attitude, his true colors. I was waiting. "No, you don't understand," he said aggressively, looking at me straight in the eyes with his face close to mine.

He wanted to have a go and was just waiting for an excuse. There were still many normal customers waiting in the queue, all watching what was happening.

"I said they're all okay, they're with me." Then he motioned to them. "In you go, lads."

It was getting tense. They had surrounded me, all ready to prove themselves to AK, and AK was ready to show them that he was a head, this was his place and he could do what he wanted.

"Sorry," I said loudly, "they're not coming in." I was standing my ground. It was suicidal, but I was prepared to take it as far as I could. "Don't fucking disrespect me," he shouted close to my face. "I run this fucking place, so what I say goes do you hear?"

I could see his fist clenching he was raging and ready to strike. The others closed in around me and I could see that many others also had clenched fists. They were preparing to storm the door and there was little I could do. I was worried, as it could turn into a massacre. Even if we fought like troopers there were just too many of them.

Dave was standing directly behind me. I wasn't watching him, but he was unusually quiet a rare thing for Dave; he'd never been shy with words. While I stood my ground and blocked the entrance, Dave quickly beckoned AK to one side as the scumbags surrounded me. They were all watching AK, moving their heads nervously from side to side and waiting for his nod. I was scared. I didn't think I'd be going home to my daughter that evening; I didn't think I'd see her again. Once they got going there would be no stopping them. I would battle for as long as I could, but it wouldn't take long for them all to overpower me to the ground, and that would be it; there would be little I could do. I really wasn't bothered about myself; I was just thinking about my lovely little daughter and didn't want her to wake up on Sunday morning without her daddy.

I wasn't listening to what Dave was saying, but after a few minutes he looked at me, nodded and waved AK and all his scruffy scrotes through the door and into the venue. I was really angry, but in a way I completely understood there was simply nothing we could've done. Once inside, the manager appeared and we explained the situation and discussed calling the police, but we had 500 other well dressed, decent customers and getting the police to remove the scumbags quietly might've been a problem.

I was seething and vowed to take revenge. They had no place in the venue, no right to be there and no right to walk past us on the door. They were taking the piss and it annoyed the fuck out of me. I was proud and I was thinking, illogically, that a battle would have been preferable to having these scrotes in *my* club. That evening I decided I was going to kill him. He wasn't an innocent, a one night drunk going just a little too far, but a criminal that had respect for no one and nothing. He deserved to die. I could think of a dozen ways in which I could kill him without any comeback on myself. He deserved all that was coming to him.

On his way out at the end of the night AK passed me, shook my hand and said, "Everything's cool," while I was thinking, you're going to die you fucking scumbag bastard.

For a brief few seconds I considered taking him out there and then, shoving my fingers deep into his eyes, biting off his nose and ears and ripping off his bollocks. But as he walked straight past me and out into the cold I decided that the very next time I saw him I would rip his eyes out and shove them down his throat. I wasn't going to back down next time, no matter how many of them there were and no matter how violent it got.

The following weekend we were expecting them to turn up again and I wanted to be the one that was going to tell them that they were not coming in. Tony Hill also came to help out. Everyone that goes into battle is nervous; anyone that says they don't have any fear is either an idiot or full of shit. Everyone should be scared; it's good to be scared. Fear makes you stronger and able to fight harder. We were all scared, but we were prepared.

But they didn't turn up. Not that week, nor the week after.

I was chatting to one of the doormen at another club in Wilmslow and he told me that they had also been having problems with AK and his crew. They had been at their venue causing trouble, biting and headbutting customers and being abusive to women. I felt sorry for that door crew, but my thinking was: so long as they don't come back to The Rectory and cause me any more problems.

As the weeks and months rolled by, with no sign of AK, things calmed down and we were all feeling very relaxed. The Rectory was continually full of the trendiest people in the area and it was a pleasure to work there. Dave Powers eventually left and moved back into Manchester, to a large 1,000-capacity venue, and a guy called Andy took his place on The Rectory door.

Although for a long time I had wanted to move off the doors and on to a more settled and less violent lifestyle, on the door I was the boss; I controlled my own territory. On the doors and as a bodyguard I was somebody and I enjoyed that feeling. I was unique and an individual and could never imagine being just a number in a big company somewhere pushing paper all day. There had been times in my life when I was younger that I would come away from a fight covered in blood not mine. There had been times when my rage was so great that no one dared to stop me and I had beaten people unconscious. But now I saw The Rectory as my retirement venue. I was over 40 and didn't want to brawl and fight anymore. I knew that the only way I was going to change my life, to move away from my constant violent thoughts and feelings, was by leaving the doors once and for all and looking for an alternative life, before it was too late.

However, I never imagined that I would be leaving the doors as suddenly as I did.

It was a Saturday night and The Rectory was packed as usual. I was working the front door with Andy, while another doorman. Steve was upstairs on the balcony keeping an eye on both the front door and the upstairs section. The DJ was upstairs and, although there was no dance floor, people were dancing. The manager had just done his own small tour of the club and had noticed two knobheads making an arse of themselves near the DJ console dancing aggressively, banging into other customers nearby and generally pissing around. Steve was nearest, but the manager came down to the door and requested that I ask them to leave. I didn't think there would be a problem, so I told Andy that he could stay on the door alone while I took Steve with me. As we squeezed through the crowd, I immediately clocked the two arseholes in question. The manager asked one of them to leave, but he ignored him. The manager asked him again, and for the second time he took no notice. So the manager then grabbed one of them and turned him in the direction of the stairs. Steve then took over and started to escort him downstairs.

"You have to go as well," I shouted to the second one.

"Fuck off," he replied, and he turned slightly away from me as though I wasn't there.

"Listen, I'm not going to argue. Will you leave by yourself or will I have to escort you out?" I was being patient, but I could feel the anger rising.

"You? Throw me out?" He looked at me and laughed. "Fuck off."

I took his arm, intending to guide him downstairs. As I grabbed his arm I could feel him tense and, in the corner of my eye, I saw his fist clench. He stepped back slightly, ready to throw a punch, but I grabbed him hard by the throat and threw him onto the floor. Something inside me snapped.

I grabbed him by the hair and screamed, "Fuck with me, will you? Fuck around in my club?"

I punched him again and again in the face while I was dragging him down the stairs by his hair. The manager tried to pull me off, but I just shrugged him away. He realised that there was nothing he could do to stop me. I dragged the lad by the hair all the way down the steps, punching him repeatedly in the face and the side of his head. I could feel great chunks of bloodied hair coming out in my hands, but then I would drop him for a few seconds, grab another handful and continue to drag him down and out of the front doors, all the time screaming, "Fuck with me, will you?" Everyone in The Rectory could see what I was doing.

After that incident I realised that it would soon be my last night on the doors. I had snapped and lost all control. I was crazy.

The following weekend I went back to Moscow. I had a one week bodyguarding contract and so I was away from The Rectory for just one weekend, and on that Saturday night, after an absence of 12 months, AK decided to visit the venue again. None of the doormen stopped him. He came in with all of his friends, drank two bottles of champagne and left without paying.

Tony Hill promised a strong team on the door the following weekend to stop AK coming back in. Tony planned to be there again, along with Darren from Warrington another hard looking doorman who didn't give a fuck about fronting anyone. We would tell AK to his face that he was barred for good, and if he wanted a war we would give him one.

While I was away I had made the decision to leave the doors once and for all. I knew, after that previous weekend, that my time on the doors was coming to an end. If I stayed on the doors things would never change. I would be going nowhere, struggling by week after week. I had decided to work that one weekend and then quit. I would find another life, wherever that may be.

As soon as I got back I was briefed about what had happened in my absence and I decided that I would not let the guys down and would work through the confrontation. I would stand fast and do what I had to do this one last time and then leave the doors for good.

The following weekend Darren and I were manning the front door. Tony had popped off briefly to drop off another doorman at a club nearby and would be returning and staying with us until the end of the night. I had an awful feeling that AK would turn up again and hoped that Tony would be back in time. We had arranged to call Tony if AK turned up before he returned, and he would then gather up an army of Manchester doormen to teach this scumbag a lasting lesson.

While standing on the door I noticed the imposing figure of AK with about five others behind him, sauntering across the car park towards us. Just as he reached the door, Tony Hill pulled into the driveway. There would be three of us against six of them. It would be a war, but a good war nevertheless.

AK grinned and held out his hand, so I grabbed it as if to shake it and looked him square in the face. "Sorry, AK, you've been barred."

The smirk quickly turned to rage. "What the fuck for?" he shouted.

I still had hold of his hand. His other hand was in a cast following a gunshot injury, so I knew he could only punch with the hand I was gripping.

"Because you left without paying your bar tab and the manager doesn't want to let you in anymore."

He slammed his injured arm across my chest, pushing me away from him.

"I'll give you the fucking money now," he shouted. "I have £2,000 in my pocket. Go and get the fucking bill."

"Sorry, but it's too late," I said. "The manager doesn't want you in."

"Go and fucking get him!"

"He isn't working tonight."

'Go and fucking get him… I'm coming in."

He tried to walk past, but we blocked his way.

"You're not coming in," I said.

"And *you* are going to fucking stop me?" he screamed.

My legs were shaking, but I went up to his face. "If you want a fucking war, I'll give you a fucking war," I said. "You take the piss out of us and you've got a shit attitude. Who do you think you are? We don't want you here. Now if you want to fight, let's do it now and get it over with. Either way you're not coming in. I'm too old for all of this and I don't want a war with you, but if you want a war I'll give you a fucking war you'll wish you'd never started."

He slammed me hard in the chest, pushing me away from him.

One of his friends said, "Come on, they're not going to fucking stop us, we're going in." But the others crowded round and pushed him back.

We stood our ground. AK was straining forward, the veins in his neck bulging, his face contorted with anger and his fists clenched. We stood ready for battle. I was just on the verge of jumping in, grabbing at his eyes and tearing them from their sockets when a police van pulled into the driveway.

AK turned and ran, yelling, "I'll be back! I'll return, and you, Robin, are fucking dead!"

I knew this time I was marked. I understood it completely. He was a head amongst his own small gang. He had things to prove and he would never leave it.

I was too old for a war; a war I knew I could never win. So I left the doors, not knowing what I was going to do or where I was going to go.

PART TWO
GOING INSIDE

Written by Robin Barratt and Charlie Bronson,
with contributions from:
Kevin Lane (www.justiceforkevinlane.com),
Terry Field and Robert Etchells.

Introduction

By Charlie Bronson

When Robin asked me to come in on this project I thought: fuck me, what do I know about door work in this era? I've been on Mars for almost four decades. Why ask me? Then I thought: fuck me, why not me?

So here I am, yours truly. Love me or hate me, I really don't give a flying fuck. My world is a million miles from yours, and you really don't want to step into my space. But please have a bit of respect for what I once stood for: a first-class doorman, a bouncer from the old school. I had a serious reputation to live up to and I took my work very, very seriously. My era was the 'real era', when we used violence against violence. There was none of today's shit of restraint and control and watch your Ps and Qs and all that PC bollocks. Our way was a sharp right hook. Problem solved. Our way was the only way.

Today's doormen are a new breed. It's a different way of life. Not that I know a lot about it; only that they all train on courses, they speak sort of posh, they look sort of posh, they wear them silly ear contraptions, and there's even female bouncers!

Fuck me, what's happened out there?

"The good old days?" I hear you say. "How many times do we have to hear this bollocks?" "What was so good about them old days?" "Why can't the old doormen accept that times have changed?" "Why can't they give us young 'uns some respect?" "Why were they so special?" "They never had a licence like us!" "We are the new breed of respect and reputation!" "Our way is far better than the 'Bronson era'!"

Yeah, and pigs fly!!

Let me tell you, guys and girls, your way bores me to death. In fact, I wouldn't wish to do it. I don't need a licence to knock out some troublemaker; I don't need some instructor to teach me how to pick out a potential troublemaker; and I'm not interested in learning how to handle a volatile situation. All the training in the world can't teach a man about how to survive in the trenches of life. I have seen 20-stone men run off from a fight!

You're born with that survival instinct; you can't learn it!

To me, a cunt's a cunt; it may as well be tattooed on his forehead – all the PC brigade can kiss my arse.

That's how it is with Charlie Bronson and men of my era. I don't mind if you hate me for what I am, but don't love me for what I'm not. Look at it this way: did the parents of the teenage girl hate me for holding her face together when some sicko smashed a beer glass into her boat? That's Respect. 180 stitches later when I pop into the hospital with some flowers to cheer her up. That's Respect. A beautiful young girl cut up like a piece of steak.

You can watch all the horror movies, all the blood and gore and chainsaw lunatics; I've seen it in real life. That good, honest blood dripped all over me. I've seen the middle-aged woman nutted in the face and watched her nose splatter and crack, and I've grabbed the attacker and given him a hiding never to be forgotten. I've pushed in a man's kidney hanging out of his back. I've held a man's cut throat together. I've picked up a man's eye from the floor. I've picked up two fingers and put them in an ice bucket. I can tell you things that would turn your hair white.

From the epileptic fit to the maniac psychotic, I handled it all!

A real doorman in my era earned his place through experience. Fuck the classes in college and instructors. It's real life that teaches the true reality of a doorman's job.

A doorman becomes a true saviour.

Do you really want to know the best part of 'on the doors?' I'll tell you the 'pussy'. There isn't a doorman on the planet that hasn't stood there for a slice of pussy. "Look, sweetheart, I can't let you in, it's full up… oh well, maybe a quick blow job in the cloakroom first… "

Every doorman has a little black book with pussy numbers, or 'fairy' numbers, as, believe it or not, there's plenty of gay doormen. Even in my time there were a lot of gay bouncers, but it wasn't in your face in them days – very hush-hush. Nowadays, it's proud to take a sausage, or six. Whatever turns you on, I say. Me, I love the pussy; even after so long in the can, I'm still a proud pussy man. You can't beat those sweet smelling, juicy, hot lips – every pussy deserves a sausage is what I say!

Anyway, where was I? Oh yes, on the doors.

It was back in 1969 when I first had a go at it; the doors I mean, not pussy! I was only 18, but I was a big lump and looked in my late twenties. At the time I was a hod carrier for the brickies. I was the best, the fastest ever; I was up and down them ladders like a ferret. It was good pay, too. I would recommend it to any youngster. Boys become men on the building sites. They're a good bunch of lads to work with. My only downfall at that time was my violent temper; I just loved a fight. In them days I would've started a fucking riot in a monastery. That's how I was; fuck with me and you fucked with the devil. I worked hard, and played even harder. My weekends were for me – I came alive; World War 3!

Don't get me wrong, I wasn't like the spineless cunts of today, picking fights with innocent people and going out in gangs to terrorise old folk. My battles were in pub car parks with lunatics just like me. Some I lost, but most I won. I fucking loved it. It was my time, my era, my scene, my thing, my buzz; it was me coming alive. Mad Micky Peterson, that's who I was then, long before I became Bronson. I was as infamous then as I am now. I've just been around a long time and I've lived as two people, and I'm proud of them both. Why shouldn't I be?

So there I was, an 18-year-old lunatic crashing my way through life with broken teeth and cut eyes and without a worry in the world. I fucking loved it. The hod carrying kept me fit and strong and at the weekend I came alive, plus my little bit of crime on the side. A guy's gotta live. Well, let's face it, our MPs today like to earn a few quid on the side who doesn't?

And then something happened; I woke up. I got a serious 'pull' from a local club owner let's just say this guy wasn't your average manager. This guy was, in fact, a very serious man of respect in the world of heavies. I was in his club when a fight broke out and a bottle hit a barmaid. I grabbed the bottle thrower, dragged him outside and gave him a good bashing. I was grabbed myself by three guys and ended up in a room in the back of the club where the 'Boss' had a chat with me. That was the beginning of my world on the door; I no longer went looking for a war, it all came to me! It was fucking brilliant (bees to a honey jar). Muggy old pissheads taking a swing at me; a quick step aside and – bang straight into the solar plexus, Crack, one on the jaw. Goodnight.

And I was getting paid for it!

The talk that the Boss gave me that night has stayed with me right up to this day, 40 years later. I'll tell you something now: that man spilt tears when I got put away and for 30 years he never missed an Xmas card with a few quid in it. That's Respect. The only reason I'm not saying his name is that in my game I have to protect the guilty. 'Mum's the word'.

It's just one of many graves that I have yet to show my respects to.

I was a good doorman; 'fair'; a decent chap. Maybe at times I was a little 'heavy', but all in all I learned fast. I could smell trouble before it started. Like I said, a cunt's a cunt in my book. It's in capital letters, big black ones, across his head: "I am a cunt." "Who the fuck are you? Let's get it on… "

It was about 11 p.m. on a Saturday and the club was rocking. There were four of us working the door and everything was sweet. I shot off for a piss. No sooner than I was stood at the urinal pissing, two guys rolled in, both arguing and getting well over the top. I'm having one of those pisses that goes on forever – you know the ones, like a rhino; it just didn't seem to stop! "Fuck me, you two, shut the fuck up will you!" They stopped arguing. All went silent, then – bang this cunt hit me from the side. Fuck me, I'm still pissing. My hands were now shaking and I'm thinking: cunt! I can't believe it! What a position to be in. Do I start up and piss all over the place. What would you do? Bear in mind that this all happened so fast. So I spun around with my cock in hand and pissed all over him. "You cunt, hit me from behind." A flick of the dick, back in my pants, zip, zip, and those two never knew what hit them! Not a bad night's work not a piss stain on me!

That brings a crazy memory. I once walked into the club toilet and caught 'Big Ernie' – all 20 stone of him – having a blow job. No big deal, you might say. Yeah, but it was with a geezer. All I got from Ernie for a month after was, "Please, Micky, don't say anything." That's what I say – it's a funny old game, this door lark. It really does take all sorts, and even more so today.

I couldn't see me working a door with a woman. I know I'll probably upset and offend a lot of women bouncers with my views, but I'm just being honest. Women, to me, are beautiful, wonderful people, with bodies to die for. Why does a woman even want to work the door? Look, sweethearts, just be a woman, be sexy, be true to yourself. It's like me going up on stage to do the pole dance. Could you see me as a pole dancer? Come on, wake up. I know it's 2009 and I'm a lost, fucked up soul; I know I'm an old fashioned sort of guy with a strong moral code… I best stop there before I dig myself into a bigger hole! And please let it be a pussy hole! What would I do right now with a nice, fresh pussy? God, why do I have to live this hermit's life? I'm only human… well, almost. I've got my needs, like any man.

Why be so cruel and nasty to me? CUNT a cunt's a cunt in my book, okay? And that includes God nasty bastard.

I hear that today most doormen and doorwomen search the customers. We did none of that. There were no metal detectors or radios, we just used our own instincts 'experience of life'. Sure, today's a more dangerous time, with drugs and weapons, but again I wouldn't want to work the doors now. And I also think that today's doormen are too close to the Old Bill; they even act like them, and at times look like them. My era did not have it with the enemy. Look how many doormen have come unstuck when the cops get involved. Loads end up in jail. The Old Bill are a slippery lot in times of panic; I would sooner trust a king cobra than the law. Sorry, but that's how I am. You doormen seem to be right up the law's arsehole today. In my era we were the law: we gave out our own punishments; we never needed a judge to do that. A car park was our courtroom! Fuck the Old Bill. I used to go and have a pot of tea in the back room when the cops arrived at our doors; I can't even look at them, let alone talk to them. I'm like the Three Brass Monkeys: speak no bollocks, hear no bollocks, and see fuck all! "I was having a cuppa, Officer, so how do I know how his jaw got broken? I'm going for a shit now, so unless you want to wipe my arse you best fuck off." That's how I am, today, and yesterday.

Tomorrow...? Who gives a fuck.

"You can come in my club anytime, sir... but you may not get back out."

One thing that put me off the doors is sick! Why did people have to spew up near me? Why couldn't they just leave fast and be sick outside? Go spew up on a policeman, or all over their cars. The dirty sick bastards no consideration for people like me who have to witness it. And, sadly, it's mostly girls who do it.

I hit a geezer one night. He was getting a little silly, acting like a prat and showing off to his girlfriend. He kept creeping up to me and saying, "Hi, Mr Penguin."

"Ha, ha... fuck off, cunt. Don't push it. Go away."

Would he listen? Would he fuck. So I grabbed his Adam's apple and hit him in the solar plexus not hard, but hard enough to tell him, "Stop now, cunt."

Would you believe he spewed up all over my shoes, my favourite black brogues? That's the story of my life: blood, snot and spew. I could've killed him. I should've killed him. Lucky bastard.

I took off my shoes and told his girlfriend, "Go and clean them or I'll rip your fella's face off."

Those shoes were never the same again. You don't forget; it's a bit like a smelly, fish paste pussy. Who needs it? Take a tip, girls: keep that pussy of yours sweet. There's no need for an unhygienic body. Face facts: if you can't keep yourself clean, then you best crawl back into a hole and die. I hate bad breath too. It stinks! It makes me feel dirty. I brush my teeth six times a day. You can kiss me anytime; I'm as fresh as a daisy try it one day later; you can kiss me for free. Respect your body and hygiene. I actually wash my bell end every time I have a piss. Not many guys do that. Unlike me, they haven't got the time – I've got all the time in the world. My bell end shines with pride. It lights up in the dark, and nobody on this planet knows the dark quite like me. I've lived in this bottomless hole for so long that it's now my heaven. To you it's hell. You couldn't survive my life for one single day; you'd be on your knees. "Please, God, free me from this madness."

That would be me on the door today: "Please, God, free me from this madness."

I just couldn't do it; it's not me. I'd feel a total prat having to wear the earpiece and mike, using a metal detector and rubbing down men's bodies. I wouldn't be allowed to call a cunt a cunt anymore. How long would I last today? Even other doormen would grass me up to the Old Bill. "Officer, I saw Bronson headbutt that poor man, then kick him in the bollocks."

I'm sorry, but I just feel so sorry for you lot today. It breaks my fucking heart what's left of it. It's crap. I wonder if they still get a lot of pussy? What about women door staff? Do they get a lot of cock or do they just shag each other on the doors?

What's going on out there in that mad, crazy world?

The greatest part of a doorman's job is meeting all the wonderful characters. That, for me, was all worth a punch in the head, and let's be honest about this: nine out of ten punches ever thrown are by drunks who, when sober, are nice, decent people; the drink just turns them mental. But a good doorman can work out the real nasty fuckers. The drunks are two a penny, easy to sort out; it's the nasty fuckers that cause the big problems. That's when we have to get nasty back. "Okay, buddy, let's do it. You want some, you'll fucking get plenty!"

I'm not quite sure how today's bouncers sort that out. Probably restrain and wait for the fuzz to arrive. How fucking boring and time wasting! I just couldn't be involved in such pathetic rules. It just spoils all the fun for me. But that's your PC bollocks for you. That's what you get when you let the councils and MPs get involved: silly rules. Do this, don't do that, don't hurt him, sit on him until Mr Plod comes. Fuck all that – our old way worked so much better.

And I think the public respected us more for our fast work. Come on, let's be honest here: nobody wants to see violence erupt on a good night out, especially happy couples out for a great time. Us guys only rushed in to stop good, honest people from getting hurt. Me, personally, I hit hard; I hit with a lot of hate. When I punch I smash bones – I punch to hurt; I punch to take out, and fast. It's not a game. The troublemaker may have a tool, a blade, a cosh. I had one nutter with a test-tube full of acid. Obviously, I didn't know at the time what the fuck it was, but when he pulled it out of his jacket and threatened to chuck it in my face I knew it wasn't cream soda. Cunt. Once I'd touted him 'outside' I broke the evil bastard's nose. "Fuck off." That's the sort of evil fuckers you can come up against. What sort of prick goes for a night out with a tube of acid? Why? What reason? What would doormen do today with that situation? Hand him over to the fuzz? A broken nose does it for Bronson, and a kick in the arse. If he comes back for more then I'll put the cunt in hospital. I'll break his arms and legs. No slag throws acid at me and gets away with it. Nasty bastard.

I think one day I'll write a book on the wonderful characters I've met on the doors. I used to love the dwarfs, not that I've come across loads of them, but the ones I have met are treasured memories. I just love a dwarf. They're wonderful, lovely people. Again, the PC brigade stopped dwarf throwing. Why? Cos they're fucking idiots. Dwarf throwing was a great event and I'm proud to say I've thrown my share. In fact I was the champion back in 1971. Come on, even the dwarfs loved it. They wore helmets and padding, and they got a drink out of it. Everybody enjoyed it; it was a great event. I slung one little fucker 28 feet. Thank fuck he had a helmet on, cos he went flying. Laugh? We pissed ourselves. The PC brigade have a lot to answer for. So what do the little people do now? They're all at home feeling depressed, with no fun in their lives. It's a national disgrace. They loved it as much as we did, plus there was a nice few quid for them. I say, bring it back. Fuck the PC brigade. If you're with me on that, then log onto my website, BronsonLoonyology.com, and let's get a serious petition going to bring it back. Why not have it in the Olympics? Well, why not? It's a brilliant sport, plus it will liven the games up and bring back some humour! I don't know anybody who wouldn't love to watch a dwarf fly through the air screaming. It's so funny and exciting. It's a bit like all those freaks that watch the motor races hoping to see a crash. It's the same thing to see a dwarf fly.

Sadly, some do break bones; but come on, what's a bone or two for a gold medal and a chance to be famous? The dwarfs deserve a bit of fame. With fame comes dosh and a great change of lifestyle. Why shouldn't our little people get rich before the PC brigade step in and stop it again? Let's hear from all the dwarfs; let's hear what they have to say! Are they not entitled to a say? Fuck the PC bollocks, it's the little folk who decide. I'll be very interested to see the response on this. Don't be afraid to air your opinion and stand up for what you believe in. If we all stand as one we can get this sport brought back. Come on, let's do it! If I were a dwarf I'd love to be in the Olympics. Fuck me, I'd do it without a helmet!

Hey, did you know these little guys have massive cocks? It's true. There's a blue movie out there called *Snow White and 7 Large Cocks*. I'm not making it up; it's unbelievable. One of the dwarfs that came into the club where I worked used to flash his meat to the girls. They all loved him and plenty got it on with the little fella. I was told by more than one of the girls that he was the best shag they'd ever had. With his tool, it didn't surprise me either. His bell end was the size of a tangerine. But, getting back to the blue movie, I've got to say that Snow White must've been sore for months after. She took some serious cock. It's years ago I saw it, but I've never forgot it; it's just one of those films you never can forget. No wonder they called her Snow White!

I've met so many wonderful people. Us doormen are blessed. It's an absolute privilege and honour to be in such a position to meet so many interesting people. I won't name names, as you'll just call me a 'flash cunt', but I've rubbed shoulders with all sorts from every walk of life and I've loved every moment of it.

In 1974 I took a serious dive. For those who don't know about what went down, I'll tell you. I lost the plot. I finally hit the black hole, and I'm not talking pussy here. I fell into hell, where I stayed till 1987. That's 14 years of porridge and madness. The door slammed shut in my face and the bolts went on. My best friend would become a straitjacket. 'Respect and Reputation'? Fuck me, this was more like 'Insanity Gone Mad'. It was the bouncer being bounced. I smashed into every cell wall from Parkhurst on the Isle of Wight to Frankland up in Durham. To name but a few of my hotels along my journey of madness: Brixton, Wandsworth

Scrubs, Pentonville, Belmarsh, Winchester, Norwich, Albany, Camp Hill, Parkhurst, Bristol, Oxford, Rampton, Broadmoor, Ashworth... Are you getting bored yet?... Armley, Durham, Wakefield, Risley, Full Sutton, Long Lartin, Strangeways, Wilson Green, Woodhill, Hull... I'm getting bored now... Lincoln, Leicester, Hickdown, Bullingdon, Whitemoor... Fuck me, I'm falling asleep. Let's just say I've moved around a lot and I'm about to tell you all about Respect and Reputation. It's best you go and put the kettle on, make a nice pot of tea and I'll meet you back here for the next chapter... You're gonna fucking love it!

Going Inside

By Robin Barratt with Terry Field and Bob Etchells

'Prison': any place of confinement or involuntary restraint. At the time of writing this book a Norwich doorman, Steven Hopkins, is on trial for killing a customer. During the trial the court heard that on 30th May 2008 28-year-old doorman Hopkins pushed 46-year-old Phillip Ward as he was leaving the Chicago Rock Café in Prince of Wales Road. Mr Ward then fell backwards and hit his head, suffering a fatal head injury from which he never regained consciousness. A friend of Mr Ward's told the court that she was waiting with Mr Ward to leave the nightclub when the doorman told Mr Ward to shut an internal door he had opened, to prevent noise from reaching outside and disturbing the residents living nearby. She said:

The doorman approached Phil and swore at him to keep the door closed. Phil let the door close, and then the doorman asked him, again swearing, whether he had a problem with that (closing the doors). The doorman repeated that two or three times. I tried to calm the situation and just said that Phil was waiting for his wife, Mandy, who was still somewhere inside the club. The doorman was being unnecessarily abusive. When I turned around again Hopkins was squaring up to Phil. He grabbed hold of Phil with his hands on Phil's front the upper part of his chest and shoved him backward through the door. I asked him what he was doing and said there was no need for that. My partner, Glen Lambert, then said to the doorman "I think you are in trouble, boy," or words to that effect.

Prosecutor Christopher Morgan told the court that the incident had lasted no more than two or three minutes but that the end result had been the death of Mr Ward.

In his defence Steven Hopkins claimed that Mr Ward had pushed him and sworn at him. Hopkins told the jury: "I decided he was a threat to myself. I decided he needed to leave the venue." He said that he could not remember how he held Mr Ward but thought he had hold of his left arm. Hopkins said that Mr Ward had been compliant but suddenly shoved back towards him as they reached the foyer. He was concerned that the situation would escalate, so he pushed Mr Ward away: "I wanted to clear my space. It all happened so quickly."

By the time this book is published the doorman will have been found either guilty or not guilty, and he will either be free and back with his family and friends or in prison behind bars for a very long time.

In another incident a door supervisor at Bristol's Lizard Lounge nightclub was sentenced to five years in prison for ramming his walkie-talkie into a customer's face so hard that it caused his eyeball to explode. Doorman Martin White drove the walkie-talkie into the eye of a law student, who had fallen asleep in a club when celebrating the end of his exams. Judge Stewart Patterson said: "You were on duty, your job was to keep peace in the club; but instead you attacked one of the customers without the slightest provocation." Sentencing White, Judge Patterson said that the attack "sickened" those who witnessed it and described the consequences as "appalling". The law student needed four hours of eye surgery and was left blind in his left eye. Judge Patterson said that the student was then dragged across the club by White, with his head "bouncing along" and leaving a trail of blood along the route taken. White then "dumped" the drunken student at the bottom of the stairs before verbally threatening and swearing at him. Two other bouncers then helped him to get out onto the pavement.

And, more recently, a door supervisor from Birmingham who was working towards a law degree was being sentenced to 18 months in prison for killing a construction worker with a single punch to the head. Mohammed Waqar pleaded guilty to the manslaughter of Simon Bampton, who suffered a brain haemorrhage after his head snapped back from a single punch. At the time of the attack, Waqar had completed the first year of a civil engineering course at Birmingham City University and was in the process of transferring to a law degree.

As a door supervisor today, if you are unnecessarily violent or use any unreasonable force you will almost certainly lose your job; it's inevitable. New licensing and the tough conditions imposed by the government and the SIA mean that your badge is immediately suspended if you are arrested for any violent act and you will lose your licence if found guilty. Also, depending on the nature and result of your actions, or if you then continue to lead a violent life, it is almost certain that you will end up inside. And then, of course, if you continue to lead a violent life inside prison, it is almost certain that you will go on to spend most, if not all, of your life inside.

Put very simply, if you are arrested for an offence, you will be taken to a police station where the custody officer on duty will determine whether there is sufficient evidence to charge you for that offence. Currently, the police have the right to keep you in custody for a maximum of 96 hours until that decision is made, although in terrorism cases you may be detained for a maximum of 28 days (but I hope this will not be relevant to anyone reading this book!) If there is sufficient evidence to provide a reasonable prospect of conviction you will be charged, and if there is not sufficient evidence then, of course, you will be released. On expiry of the maximum time limit you must be released anyway and you cannot then be rearrested without warrant for the same offence unless new evidence has come to light since the original arrest. If you are charged with an offence, you will either be released on police bail or detained in custody pending your trial or during your trial and before sentencing. The term 'on remand' is generally used to describe the process of keeping you in detention rather than granting bail. If you are denied, refused or unable to meet the conditions of bail, you may be held in a prison on remand and the reasons depend on many things including the seriousness of the offence, having previous convictions for similar offences or likely to commit further offences, the possibility of you leaving the country or destroying evidence or interfering with witnesses, or if you are likely to be targeted in any way. When in prison on remand you do get a few extra privileges, such as extended visiting times, as in the UK remand prisoners are considered innocent until proven guilty by a court.

All adult prisoners (those aged 21 or over) are given a security categorisation soon after they enter prison. These categories are based on a combination of the type of crime committed, the length of sentence, the likelihood of escape and the danger to the public if they did escape. The four categories for male prisoners are:

1) Category A prisoners: those whose escape would be highly dangerous to the public or national security.

2) Category B prisoners: those who do not require maximum security, but for whom escape needs to be made very difficult.

3) Category C prisoners: those who cannot be trusted in open conditions but who are unlikely to try to escape. 4) Category D prisoners: those who can be reasonably trusted not to try to escape, and are given the privilege of an open prison.

Prisoners at 'D Cat' (as it is commonly known) prisons are subject to approval and given a Release On Temporary Licence (ROTL) to work in the community or to go on home leave once they have passed their Full Licence Eligibility Date (FLED), which is usually a quarter of the way through the sentence. Category A, B and C prisons are called closed prisons, whilst category D prisons are called open prisons. Category A prisoners are further divided into Standard Escape Risk (SER), High Escape Risk (HER), and Exceptional Escape Risk (EER), based on their likelihood of escaping.

Women prisoners are also classified into four categories:

1) Restricted Status: similar to Cat A for men. 2) Closed: for those who are not trusted not to attempt to escape. 3) Semiopen: introduced in 2001 and mainly for those prisoners who are unlikely to try to escape, although some prisons are now being recategorised; for instance, in March 2009 HMP Morton Hall and HMP Drake Hall had their status changed from semiopen to closed. 4) Open: for those who can be trusted to stay within the prison.

When offenders under the age of 21 are sentenced to a custodial term, they may be sent to one of four types of establishment:

1) Local Authority Secure Children's Homes (LASCHs): run by Social Services and focused on attending to the physical, emotional and behavioural needs of vulnerable young people. 2) Secure Training Centres (STCs): privately run, education focused centres for offenders up to the age of 17. 3) Juvenile Prisons: run by the Prison Service to accommodate 15 to 18-year-olds. 4) Young Offender Institutions (YOIs): run by the Prison Service to accommodate 18 to 21-year-olds.

Remand prisoners are normally held in closed prisons.

Whilst you may think that going into prison is cool and will raise the level of your status amongst your friends and peers and give you respect, take it from the majority of prisoners who have served long stretches inside: it definitely is not. Prison life will ultimately destroy you and the world around you. This is almost guaranteed.

After a few years inside, the friends that you had on the outside are no longer friends. Hopefully, your family will continue to visit and support you and help you, but even this will diminish after a while. You will no longer be able to support your wife and kids financially if you still have them, that is. And if you didn't have a partner, wife or kids before you went inside, don't forget, if you go in when you are young on a long stretch you will probably never have them, as you will come out an old man! And if your sentence is extended for violent behaviour you will miss the best part of your life: your youth, the clubs, the cars, the girls (or boys, or whatever), the holidays in the sun, the getting pissed, the good times with your mates and family and friends. Everything will end. Everything. And getting an extra potato for lunch will become the highlight of the day and something to talk about. Take it from Charlie Bronson, the man who has spent 35 years in prison: "Be someone, do something, but whatever you do, don't fucking waste your life inside."

Terry Field is a former HMP Whitemoor prison officer. He has also worked as a bailiff and has spent ten years working on the doors, three of those years as an area manager for the security company Capes UK. I talked with him about what it's like to be inside, and he spoke of his experiences in dealing with Charlie, sentiments shared by many other prison officers:

The prison service created Charlie Bronson, and now the prison service has no idea how to deal with him. Charlie is a top, top man who deserves much respect. I used my mouth instead of a riot shield. Why open him [his cell door] with six screws ready to fight when one officer ready to treat him normally and with respect could have dealt with him? It's not rocket science, is it? When you can, be nice to people and most of the time they will be nice to you back. I was always nice to Charlie and Charlie was always nice to me.

Having never been in prison in the UK, I asked Terry what happens once you get sentenced:

After sentencing you will get taken to one of the holding cells to await your transfer to prison. Usually the holding cell is downstairs in the courthouse. It's at this point that the clever ones expecting a prison sentence will have packed a bag ready to take in; writing materials, lots of stamps, trainers, but remember, if you can't have it in jail they will take it off you and put it in your property box, but it is always best pack it anyway and take the chance. From the court you will be cuffed, locked in the van and escorted, usually by a private security firm, to the local prison. Depending upon your crime, these prisons are normally Category B, such as Lincoln, Pentonville, Bedford, etc. The first point of call on arrival at any prison will be Reception. At any prison the Reception area can be very busy, so remember you are now a convicted criminal and moaning about getting locked in a room, or moaning about a less than friendly officer, won't do you any good. Your warrant that enables the State to keep you in prison will be checked and all your personal details taken. You will be issued a prison number and this will stay with you even if you are transferred out to another jail. Photographs will be taken and any tattoos you have will be logged. All new entries to prison are strip-searched. This should be by officers of the same sex and out of view from other inmates. You should never be naked and you should put your T-shirt back on before removing your trousers, which is often seen as degrading but don't refuse to do it as it will happen whether you like it or not and being carted off to the Seg Block under restraint is probably not the best start! Your clothes will go into your property box and you will be issued prison clothing and some really nice shoes! This is where the pre packed bag could come in handy. All your property will be listed and anything you are not allowed to have will go into the box as well, and returned when you leave. Different prisons have different rules, so what you can't have in one prison you might be able to have in another. Make sure both you and the officer sign for your property. The medical check is mostly to identify if you are a suicide risk, but take the opportunity to raise any concerns you might have and ask anything you want to know. Once you are done in Reception the wing staff from your allocated wing will usually collect you and escort you there. If it's your lucky day you might get some kind of wing induction, but don't hold your breath as most of the staff will probably be either too busy or not interested. As the new arrival, it's a good chance you will get either the shittiest cell or the smelliest cellmate; both if you are really unlucky. Again, don't kick off, stay cool, be nice and let the door shut and try to sort it out in the morning with a decent officer there are some! Facing prison for the first time is something we all hope will never happen to us, but the reality is we are all just a mad minute away from facing that horrible prospect. Most people, when facing the real prospect of a prison sentence, will be anxious and have a real fear of the unknown. These are normal feelings, but try not to let them affect your normal behaviour as you enter prison for the first time. Many screws are good guys and are not your enemy. However, they are human and will react to and mirror your behaviour, so if you act like a scumbag, you will get treated like a scumbag. A big reputation outside means nothing in prison, as the staff and time served cons have seen it all before and won't be impressed by a 'new boy' giving it the big 'un and mouthing off. The bad impression it leaves will follow you all around the jail like a bad smell, so just be yourself. Keep your sense of humour, as you will need it time and time again: don't make yourself into something you are not. When the door shuts for the first night of any first prison sentence, the new inmate is at their most vulnerable. It is at this time that self harm and suicide are the greatest risks. Feeling unable to cope in unfamiliar surroundings, self harm is commonplace and it's not always the weak inmate that actually does it. These feelings can affect anyone, so don't suffer on your own: talk to someone. Officers and other inmates will get you through it and help you to settle in. Give yourself time, as it does, and will, take some time to adapt to prison life. Don't do anything silly; you will adapt. Once settled in, don't be aggressive but be assertive and stay alert, as this will help deter bullies. Use basic manners with everyone and stay out of prison politics, as gossip and bad-mouthing people will bring trouble to your door. A big mistake many first timers make is lying about their crime by bigging it up or exaggerating about past crimes or people they know on the outside. Don't do it; you will get found out. Respect can be earned and lost quickly in prison. Something as simple as entering another inmate's cell uninvited can be seen as disrespectful. Remember, it might be just a cell to you, but it's somebody else's home, so don't just sit on the bed, etc. Use basic manners. The biggest no-no is drugs: don't get involved. It's not just dickheads that end up in massive debt, selling their arses for a fix, literally. Drugs. Gambling. Borrowing. No, no, no. Stay out of debt; it will lead to no good and, if you do manage to escape the wing unhurt, it will only be to a vulnerable prisoner wing for your own protection, where you will have to serve out your sentence with sex offenders, rapists and child murderers. Do you really want that? Keep yourself drug free and debt free, as in prison your actions will decide what friends you attract, so respect yourself and pal up with decent, like-minded inmates and you won't go far wrong. By far, the best reputation to have is 'He's a nice fella. He won't cause trouble, but don't take liberties with him.' Prison can be hard, so do your time the right way and remember: it is impossible to beat the system. The Government and Home Office are a big, big firm, so don't get into wars you can't win. Yes, there are some horrible Nazi screws who will try to wind you up, along with a great many dickhead inmates. But remember that a little respect to the good staff and like-minded inmates will go a long way. Be yourself. Do it the sensible way and stay safe.

Former prisoner Robert (Bob) Etchells started working the door in the late '70s, when he was just 17 years old, at the Festival House, one of the toughest pubs in Norwich at that time. He ended his career in 2005 when he was charged and found guilty of possessing a firearm. For almost 30 years Bob ran some of the toughest and busiest clubs and pubs in Norwich, as well as following his managers to work the doors with them in Plymouth and the Welsh borders. However, Norwich was his home and he always came back. Bob also ran a number of door companies, at one time employing over 50 doormen throughout the region, as well as providing debt collecting and other 'related' security services. Bob went inside before SIA licensing and so he has never applied for his SIA badge, nor is he ever likely to. Undoubtedly, Bob is a hard man, but he found prison life difficult and vows never to return:

Waiting for my trial consumed my life. Every time I read the paper I looked for crimes and sentences; three years, eighteen months, seven years for this and that, and never thought I would cop a five year stretch. The court case lasted about eleven months in total, as it kept getting put back. I had pleaded guilty at the very beginning, but if I had known how courts run and how the seasoned criminals did it I would never have said anything at the very beginning when I was first arrested. I didn't have a history of violence. I had been doing the doors for almost 26 years and had a successful door agency, but I had never been to court or been arrested for any violent crime and thought I would be spared prison. At that time I had a bit of money and thought, I can pay any fine I might get and that will be the end of it. At the time of sentencing my mum and my brothers were there as well as my sister, her son and some friends. The judge slagged me off completely. He told me I was a professional 'enforcer' and I ran a door agency known as 'bouncers' – I felt fucked when he said, "I am giving you five years." "Five years, for making a mistake?" I shouted. A security guard tried to grab my arm. "No," I shrugged him off. "Five years?!" I shouted. The judge said, "Mr Etchells, you have nothing to say that the barrister hasn't already said, now go downstairs." And they took me downstairs. I was astounded. I just couldn't believe it. I'd lost everything; my house, my job, money, everything. As soon as I went downstairs I was in shock; it was all double Dutch. I didn't really understand what was happening to me. It was such a numbing pain. As I sat downstairs in the cell, my barrister said that we would try to appeal it. And then I thought: great, I'll be out on bail until it goes to appeal, as I was on bail while waiting for trial, but no. I didn't even get to say goodbye to my mum or my family. I didn't go to prison straight away; you have to wait until there are six or seven of you, until the van is full. I was sentenced at about

3.30 in the afternoon, but I didn't end up getting to Norwich prison until about

7.30 that evening. My girlfriend at the time rang my brother at about 5.30. He said he was so sorry but I'd got five years. She was devastated. She broke down. Luckily, my family all rallied round her, and went round to see her as often as they could. Because I wasn't there I was really lucky that I didn't know how she felt or what had happened to her. Seeing her upset would have made things even harder for me. On the way to Norwich prison I sat in the van handcuffed, trying to reach up to look out of the window. I saw people I knew, but they couldn't see me. It was like trying to cling on to something you know. We drove through the main gates, and heard the gates slam shut behind. It is a horrible, horrible feeling. You feel like a wound up piece of string; all the 'not knowing' and the fear of what was ahead. You are then taken to the reception area where the guards uncuff you and process your admission. The screws started talking to me, but it was all just a mist. One minute I was surrounded by my family and friends and the next minute handcuffed and in prison. From reception you then go and get strip-searched, and then you get your clothes given to you. You don't get new clothes; you are wearing someone else's boxer shorts, someone else's shoes. They are all grey or mauve. It's cold, it's damp, it's dirty, and it's musky. You then go into another cell until all the other new prisoners are processed and then you all go up into the main prison. Fresh meat. It is exactly like the film 'Escape from New York', where everyone is hanging around the landings. You are like a rabbit really. I was looking up at everyone staring down at me, thinking: who the fuck have I thrown out; who have I given a good hiding to? There are a lot of drug dealers in prison, and over the years I have thrown a good few out or stopped them from getting into the pubs and clubs I have worked. I wondered if there were any staring down at me. I was lucky at the beginning, as I went straight onto the Fours, which was one of the better landings, and at first I got my own room, sorry, cell. I didn't come out of my cell for about three days. I didn't eat. I didn't do anything. The thing about prison meals is there is a sheet with three choices: shit, shit, and more shit. It is disgusting and if you don't put in your food slip you get the vegetarian choice, which is even worse. Because I didn't come out of my cell for three days I didn't know about the food, about letters, about visits, about applying for work to stop getting bored, or about the gym. I didn't know about showers and when you can go for a shower, or about the phone, the phone credit, registering your phone numbers, so when I did actually ask about these things I was three days behind. They did tell me all of this when I first went through reception, but because you are in so much shock nothing sinks in or registers. It is hard to explain what happens to you; barriers go up and you just go into a very basic survival mode. After three days I came out of my cell and started to talk to people. I got chatting to a young lad whose dad was a best mate of mine when I had a flat in Norwich. I knew him when he was a boy. He was in for stabbing someone and had already done four years. He obviously knew the prison routine and told me what I needed to know. To use the phone you have to register who you want to call and obviously you have to know the person's telephone number, their full name and address, as well as their date of birth, but you just don't know that sort of information for everybody you want to call. So a small problem like that suddenly becomes a mountain. You get given an initial £2.50 phone credit; after that has gone you don't get given any more. Norwich prison is exactly like the series 'Porridge', with the cold and the bleakness and the brick walls and the screws who don't really want to talk to you much. Everything is by your last name: Etchells this and Etchells that. There is nothing personal. You then have to settle into a routine. At the very beginning you have to decide whether you are going to be one of the majority of prisoners, or one of the minority. The majority are those that know prison very well, know the system and feed off the minority. If you want to be fed off, you stay in the minority; and if you want to be a feeder, you stay in the majority. You definitely don't want to be fed off, so you feed off other people and when new people come in you abuse them. You also learn very quickly that everyone in prison is on a scam. If there were, say, 700 people in Norwich prison, in all the time I was there I met maybe just a handful of genuine, decent people. Prison is an association of criminals. You mustn't have any morals in prison. If you have morals, you are nothing. For example, people will ask you if you have a stamp and you give it to them, but in return if you need a stamp they will just say, "Sorry, mate, don't have any," even if you gave him one last week. And then you think to yourself: hang on, I am asking for and getting wound up over a stamp! I was earning £1,200 a week running my door agency in Norwich and now I can't even have a stamp! And when you do finally settle in and settle down to prison life, you really see what is going on. You see the bullying and the intimidation and the threats and the fear. Norwich prison didn't have any one particular hard bloke that ran the place. People generally know that, no matter how hard they are, they could accidentally knock into someone on the landing who has just come in and are high on drugs, who would then stab him with the pointed end of a tooth brush or something. He might weigh just nine stone and never have fought in his life, but he would be scared and high on drugs. Or the new prisoner would take offence at being bumped into and wait a while until the so-called hard man went into the shower and then hit him hard with a coffee cup in a sock. So being someone who can fight doesn't count for much in prison. There are no rules in prison and there is nowhere you can go to hide. For instance, if you have a fight in the middle of the street in town, you might not ever see that person again, but in prison you live with them 24/7. If you ruck, you will see him again in the dinner queue, and again in the queue for medication, and again on the landings or in the gym. And they can stab you, or throw hot water and sugar in your face, anytime. And so there is not really a hard man of the prison, not like in the days of the Krays, for instance. There is no trust and you cannot guarantee that just because you might be the hardest bloke on the landing no one will come up to you in the shower and stab you. But, bizarrely, despite all of this hatred and dishonesty and intimidation, there are certain times when everyone sticks together. If an inmate's family member dies, you will be sad for them; if you hear that someone who has left prison overdoses and dies, the whole landing is solemn. It doesn't make sense. Where does that come from? Two days previously they were trying to fucking stab each other over some speed, or sleeping tablets, and yet the whole landing goes to church when someone they hear about dies, and then spend a few hours or sometimes even days talking about them. One minute it's all filth, and the next minute it's all soft. And the next day, filth again. I wasn't frightened of getting into a fight, but it is a different fear in prison. Prison is frightening: the noise, being next to people with hepatitis, AIDS; there are all sorts of diseases and you just don't know what to expect. I never became a parasite; I never became a bully. I wasn't in the majority, I stayed in the minority, but I wasn't bullied either. However, I think if I had gone to another prison I would have got into a lot of fights and would have been a danger. But not in Norwich, as I was known and well respected because it became known that I ran a door agency, because I didn't have anything to do with drugs or smoke, and because I stayed in my cell a lot of the time and wasn't a threat to anyone. It is all drugs now. People smuggle drugs into prison up their arses, and if other prisoners think that one prisoner has drugs up his arse, they storm into his cell, five or six guys, with a spoon to 'spoon' his arse and get the drugs out. Pretty fucking crazy. There is a lot of group violence, three or four onto one. You will frequently see a gang go into someone's cell and make a mess of someone, but you can't get involved as it could be that he owes something to someone and has not paid it back, despite several warnings. A lot of the time you have to ignore what you see; it isn't your business. It isn't like on the streets where you can help if someone is getting a kicking; inside there is always a reason. If you get involved then you are in trouble, as those prisoners will then turn on you. And it is all about what stuff you can get in prison. For instance, if you had 1½ ounces of tobacco, a ½ ounce of that is worth another 1½ ounces, because if you borrowed a ½ ounce you have to give one ounce back plus the ½ ounce you borrowed. This is where you become part of the majority and prey on newcomers, because the person that has just come into prison doesn't have anything, so he will borrow. That is when you start to get the intense intimidation and the bullying. For example, you would also be intimidated into to pretending you have backache to get the doctor to give you medication. Some prisoners do little things to frighten and intimidate you, like walking into your cell and picking up your things. I told one person to fuck off when he tried it; he did, but many people are frightened of telling another prisoner to fuck off and so the intimidation for stuff begins. Prison teaches people how to improvise. Prisoners make their own 90 per cent proof alcohol. I have met people who are doing their sentence brain dead because they have been drinking hooch, or moonshine as it is known in the US. They just sleep their prison sentence away. Prison is all about drugs and medication, and prisoners will do almost anything to get sleeping tablets or painkillers or any form of medication. They walk around the landings, shouting down, asking who has got what available, and then you see people passing stuff up over the landings that eventually goes to someone for four or five times the original value. It is like bartering town. And you can go into prison for just three months and come out a complete bastard, a liar and totally untrustworthy. You can easily lose all your morals, only because you get intimated and therefore to survive you intimidate back. For instance, you can sit and be friendly and chat to someone in his cell, then leave the cell a few seconds behind him after stealing something that you have already sold for a few ounces of tobacco. There are no rules. The long termers feed off the short termers. Being a grass in prison is taboo and is just as bad as being a sex offender – in prison there isn't much difference; you will be getting beatings no matter what and people will just step over you. It is the norm. The regime in prison is degrading. You have to ask for everything: shampoo, soap, toothpaste, everything. You even have to ask for an envelope. You are allowed one envelope a day. One fucking envelope! If you have used that envelope and want another you then have to borrow, and then you have to pay it back. There are different classes of people in prison; you have the right scumbag, then the lesser scumbag, then the scumbag, and eventually down to the nearly human. It is amazing how people made a life for themselves in prison. Just sitting watching everything that was going on was sometimes amazing. Without any actual violence, there was loads of it. The 4s would intimidate the 3s. The 3s would intimidate the 2s and the 2s would intimidate the 1s. Each landing had their little crew running all the scams. If you got the job as a landing cleaner then you would be used to move drugs around, so you didn't want to be a landing cleaner. So you refused the job, which then gave pushers and dealers an opportunity to get someone they wanted as a landing cleaner. You had to try to pick jobs according to their implications. I was lucky, as I worked in the printing shop where I was treated a little bit better and more like a human being than many in other jobs. But even in the printing shop I saw people take the glue they used to put the pages together. Pots of glue would be smuggled out and sold as solvents. Norwich was such a cold prison. Visits would be just an hour, but in most prisons visiting times are two hours minimum, sometimes up to four hours. Norwich is not a nice prison; for instance, if you had to make an appointment for the dentist it might take three weeks, if not more, to get to see him, so you could have an abscess and have horrendous toothache and be in pain for three or more weeks. I made friends with John, a lifer who had killed someone and got 15 years, and then he stabbed his cellmate and got life. He had done 27 years already. His skin was sallow and grey, he had prison tattoos on his neck and arms, he was covered in scars and his eyes were dead; there was no sparkle, no life left in them. He was never getting out; a bit like Cape Fear really. We were chatting when a 'black man' came straight into our cell and interrupted us, asking if we had any 'burn' (dope). From his sock John took a blade he had made from two toothbrushes melted together with a lighter and sharpened, and told the 'black' to fuck off or he would stab him there and then and leave him bleeding. He would have killed him just because he interrupted our conversation. John literally had nothing to lose. And then we returned to our conversation as though nothing had happened. That is what it's like in prison. Lifers who will never get out, who have no family, whom no one writes to, who have nothing and who have nothing to lose, they make their life a little better by intimidation and running the prison as best as they can. Their only home is prison, which is why they are the way they are. A lot of problems with prisoners are down to the fact that they don't have anyone. They don't have anyone to keep them strong. They then get depressed. They try to hang themselves. They self harm. They don't wash. They stink. One of the most moving and emotional experiences I personally had inside Norwich prison was my first New Year's Eve as a prisoner. Because I could see out into the car park, my girlfriend told me she would come up at midnight. I kept looking for her and eventually I could see her standing in the car park waving at me. On the stroke of 12 and just as the fireworks exploded nearby she shouted, "I love you, Bob." And then suddenly one of the other prisoners shouted, "She loves you, Bob," and a few seconds later the whole of the prison were banging their mugs on the railings shouting, "She loves you, Bob," "She loves you, Bob."

Respect and Reputation

By Charlie Bronson

It's very difficult to explain the massive changes to the world after spending untold years inside. It just blows your brain away. It really is another world that's moved on without you. Time stops dead from the day you enter, and you walk out 'thinking', 'hoping' it will be the same.

When I walked out after my first long stretch I served 14 years, 13 of those in solitary in punishment blocks up and down the country the things I saw disgusted me. Sadly, the drug era had taken over our streets and out went all the morals and self-worth. Even some of my old buddies had lost their sparkle and self-respect. They looked sad and empty and sick of life. I was 14 years older, wiser and as fresh as a daisy. At 35 years of age I felt like 19. I was fit and strong and ready for anything.

It was through Reggie Kray that I went into the prize fight game, and his old mate Paul Edmonds became my promoter. My first fight was at Bow, East London. All the 'chaps' were there; it was a villains' paradise. Even Charlie Kray turned up and gave me his brother's best wishes. That's when Bronson was born! The rest is history. In 69 days of freedom I had four fights: three with men, one with a dog. I could not lose unless they shot me. Sadly, nothing lasts, good or bad, and my freedom run ended as fast as it had started.

In those two months of freedom I also did my bit on a few doors and, again, I was shocked at what I saw. The world had truly gone mad. I had never seen so many lost souls with dead eyes: young guys with haggard features, pale skin, bulging eyes, snorting all sorts of shit up their noses. They even smelled of stale sweat, or was it piss? The young lads had no real buzz in them, no flare, no charisma; scruffy looking sods.

My club life was not like this. It was so different. We didn't need drugs to have a good night out. I felt a deep loneliness come over me, as though I did not belong, as if it wasn't me and I'd never fit in. Even some of the doormen were sniffing a bit up their noses and acting like giggling schoolgirls. This wasn't my scene anymore; I really lost interest. Sure, there have always been drugs in clubs, but not like it was then. For those few weeks I worked the door I just never felt right. I never even trusted my fellow bouncers. To put it bluntly, they were a liability; a total disgrace to the trade and an insult to every decent doorman in the UK.

That's how it affected me.

I couldn't do my job the way I used to do. There was no respect. How can a guy run the security when he can't even trust or count on the guys he works with? It's impossible. A man needs to be in control of a situation. He has to know who's who and what action should be taken when needed. How do you do that when you are coked up to the eyeballs?

I really was lost in time; it just wasn't me. If you live on a farm you smell of shit. It was time I left it all behind. So I moved on to a spot of minding and collecting.

One guy I looked after was a serious jeweller who'd done a lot of biz up north. So we made a weekend of it. I enjoyed that sort of job, as I was in full control. I could weigh it all up: who was who, how safe it was, when to move, when to stop. And it pays well. I'm just a natural minder. I can smell a rat a mile off. I can spot it coming: the way somebody looks at a watch or a chain or a briefcase; how the creeps are the way they move, the darting eyes, that glow of excitement just before the hit comes. "The same way as they clock me… fuck it, I'd better not. This guy's alert, he's onto me."

That's how it works. I can snap a man's leg with one kick. There can only be one outcome (unless you shoot me). Even then you would have to be quick and a good aimer, otherwise I would be onto you so fast.

You learn only by life's experience, not through books.

It's like all these guys who work out in gyms and on punchbags. Real life is not a bag or a dumbbell. Real life hits back and it fucking hurts. Sometimes it kills you.

When I arrived back in jail after those two months I don't really know how I felt; obviously low and confused and very angry. I also felt a bit guilty that I had let down both myself and my family. It also felt as if I had never been freed. The prison stench soon takes over. The routine sets in. It's as if it's in your blood, meant to be, meant to happen. The prison world sucks away all your hopes and dreams and fills you up with hopelessness.

But the truth is, I'm still alive and kicking. I've still got all my morals and self-respect. So I must be winning!

Respect and reputation don't stop when the prison gates slam up and cut you off from the free world. Fuck me, it never stops till the heart refuses to beat. Even in death you reap what you sow; some are buried and long forgot, and others still live on. But prison is another world: cruel, cold and insane; and the colder and crueller and madder it becomes the more 'I love it'.

Did you know, back in the 1960s and '70s in jails like Parkhurst and Hull we had cell parties with our own doormen on guard? Yes, hard to believe, but a fact. A heavy is a heavy, in or out.

Take the celebrity cons such as Jeffrey Archer, Lester Piggott, George Best, Tony Adams, Boy George, Jonathan Aitken… I could go on, there's so many. Most of them were like fish out of water, lost and afraid, so a heavy appears and makes sure they're safe. And that's how it all works smoothly. A bodyguard can be a very useful protection and every jail around the world will have one. Some 'faces' may need a 'meetup' and don't want to be disturbed, so they put two heavies outside the cell door problem solved.

Ronnie Kray always had a couple of heavies on the scene at Broadmoor not that Ron couldn't sort any shit out himself, but as you age, who needs it? Bear in mind that Broadmoor is a madhouse full of crazy people. A lot used to pester Ron, always asking him for things favours, tobacco, food, etc., etc. Once or twice a day is no problem, but 30 times a day can drive you nuts, so the heavies would step in. And that's how it works, even in the asylum.

Just because a guy is locked up, he still has to live by a strict code of conduct, morals and self-respect; unless, of course, you are a fucking hobbit, or some cracknut, snorting moron, with no dignity left. And, sadly, prisons are full of these muppets, these soulless characters. It's really quite sad to witness, but that's life.

You don't get nothing from nobody inside; it's the survival of the fittest. Eat plenty, train hard and get lots of sleep. You will live to a hundred (if you want to).

My reputation lands in a jail before I even step inside. My respect was earned long ago. And, although the penal establishment hate my guts, in a strange way they also respect me. After all, my survival has been a very long, solitary existence, and there ain't a prison governor or guard or convict that don't know me, or of me. A man can't spend nearly four decades in hell and not be the devil's minder. That's me, that's what I am: the devil's right-hand man.

Since 1974 right up till now (2009) I have been caged up for all but three poxy months of freedom, so that's why I am what I am. What else can I be? What would you be after so long behind a door, I wonder?

A reputation can bury a man. It begins with the Jesse James syndrome – the fastest gun in the West, or the fastest fist; some young con waiting to knock out the old con, the old has been. That's what happens, but it's disrespectful to the old chap! It's the same as the old boxers in the ring, who went on to fight one too many. It's sad to witness such a beating; it's not nice, it's cold, it's cruel and insane, however you look at it! Some young cons probably dream of taking me out.

I done Bronson He was a pussy Tough as a slab of butter He bled like a pig He's eating his food through a straw His nose is sticking out of the side of his head Dreams

So life inside can be very like life outside: the same code of honour, the same morals and the same rules. A heavy is a heavy, and they do a fucking good job when needed. They're a special breed of man. Most of them are decent, respectful and honest guys, smart too. They know how to dress, they know how to behave, they love what they are; professional. They stick out wherever they go. I can pick them out a mile away: the walk, the posture, the look, that stare. The planet would be a mess without them and jails would crumble; they keep life neat and tidy. They do what needs to be done; they do what most guys could never do; they sort it out, and fast. Sometimes just a little word can often stop a fullblown riot. Most heavies are actually intelligent men; they have to be or they wouldn't last long in the biz. Who's going to employ a gorilla with no sense? Psychos are three a penny in jail, but a good heavy is worth his weight in gold. Bear in mind, the object of a prison sentence is getting out 'fast'. I just lost my way; some fucker switched the light off and the darkness sucked me away. I should have known better after all, I am a professional heavy. But I make no excuses, I've no regrets – my fall was my own doing. I fell alone. That's what a good heavy must do: go alone; never take nobody down with you.

Drowned alone in the insanity of life!

Years ago inside we had to wear 'greys' (jacket and trousers) with a blue and white striped shirt. I even had a red tie and shining boots. My shirts had starched collars and I used to lay my trousers under my mattress to put the crease in. I was smart in prison rags. Respect and reputation must continue. If a man looks like a bag of shit, he smells like one. Sleep in a pigsty and you become one. A bar of soap costs nothing. Cleanliness is godliness (remember that).

I used to march around the wings and the yard like a captain on parade. Some of the cons used to shout, "Here comes the guv'nor." It felt good; it gave me a sense of pride. You can't buy that. You're born with it – pride, self-worth.

That's why I salute all the doormen, bodyguards and heavies, cos they're all the same, from the same firm; solid, staunch and fearless. All have had to earn their respect and so many have ended up in jail. Many were just doing their job and may have hit some prat a little too hard. They're soldiers, that's what they are; fighting men in suits and shades.

Inside we become a bit like 'social workers', sorting out everyday problems: a bit of collecting needs to be done; stop a bit of bullying; have a word here and there; sort this out, sort that out. There aren't enough hours in the day, it's endless. On top of that you can't miss out on your workouts. A man must keep fit and strong (especially inside). The old jails were the best for a bit of biz: the Scrubs, Wandsworth, Walton, Winson Green, Durham, Leicester, Strangeways, Parkhurst, Hull. Those were the places where real cons earned respect, the proper jailbirds, when porridge was porridge and cockroaches were cockroaches.

Lovely memories!
Treasured!

Prison Life

By Kevin Lane

The difference between respect and reputation is that respect is earned but reputations are given, and they can both take on a life of their own within the confines of the prison system, way beyond the control of the individual involved.

I am a 41-year-old man entering my fifteenth year in prison for a crime I did not commit. I have always maintained that I am victim of a terrible miscarriage of justice and that the leading investigator and disclosure officer in my case, Detective Inspector Spackman, fabricated evidence with police informers Roger Vincent and David Smith and withheld other vital evidence to secure my conviction. I was arrested and subsequently convicted of slaying Robert Magill in a Hertfordshire lane in 1994. The background to the case is that 44-year-old Robert Magill was walking his dog at 8.15 a.m. on 13th October 1994 in rural Chorleywood, Hertfordshire, when he was ambushed by two gunmen who blasted five rounds from a pumpaction shotgun into him. Mr Magill died instantly.

I am serving life with a tariff of 18 years and have witnessed a great many events in prison. Whilst on remand, I have also been held at the highest imaginable Category the Prison Service can throw at you: Exceptional High Risk Category AAA. Inevitably, this has given me an insight into prisoners and how they will behave under extreme pressure, including solidarity, honour, courage, cowardice and deceit. The strengths and weaknesses of men, myself included, have been exposed along the way. However, I am proud to say that I have learned from them all and I hope my opinions and tales will be considered in the context of intending to inform the reader fully without seeming egotistical.

It's a difficult subject to set out elegantly, moralistically or from a common, sensible point of view. What is about to unfold in these next few pages was forcibly extracted from me in times of extreme pressure; thankfully, they are now behind me. However, social policies will never understand the contributing factors and methodology in relation to some of the events that I have suffered, and that are soon to be told. I hope that this will be a factor you'll keep in mind when you try to imagine how you would feel if you had been ripped from the warmth of your loved ones as an innocent young man and imprisoned deep into the belly of the beast, in Britain's most severe penal prison.

Some psychologists believe that innocent people behave in a bizarre, violent manner. After all, what coping mechanisms does such a person have in place to deal with an unnatural environment? I found that it took a number of years before I was able to control the explosive, erupting anger about my situation and realised that the way forward was not with my fists but turning solely to the pen. I sympathised with The Count of Monte Cristo. Respect and reputation are sometime thrust upon an individual, while others purposely strive in all they do to obtain the same. It's those who obtain the title and aura without setting out to do so that are inevitably the real gentlemen in life, who generally have good morals for the betterment of everyone and, more often than not, stand up to bullies and the like. Then there are those who want to use 'respect and reputation' as a springboard for nefarious objectives, mostly for their own illgotten gain, causing pain and suffering for others along the way. These are the arseholes of life.

So what is the difference between the two? A gentleman with a reputation can be introduced to anyone and will be warmly welcomed because they are the John Waynes of life; people love their company because they offer no cause for concern. The person considered to be a real nasty bastard (the arsehole) will generally find that people don't want to be in their company, will be nervous around them and cannot wait to distance themselves.

I know which one I would prefer to be.

Respect is given for a variety of reasons: the way you conduct yourself, how you treat those around you, and how you treat yourself. Being a gentleman and having good manners goes a long way in prison and earns you the respect of those around you. Often, cons may not necessarily like you, but they afford you that respect due to your own actions. A reputation, however, is built on how others perceive you and the things you have done. Prison is not unlike a shark infested sea, with everyone circling each other, looking for any weaknesses and opportunities to advance through treachery in the pecking order. The closer you are to the top, the more people will avoid confrontation with you. If you are willing to stand up for yourself, to stand by what you say, to believe in your own convictions, then you will gain that reputation. For instance, if you get rushed by the mufti/screws (for whatever reason, and there doesn't always have to be one) and you fight back with everything you've got, if you won't back down from confrontation with other inmates, you will gain a reputation. At first, whatever happened during an incident will get passed on reasonably truthfully for about a day. Most cons love a bit of embellishment in the recounting of a fight or incident to make it more spectacular. So a 'clash of The Titans' quenches the thirst of the bloodthirsty pack and will be retold with force and recounted blow by blow. Thus legends are born, as everyone claims to have been there, and known the protagonists personally. A couple of incidents like this and the reputation will grow and establish itself; it's beyond the control of the person concerned, and both respect and reputation increase exponentially when stories are retold in other people's selfdreams keeping the story alive as if it took place yesterday.

A common mistake that people make in their lifetime is equating respect with instilling fear. Whilst fear can feed respect, it can never govern respect. An inmate who is a bully a nutter willing to stab, scald, clump anyone with an iron bar, etc. will to a certain extent be feared, but this is not respect. Respect through fear inevitably only lasts until the perpetrator confronts the wrong person and comes unstuck, and it always happens sooner or later. So a few will gain a reputation, but no respect. An inmate who is steadfast in doing the right thing by the 'laws' of our society, in here can do the same things, for the right reasons, and gain respect. If a less physically able con bangs a 'liberty taking' bully over the head with a dish, or defeats him by whatever means, he will gain respect. He has stood his ground and not allowed the bully to exercise power through fear, and if he does this on several occasions he will gain a reputation of being particularly hard (adept at fighting). So, in this mad, twisted environment we live in, you do not have to be the best fighter, the biggest bloke on the wing, the fittest in the jail. If you treat everyone fairly and with politeness and don't take liberties, you will earn respect. If you add to that a willingness to stand your ground when you're not in the wrong, you will gain a reputation as well.

Respect is not something that you can buy, or build, by beating up those around you. It is earned through the mixture of small interactions you have from day to day with your fellow cons.

Behave like a gentleman and you will be given that respect. If, however, you want to punch your way through your sentence by attacking those weaker than you, either physically or verbally, you will never gain respect. You will be despised, despite what some may say to your face, and one day in a TV room, a cell, the showers or wherever some angry nine-stone nobody is going to take you out.

It is not in me to lie down and roll over in any situation that I believe is wrong, and standing your ground is everything in here. Throughout my time in prison, I have witnessed and been part of just about every situation you can imagine could be thrown up by such an oppressive, negative environment. People's behaviour is dictated often by the pressures that any given environment exerts on them, and their strengths and weaknesses are laid bare. No one is exempt from this. It is an uncaring, ugly and, at times, vicious and brutal environment, and negativity will, 90 per cent of the time, produce negative responses. Yet, against all reason, there are moments of such shiny positivity that hope is kept alive.

Prison life is such a complex subject to describe both briefly and coherently to the layman. There are so many factors to be considered. The effect that prison has on your emotional state is multifaceted: being removed from your loved ones, your life, your liberty. Having all control taken away from you is a traumatic and psychological shock. It is extreme, and extremes will affect severely how you react. We are all individuals and will react differently to different situations. Some come to prison and can't cope; some cope all too well; but most of us just survive. What concerns us here is the course of actions you take to ensure that survival. You are, in essence, defined by your actions, and respect and reputation are manifestations of others' perceptions of your actions.

Whilst both of these attributes allow an individual a certain amount of control, they are largely established by your peers. Some people actively seek reputations for a variety of ulterior motives, oblivious to the liberties they take or the hurt they cause others. These are the bullies or arseholes, who inevitably gain nothing and eventually come unstuck and get their comeuppance. As true respect and reputation are bestowed according to others' views of your actions, once given these endure. The man that conducts himself as a gentleman, employing decency, good manners, a good moral sense, a willingness to stick up for himself and defend those unable to do so, will earn the respect of others. Similarly, if he has also had a few fights and 'runins' with the screws/mufti, displaying the fighter's spirit and a willingness to 'have a go' whether the odds are good or bad, he will also gain a reputation. The bully utilises fear to gain these things, but he will always ultimately be unsuccessful. He will inevitably meet his nemesis and should be mindful that 'just because the waters are calm, it doesn't mean there aren't any crocodiles in it'.

I have endeavoured to instill in my sons the value of acting appropriately in life, towards themselves and towards all those they deal with.

Both respect and reputation increase exponentially as time goes on. Once earned, respect can be difficult to maintain. You must be consistent in your dealings, steadfast in your convictions and fair and well mannered in all you do. If you deviate from this philosophy, you can lose respect easily it is a powerful yet fickle thing.

A reputation is not quite so easy to shake off should you so desire, and it is subject to the 'Chinese whisper' effect. I recall an incident very early on in my incarceration when I was held in the Special Secure Unit (SSD) at Belmarsh Prison. I had been attending my trial by way of a Level Two escort, which entails all the trimmings: helicopter, police outriders, sirens, guns, blues and twos, and enough guards to form a battalion! This procedure is often used by the authorities in order to attach a dangerous reputation to the prisoner for the benefit of the court, whereby Joe public and the jury develop preconceptions about who/what you are and consequently your guilt before the trial has even started!

Anyway, one of the screws, evidently a power lifter or body builder from his build – subjected me to a constant stream of threats and aggressive behaviour all day, informing me of his penchant for violence, and all of this whilst I was shackled like Houdini. A former screw, George Shipton, an unbelievably decent bloke, told the meathead to leave me alone, but it made no difference. Back at the prison, whilst undergoing the obligatory humiliation of a strip-search, he once again told me of his of love for violence and asked to look at the soles of my feet, even though he'd just watched me take my socks off. That was the last he had to say on the matter. It took a few seconds for the other officer to react, hit the alarm bell and secure my arms, as in stunned fascination he watched his bodybuilding colleague sliding, unconscious, down the back wall.

What a surprise. I had been goaded and provoked all day. I subsequently received further police charges for Grievous Bodily Harm. George retold the day's events to the Governor of the SSU. I was removed from the block after just three days, with pending court charges for the offence.

In this environment you cannot allow such threats to pass unchallenged, otherwise some screw, con or lackey will believe they can treat you inappropriately and with impunity. This type of incident spreads around the prison estate like wildfire. The SSU has a small 'community'; nevertheless, people come and go from the high security prisons, so news travels quickly. I suddenly found that my name was being bandied about by people I'd never met or even heard of. I was later convicted and placed in the SSU at Whitemoor. The unit had recently opened after the infamous escape of the IRA and the East End baddo, Andy Russell, in 1994. Andy was also the mastermind behind the helicopter escape from Gartee Prison. SSUs operate a regime that is even more regimented and oppressive than the prison estate as a whole:

closed visits with family and legal representatives; complete segregation from the general population; caged exercise; more bolts and locks on the cell doors than were required for Hannibal Lecter; and numerous fences and cameras! Despite a pre transfer meeting with the unit staff to smooth the way, the reception committee was way over the top, complete with three Alsatians and more staff than at a POA meeting. Later, when I was let out of my cell, I bumped into and engaged with a con known to be a real 'wrong 'un', whose former wife and children had been subjected to the most severe abuse. As the staff took me to solitary, leaving the con sleeping soundly on the floor, I stated, "No one can say that I've ever told him anything, can they?"

Boundaries had been clearly set out.

Shortly after, I had my first 'meeting' with the mufti. There was a peaceful protest in support of concerns over the running of the unit. Seven of us were asked by John Sayers (one of the North East Godfathers) to refuse work, which we all did. The staff spent the whole day in riot gear and fed us at our doors with polystyrene cups, plates, etc. It went thus: a full compliment turns up with your meal, screaming through the door for you to listen carefully to the instructions, "Remain still at all times, keep you arms by your side and don't move." Fuck me, I was making my bed at the time! My meal was placed on the sink near the door whilst still being shouted at by another screw. Because this lot had earlier attacked Matthew Williams (who had previously escaped from Parkhurst prison in 1994), I felt threatened, and having always being taught by my dad that the best form of defence is attack, I waded in.

I was fortunate enough to take out the 'shield man' not an easy feat; the others continued to rain punches and kicks on me as he was removed from the cell by his feet. I traded punches for at least a minute, which is an eternity in a situation like this, but unlike them I was fit and could maintain that explosive energy. Fortunately, the layout of my cell furniture hampered the onslaught. Then, suddenly, I noticed that my budgie Joey had escaped and was flying about the cell. My immediate concern was that he would get hurt, and my fear of Joey's impending squashing induced me to stop fighting and shout, "Watch my budgie, watch my budgie!" Both me and Joey were immediately pounced upon and relocated, Joey to his cage and me to a strip cell with cuffed arms and legs. Many hours later the legion of Manga troops returned with a doctor in tow. I was given a prison garment to cover my nudity whilst the open gash above my swollen eye was sewn up under torchlight! Not only was this procedure done on a cold concrete floor, but also they fucked it up and had to remove the stitches and do it all again without any anaesthetic! The recording of this incident has been viewed as a staff training video, and so the reputation grows with the retelling.

Not enduring threats will, along with good manners, accord you a bit of respect with staff and inmates alike.

After 27 months I was placed back in the general population, albeit within the dispersal system, but the damage was palpable. I was soon to cross paths with Gary Nelson.

In 1994 Nelson was charged with killing PC Dunne in 1993 at Catford, London. Nelson was acquitted of the murder charge at that time but was rearrested and recharged with the offence a decade later, and in February 2006 Nelson was convicted and sentenced to life imprisonment for murder. The sentencing judge described Nelson as a 'premier league criminal'. News headlines claimed that Nelson was responsible for several contract killings and was one of the nation's most dangerous criminals. Nelson met the police informer Roger Vincent in 1994 when they were both held in Wormwood Scrubs. Roger Vincent and David Smith were both arrested on suspicion of murdering Robert Magill on 16th December 1994. Both Vincent and Smith are recorded in the police evidence as supplying information to the police upon their arrest, which led to my arrest.

Vincent and Nelson hit it off immediately in prison and soon became friends. In 1999 I received material from the CPS informing me that Vincent had named me for the murder of Robert Magill. Naturally, I took this up with Nelson, who by now had struck up a strong bond with Vincent. The next time we clashed was on a football pitch, and this time it wasn't verbal. With over a hundred inmates looking on, I took him to the cleaners. Had people not restrained me he would have received the hiding of his life. The legend grew; 'major player Nelson gets his arse kicked by college looking boy from the countryside'. The sad thing in all of this is that to a great extent violence is often the language of the prison estate and it undoubtedly gives you respect and a reputation; but the pedestal you stand on in here is like all pedestals stationary and you fail to progress through the prison system. The powers that be frown on such events, illustrated by the fact that you see people come and go over the years whilst you stay still. The Prison Service never forgets.

My advice to anyone coming into prison is always be mindful of your actions so as not to cause concern to others, without compromising your beliefs and convictions. Try to avoid confrontations; they are almost always solvable by talking, as most disagreements in here are over nothing. If you treat people well but firmly and go about your own business, no one can say anything about you. Reputations are born of adversity and can work against you. Respect, on the other hand, is hard earned and will gain you the courtesy we should all strive to live by both in here and out in the big, bad world.

The type of person entering prison these days has changed. They have very little consideration for others a sad reflection on today's society. There is a distant lack of common decency and, although it may sound strange, decency counts for a lot in prison. Fifteen years ago, at weekends you were mindful not to make a noise in the morning. Now, the young cons shout first thing in the morning from one end of the wing to the other, "Yo' blood, my man last night, yeah, he was chilling, you get me." As daft as that may seem, that replicates the average dialect in prison. I often think I've landed on Mars. Prisoners these days have attitude; most of them walk with a pebble in one shoe, causing them to limp! Respect has a different meaning these days. The most important advice I can offer is: keep a closed mouth and don't be lured into prison politics; and if you've reported an opinion on someone then you've made a verbal stand and you'd better be willing to stand by it. Things like this are life and death in jail. I suppose cons have very little else to concentrate on without realising, and they're directing their anger and hurt towards others as a result of what they feel themselves from being in prison.

Keep your numbers small and you won't have everyone's problems, and hopefully you'll move through the system under the radar of the security department. Steer clear of those who attract attention to themselves, those who bring trouble to their door, and stay away from the drug culture. The prison security department knows almost everything, as the wings are full of prisoners receiving privileges for information. Be warned and take notice. Use your time constructively. Take up an interest that you may have, use the gym, even if it's simply to walk on the treadmill, and get out on the exercise yard or off the wing as often as you can. Fresh air in your lungs and the wind on your face does wonders for your health, both in body and soul. Consider undertaking a distant learning course with a college you'll be amazed to see what courses are available. Don't sit in front of a TV or Game Boy for hours on end. Read a good book you'll enjoy it more.

The reality of the situation is this: this is your life now, so create a life within these walls and keep busy.

In prison there are many good people on both sides. You will do well to remember that and be thankful for them. Imagine if the place was full of spiteful bastards causing grief all the time. Thank God for the good who make life somewhat easier. Prison staff, like most people, simply want an easy life; they like manners and prisoners who know how to conduct themselves accordingly. Be aware that most prisoners do not have social skills, so if they don't get what they want they resort to temper tantrums, raised voices or even violence. It's almost like a baby who spits out his dummy: I want it I will have it. A fact of life is that we can't always have what we want, and consequently we must address our childlike behaviour to be able to fit into a normal society. Some prisoners will take umbrage with my comments, but being able to sit back and understand another person's view is something I have gained from listening to all sorts of people over the years.

When I was held with the IRA and Andy Russell, one of the IRA told me that if the IRA wanted to hurt innocent people they would plant a bomb in the middle of a football stadium, but this was not their intention. I was told how all the IRA bombs are reported to the police well before they are due to explode in order to ensure the public's safety, and that it was the government that allowed the bombs to go off – guaranteeing public opinion in favour of the politicians' cry for support against the IRA. It's worth considering when you think of the weapons of mass destruction that Iraq was reported to have by our own government.

I would like to tell you a real life story relating to something that took place recently within these walls. You may be aware of the plot to blow up Glasgow Airport by Balal Abdul, a qualified doctor, and another man. My story relates to a fellow prisoner, Terry Conneghan, a true, staunch Glaswegian. Terry suffered terribly with asthma and he had a severe attack as a result of being prescribed the wrong medication. Terry's breathing was laboured, his eyes were popping out of his head (like Golem's) and he was in a bad way. The prison doctor was summoned, but 20 minutes later he was still nowhere to be seen. Jimmy Johnson had a 'brainwave': "I'll go and get Abdul". He ran off and returned quickly with Abdul in tow. Abdul promptly sprang into action, almost as if he was in the accident and emergency department of his local hospital. Terry was in terrible distress, as his attack had worsened. He appeared to be looking at Abdul and then at Jimmy for help, his eyes even wider now, as he attempted to get his words out. Failing miserably, he placed the oxygen mask back over his mouth. Abdul continued providing professional assistance, doing all he could. Time was swiftly moving on and still there was no doctor. The staff informed Abdul that he had to leave and return to his cell. Abdul refused point blank to leave his patient and took the higher ground of his professional expertise, stating that he was a doctor and Terry needed his help. Eventually, the staff decided to whisk Terry off to the health care centre. Terry, with the oxygen mask tightly fixed to his face, was quickly removed in a wheelchair that had a buckled wheel and was doing a merry dance as he was led away.

The following day Terry came steaming back onto the wing and marched straight up to Jimmy. "What the fuck did ya think yee was up to yesterday, bringing Doctor Death to help me? He was going to blow up 3,000 of my countrymen, you stupid bastard, and you bring him to help me!" Now we know why Terry's attack got worse.

Terry eventually did thank Abdul and they have since both laughed about the scene that could have come from a Carry On film. It just goes to show that people can get on once they've got to know each other, and I hope this story illustrates the lengths that some men will go to at times of extreme adversity.

Respect Where Respect is Due

By Charlie Bronson

So how do men in jail hold on to their respect and reputation? Believe me, it's not easy. Some lose it; they just crumble and get crushed. Some turn to drugs. Some become zombies. Others die as they enter the reception block. A man becomes a number. The number is your life; from the day you enter to the day you leave, that is how it is!

Over my three and a half decades I've bumped into 'everybody'. I have witnessed good men weaken. It's sad to see, but it's how prison sucks away your soul.

Me, I just ride my time; I don't let it take me over. I make my stay inside 'my time' and no fucker tells me how to do my time but me. It's why I'm always smiling. Some may say Bronson's institutionalised. Well, let me tell you I'm not, nor ever will be. I dislike prison as much as I did when I first came in, so that proves I can't be institutionalised.

Here's a few of the 'cons' I've met and admire for how they served their time. These guys came inside with a reputation and kept their respect. Some died inside! Others got out and some returned, but in my book they're all legends.

Ronnie, Reggie and Charlie Kray

I met the twins in Parkhurst back in 1975, and also met Charlie in Parkhurst on a visit in 1976. The Kray brothers played a big part in my life and we remained friends till they all died. I spent time with Ronnie too, in the asylum, and time in Gartree with Reg. And I got to see Charlie on visits. They all had tragic endings, but they all lived life as men of respect; men of great honour. Ronnie Kray only had to walk in a room and it would light up. Some men are special like that. Others only think they're special; they can act it all their life but never have that quality. Ron and Reg survived so many wasted years inside, but they never cried. They had no self-pity; they rose above it all. They made it work for them and I feel humbled to have served some time with them (get my book *The Krays and Me!*).

Frankie Fraser

I first met him in Wandsworth Jail in 1975 down on H/1 punishment block. From that first meeting I knew he was a serious man of respect. He was only a small man, but fearless. He did his time inside – a good 40 years his way. He was a true survivor. I've met cons that are 20 stone of solid muscle, strong as a bull, but they have the heart of a mouse. Frank's heart is that of a lion. I've so much respect for the man.

Bruce Reynolds, Charlie Wilson, Tommy Wisbey and Buster Edwards

I have met all these guys inside. They were all part of the Great Train Robbery. All were very respected and all did their time their way. They were legends in their own lifetime. I salute them all.

Harry Roberts

I've known Harry for donkey's years. He is now into his 43rd year of a life sentence. Imagine that if you can 43 years of porridge! Harry got 'lifed off' back in the early 1960s over the shooting of three coppers. He got sentenced to a 30-year tariff, so he is now 13 years over that (which must be illegal?) What a lot of people don't know about Harry Roberts is that he was a hero in the British Army (people forget things like that). That man fought for this country with pride and respect and he's now survived 43 years of a life sentence. That's respect. You can't but respect Harry, and I salute the man! Will he make it out? Bet your arse he will!

Jimmy Boyle

Nobody was a tougher, more violent man than Jimmy. His fights in jail are legendary. The man was brutalised and dehumanised, but he survived and served 15 years of a life sentence. I met him in Long Lartin jail back in the late 1980s when he came to do a TV documentary. Jimmy's a good man, a good friend and I salute a winner. The Krays always spoke highly of him. It's all about respect and reputation!

Big Ronnie Brown

Ronnie was what I call an 'old type blagger' – a proper good armed robber! Sadly, nothing ever lasts and he fell. In the 1960s he copped an 18-year stretch. He served that only to fall again and cop another 18 years. But Ronnie walked the prison yard with his head up and marched on. He did his porridge like a soldier, military style. You could eat your food off his cell floor it was immaculate! Even in prison clobber he looked smart, with his polished boots and starched shirt. Ronnie Brown to me stood out, at 6 ft 1 in, 18 stone and with shoulders like a barn door and his big shiny bald head. I salute the man. Respect.

Valerio Viccei

This Italian I met on the maximum secure unit in Brixton back in 1988. He was nicked on the £60 million Knightsbridge safety deposit robbery. He was a serious man of respect; a man who walked the walk and talked the talk. He lived how most men only dream of. He copped 20 years for that robbery (only £4 million was ever found). Valerio was later extradited back to Italy from Parkhurst prison. Soon after, he was shot dead by the Italian police. He died how he lived – dangerously, and that's how he would have wanted it to be. I rate Valerio as one of the greatest men of respect that I ever had the privilege of meeting. To me, and his friends, he was known as Gigi. I lost a good mate there. I loved him like a brother. Adios amigo.

Roy Shaw

They don't come any tougher than Roy. I've known him for years. He once came to one of my trials to support me. When it comes to 'respect', he comes second to nobody! Like myself, Roy did his porridge hard and fought every day of it. It even got him certified mad and packed off to Broadmoor asylum, but Roy kept his reputation and walked out the winner! Men like him don't dream about losing (he can't), cos he's a born fighter. Even today in his late 70s he still works out on the punchbag and does his road work. The man is a legend. Respect.

Joe Pyle (Snr)

Sadly, Joe is no longer with us. He was like a second father to me and I loved him to bits. He went back to the '40s, '50s and swinging '60s. He rubbed shoulders with every villain in London. Everybody respected Joe Pyle. You will never hear a bad word about him, cos he was a man amongst men. He helped so many men stay out of jail; he was like the criminal adviser. Joe did his bit of porridge how he chose to do it his way. You never heard him moan about it; he just got on with it and made the best of a bad situation. He still kept his dignity in jail. It was steak and chips for Joe every day! Even the screws respected Joe Pyle. Believe me, there are very few like him. He really is one of a dying breed we shall never see again. Joe was probably the biggest crime boss of the last 50 years. Some called him The Silent Man. Let's just say, you didn't fuck with him. If you did, you only did it the once, believe me. RIP.

Harry Marsden

I first bumped into Harry in Leeds jail back in 1975. He was a lot like Frankie Fraser: only a small man, but fearless. Harry and me were battling with the screws every week down in the dungeon. I'm talking about serious punchups. We were both put in body belts and straitjackets. Our world was violence. It was our life. It's only in times of great pain and misery that you find out the true qualities of a friend. Harry shone through every time. He never knew the word 'defeat'. He spent many years battling through the system till he finally made it out. Amazingly, he turned his life around and opened up a boxing gym for the youth up in Newcastle. His respect and reputation just grew. Sadly, the 'big C' cut him down; it was one fight he couldn't win. But Harry lives on in many hearts, both in the criminal fraternity and in the real world of hard knocks. A man we all loved!

Big George Wilkinson

I first met George in Wandsworth jail back in 1976. Now, I've met all the hard men, the tough guys and the raving lunatics, but nobody matched this fella. This guy was so dangerous, he made Al Capone look like a choirboy. George was a nobody outside. He built his respect and reputation inside as a very dangerous man. You did not fuck with this guy; he was the original mean machine. George was a Geordie, he stood at 6 ft 2 in and he weighed a good 19 stone. He was a giant of a man; a naturally strong man who didn't need a gym. He spoke very little and always had that 'look' about him: "Want some of me, cunt?" When I first met him he was awaiting trial for taking a screw hostage down in Parkhurst.

I thought he was going through some serious mental times, as he kept losing the plot. Some of his actions were a bit strange and he became violent just for the sake of it. I believe the system had created the ultimate madman and had lost control of him. Over the next few years there were more hostages and more violence, until he was found mysteriously dead in the strong box of Liverpool jail. Whatever you hear about George Wilkinson, take it from me: he was a smashing fella who had lost his way. And he's one of a handful of men who ripped a cell door off (I am also one of them). It's a very rare club to be in. So I salute Big George is a true legend. Yes, he was a feared man, but the respect he had was awesome. It's time someone wrote a book on the man. RIP.

Siddy Draper

Sid got nicked up in Scotland on an armed robbery where a guard got killed. He got a life sentence with a 30 rec. I met him in Hull jail in 1974. He's one first-class chap, a good man to do time with. He's always cheerful and hopeful. Sid was what he was: a proper pavement blagger. Where there was a security van Sid would not be far away. Fourteen years into his life sentence he decided that a holiday was well overdue and down came a chopper into Gartree jail and off he flew! Sadly, his holiday only lasted a short spell, but his is still the only chopper escape in England. If that's not respect, what is?

Johnny Paton

John is from my town, Luton. He copped a 12 stretch for robbery, but it never ended there. Whilst in Parkhurst jail he stabbed a con to death, all for respect and reputation. That cost him a life sentence. Then he stabbed another con to death, this time up in Wakefield jail. That cost him a second life sentence. Over the next 20 years John went deeper and deeper into himself till he found a way out: he hung himself in Garth jail. I respect Johnny cos he was a proud man who couldn't back down. He once told me, "Charlie, I'm a shit fighter, what else can I do but stab them?" And that's just what he did. You must bear in mind that a reputation like his was not easy to live up to. Imagine it. It's a bit like the Jesse James syndrome. All tough nuts want that label. Johnny was trapped. He saw his only way out: freedom in a body bag. Respect.

Linda Calvey (The Black Rose)

The media called her The Black Widow. I soon changed that. It was back in '87 when she got nicked over the murder of Ronnie Cook. Ronnie was a prolific armed robber, a very respected man, and whilst out on home leave somebody blew his head off. Linda served 20 years and then got out and married a millionaire. Come on, 20 years for a woman is like 40 years for a man! That's why I respect her so much. Linda to me is like Bonnie Parker! She was married to Mickey Calvey, another top blagger who got shot dead by the Old Bill. Linda even served 10 years before the murder of Ronnie Cook for armed robbery. Hell, she's on fire! Both me and Reg Kray proposed to her back in the early '90s. She knocked us both back. That's how the Black Rose is… unique. She's earned her respect ten times over. She's got more bottle than most men ever have. She's a wife, a mother, a grandmother and a fucking living legend. That's The Black Rose for you.

Lindsey and Leighton Frayne

Both these guys are in my movie, *Bronson*. I made it clear: if they're not in it, then don't do it! These brothers have both done time. Leighton, like me, got certified mad (it's just a label). They do it cos prison can't control you, so you're off to the asylum for a break. They both visit me. They're my Welsh brothers; they stand solid in friendship. They're good biz men and respect is their game. They earned their respect the hard way and they walk tall. You don't mess with men like the Frayne brothers. Ronnie Kray actually wanted them to play the twins in the Kray movie, but the Kemp brothers stepped in. Such is life. Respect.

Alfie Lodge

My little Welsh buddy Alfie is one of the best armed blaggers to come out of south Wales. He often pops up to visit my mother to see if she's well. He's a good, loyal friend. I first met Alfie in the late '80s in Long Lartin. He used to make a wicked bucket of hooch – he was legendary for his moonshine. I used to tell him to get out and open up a brewery: "You'd make a fucking fortune!" You don't become a top blagger overnight. It takes years of hard work to become the No 1. Alfie was the No 1. He's now retired and got his feet up. He lives for his woman Bev and all his dogs. The man is as free as an eagle! His reputation is intact and his respect undisputed. We love ya, Alfie!

Paul Edmonds

I first met Paul in Parkhurst in the early '80s. He copped a 12 stretch for armed robbery. He's a typical east Londoner proper staunch. He did his bird easy, his way – good grub and hard training. Paul was a very respected convict. He later became a fight promoter and I stayed with his lovely mum for a spell in Canning Town and met all his family. Salt of the earth. I learned a lot from Paul. He was a real man; a true uncut diamond. I soon ended up back in jail. I don't last long in the outside world and, sadly, neither did Paul he got shot dead. I don't know the ins and outs of it, but I know we lost a living legend. Even the Kray twins said Paul was a one off diamond. He lived and died respectfully; in jail and out of jail he was top dog. Well and truly missed. RIP.

Dave Courtney

I've always liked this guy, cos he always keeps the respect and he knows how to win in style. Lots of villains are jealous of him. Why? Simple: he's a clever fucker, a shrewd character; he rarely does any bird, Dave's done a lot of favours for me over the years. Nothing is too much trouble for him in sorting a problem; his loyalty is second to none. Let's face it, he put on a funeral fit for a king for Ronnie Kray. My mother and sister love him to bits. Dave has earned respect the hard way. When I'm out, look out for our show 'Chaz and Dave', and come and see us and have a fucking good night!

Dee Morris

I call her The Cockney Sparrow. Three of her brothers are in jail, all good guys, and she stands by them all. Nobody I know on this planet has as much fight as she does. She organises all the Bronson protests, she is one superwoman, and she's got a lovely arse to go with it! We all respect and love Dee; her reputation is one of loyalty. Her late dad would be so proud of her; he, too, was a diamond must run in the family.

Dave Taylor

Master of 'Chen Jin Iron Shirt'. This guy has done so much to support my fight for freedom. I consider Dave as one of the best pals I've ever had. Back to back we could take on an army, and I'm not joking. Respect and reputation are engraved in steel with this guy; he's earned them with blood, sweat and more blood. He's a true brother. A man you do not want to fuck with, believe me!

Vick Dark

I first met Vick in Brixton high security wing in 1988. He's the real deal; a born fighter and a man of rock. He can kick a man's head in a split second and punch you ten times before you blink. He copped 17 years for a robbery gone wrong and served his bird like the man he is: solid. He got out and got on with his life and he's done well. I salute a winner and Vick Dark is born to come first. Fuck me, who's gonna stop him?

Tom Hardy

Now here's a guy who's earned respect and reputation. He played me in the *Bronson* movie. I've not seen it (!) but all my family and friends have and tell me he did me proud. He even looks like me, walks like me and talks like me. He brought me alive on the silver screen, to show the world the atrocities that go on behind these walls of shame. I could die tonight in my sleep, but Tom's helped to make me live on. My respect for him is the dog's bollocks! He even bulked up four stone to play me; he put his heart and soul into it. Total respect. Tom's the man!

These are just a few – the tip of the iceberg. Read my book, *Legends* they're all in there. They show how you can still live up to your reputation even inside.

You are only what you are.

You can't be something you ain't.

Respect is in your blood, pumping through your heart.

But remember: one sneeze and your halo can become your noose.

www.ingramcontent.com/pod-product-compliance
Lightning Source LLC
LaVergne TN
LVHW011911080426
835508LV00007BA/338